POPUL

RELIGION

IN LATE

SAXON ENGLAND

The
University
of North
Carolina
Press
Chapel Hill
and
London

KAREN LOUISE JOLLY

POPULAR
RELIGION
IN LATE
SAXON
ENGLAND

ELF CHARMS IN CONTEXT

The paper in this book meets
the guidelines for permanence
and durability of the Committee
on Production Guidelines for
Book Longevity of the Council
on Library Resources.

Library of Congress
Cataloging-in-Publication Data
Jolly, Karen Louise.
Popular religion in late Saxon England:
elf charms in context / Karen Louise Jolly.
    p.   cm.
Includes bibliographical references
and index.
ISBN 0-8078-2262-0 (cloth: alk.
paper).—ISBN 0-8078-4565-5
(pbk.: alk. paper)
1. England—Church history—449–
1066. 2. Charms—England. 3. Anglo-
Saxons—Folklore. 4. Magic—Religious
aspects—Christianity. I. Title.
BR747.J65   1996   95-38408
274.2'03—dc20   CIP

00 99 98 97 96   5 4 3 2 1

THIS BOOK WAS DIGITALLY MANUFACTURED.

CONTENTS

ILLUSTRATIONS & MAPS

ACKNOWLEDGMENTS

I am often asked why, or how, I began studying elf charms and popular religion. The reasons are both scholarly and personal, a mixture of intention and serendipity. While I cannot articulate all of the circumstances leading to this book, I think it is appropriate to acknowledge how my views developed and give credit to those who influenced the choices I made.

The tenth–eleventh century is an exciting period for understanding how a religion such as Christianity made itself at home in a culture, and vice-versa, how a culture grew into and adapted to a religious conversion. Without this assimilation and acculturation, Christianity would have failed to prosper in early medieval European cultures. On a larger scale, the processes at work in this period shed light on the implications of conversion for culture, the impact of dominant religions such as Christianity on societies they encounter, and the importance of assimilation as a factor in the development of these cultures.

The emphasis in this book on confluences and interactions in part stems from the diverse influences on my career as this work developed. My research into the context and meaning of Anglo-Saxon elf charms began in the late 1970s at the beginning of my graduate career at the University of California at Santa Barbara and has continued during the time I have been at the University of Hawai'i at Mānoa. Over these years, my study has evolved along with the developing methods of cultural history.

The shaping forces of my thought originated with my graduate mentors, C. Warren Hollister and Jeffrey Burton Russell. What I owe them cannot be expressed adequately or completely here, but between them and working in concert, they brought balance to my nascent thoughts. I also wish to extend my appreciation to two of my fellow students, Cheryl Riggs and Marylou Ruud, who acted as sounding boards for my ideas. I am grateful to the University of California at Santa Barbara for its institutional support, both in the form of a Regents Fellowship in 1984–85 and through the library resources. I especially appreciate the assistance of the Interlibrary Loan staff, who often encouraged me by reading incoming materials and telling me what they found interesting.

The environment of the University of Hawai'i at Mānoa has brought a whole new set of shaping influences to my research. I would like to thank my colleagues in the history department, particularly Jerry Bentley and David Hanlon for their insights on world history and ethnography. A fellowship from the Center for Arts and Humanities in 1991 and extensive support from the Interlibrary Loan staff at Hamilton Library assisted me in completing my research.

A more unusual (but perhaps increasingly common) acknowledgment I extend to the University's Computer Center for making available Internet access to research resources. Likewise, I am grateful to the medieval electronic communities, the Anglo-Saxon and the Medieval History networks, for the stimulating dialogue they provide and for the informative advice list members give in response to queries.

The writing of this book has also benefited from the advice of willing readers. My writing group colleagues, Jane Moulin, Judy Van Zile, and Judy Rantela, listened patiently to several early drafts and contributed many wise insights. Kathleen Falvey and Peter Nicholson in the English department proofread my Anglo-Saxon translations, and colleagues in the history department offered constructive criticism of the manuscript in its later stages of development. I also wish to extend my thanks to my editors at the University of North Carolina Press, Lewis Bateman, Pamela Upton, and Stephanie Wenzel, for their encouragement, assistance, and correction. Any remaining infelicities in the book are mine.

Last, but not least, I am most thankful for my family. I am grateful to my parents for bringing me up in a house dominated by books. I wish to thank my husband, Jim, for his patience and support throughout my academic career. To my daughters, Alice and Laura, and my son, Jamie, I give thanks for reminding me of what is truly valuable in the world: knowing and loving one other.

POPULAR
RELIGION
IN LATE
SAXON ENGLAND

INTRODUCTION
CROSSING BOUNDARIES

Bald's Leechbook, a mid-tenth-century medical manuscript copied in an English religious foundation, recommends two prescriptions for an animal shot by an elf. The first is an ointment applied on the afflicted beast; the second is a purgative treatment. The enigmatic quality of the affliction and the two treatments highlight the difficulty of entering early medieval worldviews.

> If a horse or other cattle is [elf]shot, take dock seed and Scottish wax and let a man sing twelve masses over [them]; and put holy water on the horse or cattle. Have the herbs always with you.
>
> For the same affliction, take an eye of a broken needle, give the horse a prick with it in the ribs; no harm shall come.[1]

In a world where everything was alive with spiritual presences, where the doors between heaven and earth were open all around, then saints, demons, and elves were all equally possible. Such was the world of late Saxon England. Remedies in Christian medical texts using liturgy to cure ailments known from Germanic lore were not a bizarre aberration at odds with the Christian tradition. They were, rather, practical expressions of some of the most central Christian ideas about spiritual and physical well-being. The mutual assimilation between Anglo-Saxon culture and the Christian religion resulted in a unique cultural creation by the tenth and eleventh centuries—an Anglo-Saxon Christianity or a Christian Anglo-Saxon England in which elves were nicely accommodated.

Charm remedies, such as the ones above, copied by Christian scribes, are one type of evidence of this kind of assimilation that appears, to the modern eye, to be quite strange and not exactly "Christian." However, put in their context, these practices make sense as expressions of popular religion. Several contexts overlap to demonstrate how these charms contain a logic of their own, representing one aspect of early medieval worldviews. The increasing number of churches, evident in documentary and archaeological sources, reveals the spread of Christianity on a popular level and hence the rising level of contact between the folk and Christian ideas. The outpouring of laws, homilies, and letters from church leaders on what Christian society should be like also reflects an awareness of the consequences of this increased contact. The evolution of medical and liturgical texts in relation to this developing Christian folklore provides a rich, multilayered field of ideas and crosscurrents that produced the late Anglo-Saxon charms. These texts, seen in that dynamic context of growth and reform, demonstrate how assimilation occurred between the Christian religion and early European cultures in a much more subtle way than the more obvious conflicts between paganism and Christianity usually attracting attention.

The aim of this book is to use the Christianized charms against elves to show one aspect of how, in this critical cultural transition in the years between 900 and 1050, Christianity and Anglo-Saxon culture intermingled. These charm texts become comprehensible only when they are placed in the context of late Saxon popular religion and when they are examined using both traditional and popular sources. Traditional sources, those issued by rulers and religious leaders, reveal tensions and oppositions, such as pagan versus Christian, miracle versus magic, or God versus the Devil. Popular sources, or ones that give us a glimpse of everyday life, however, reveal the gray areas—the in-between practices that demonstrate a considerable amount of assimilation between these opposing categories. In these in-between or "middle" practices we can best see how Christianity and Anglo-Saxon culture were fused. Christian charms, particularly those aimed at elves, are the middle practices that form the focal point of this analysis, texts that are so opaque in their worldview that they require a contextual analysis to understand how they came to be what they were.

The first four chapters of this book build the context for understanding the Christian "elf charms" examined in the fifth chapter. The first chapter establishes a model of popular religion, not as the opposite of formal "elite" religion, but as a fruitful middle ground in the interaction between the formal church and popular experience. The second chapter examines the grassroots context for the development of popular religion, locating it in the environment of the local, proprietary church and in the relationship between priest and laity, with special reference to the impact of the Viking presence in the Danelaw. The third chapter explores the formal church's view of popular religion through the efforts of such reformers as Ælfric and Wulfstan and their attempts to mold popular belief and practice. Chapters 2 and 3 function together to develop two interacting points of view on popular religion in order to establish the confluence of ideas that produced Christian charms; Chapter 2 is the view from the ground of local reciprocal bonds, and Chapter 3 is the aerial view of the church hierarchy. The fourth chapter addresses the specific context of the charms and the mixture of sources present in these remedies. The fifth chapter analyzes the Christian elf charms as particularly revealing phenomena expressing the dynamics of conversion, acculturation, and popular religion in late Saxon England.

The prevailing theme in all of these chapters is the idea of overlap, or crossing boundaries, between the dualities inherent in European worldviews. The tendency in western thought to propound mutually exclusive opposites — whether it be Good and Evil, God and the Devil, Magic and Religion, or Civilized and Barbarian, Christian and Pagan, Religion and Science — is useful only as a means to understanding the dialectical interaction between these forces or tendencies.[2] As ideas these extremes are quite powerful, but the realities of human existence range between them. It is this range of what I call "middle practices" between popular and formal, between magic and religion, between clergy and laity, and between liturgy and medicine that interests me as evidence of how conversion to Christianity took place in the everyday world through a process of acculturation. Christian charms fit exactly there, in the middle, not at either end of the spectrum stretching between these dualities, but as a shared product. Consequently, I resist efforts to label these practices as one thing or another — as magic, for example — because they exist at an intersection of ideas. My goal is to reframe our image of late Saxon religion, to place these every-day practices in the middle of the picture and put the extreme dualities on the margins so that the depth and diversity of popular religious belief and practice come into focus.

Getting at this range of experience in a long-dead period requires using a combination of diverse sources—documentary, literary, liturgical, and archaeological—that scholars often treat in isolation from one another. A work focused ultimately on a set of texts commonly called "the charms" cannot do justice to all of these sources; rather, I use them as background for the charm texts. In that sense, this study is both wide ranging and narrow, moving between specific texts and a larger context. I use popular religion to make sense of a relatively obscure phenomenon, elf charms, and—vice versa—I use this specific set of texts, elf charms, to elucidate popular religion in late Saxon England.

Because these primary sources for popular religion stand at the center of this analysis, they are translated and quoted in the fullest possible manner, in order to show the wholeness of each piece and to give primacy to the voice of past experience. I have translated the medical remedies and rele-vant homilies from critical editions and consulted other translations, with reference in some cases to facsimiles.[3] In these translations I have endeav-ored to use language as close as possible to the Anglo-Saxon, even if it is rough sounding, in order to give the feel of the ideas in the vernacular. I have left any Latin intact in order to show the contrast in language in the texts, although I provide translations of the Latin in brackets at the end of the section (with certain commonly used Latin titles, such as the Pater nos-ter [Our Father] and the Benedicite [Blessed], I have indicated the meaning only in the first instance in the text). All of these Latin and Anglo-Saxon words used in the text are included in the index so that the reader may check the definition or locate other passages containing the same words. I have used brackets throughout the translations to indicate words added to clarify meaning or to suggest alternate translations. In a number of places I have included an Anglo-Saxon word in brackets after the English where I felt the original word was of interest or formed part of my analysis. A few Anglo-Saxon and Latin sources used as background in the early chapters are quoted from modern, definitive translations.

The use of long block quotes is, I fully realize, controversial. Some readers may be tempted to skip over them (others, like myself, may en-joy reading long excerpts from primary sources in a scholarly work). This choice, however, is intimately connected to my thesis and method. Eth-nographer Richard Price, in his book First Time, takes the radical stance of physically separating the transmitted text and his own commentary on the page in order to highlight the interaction between the source and the interpreter. Like Price, I ask the reader to peruse the quoted source-text (even if it is familiar), read my analysis, and then reflect again on the text. The texts, of course, stand on their own for any who choose to read them. But because these texts are so opaque to modern sensibilities, they require explication. My task as the interpreter is to present ways of understanding those texts by bringing together the different strands I think intertwined in their production and reception. This method of moving back and forth between text and context is at the heart of this endeavor and is the reason for my inclusion of whole remedies or stories in this book. The charm texts reveal a worldview very different from our own, one worth exploring in all of its richness and diversity.

1

POPULAR RELIGION
THE PROCESS OF CONVERSION

Consider the following ceremony for blessing the fields, found on a few
folios from the late tenth or early eleventh century, and ponder the contexts
in which it was developed, performed, and written.

ÆCERBOT [FIELD REMEDY] RITUAL[1]

Here is the remedy, how you may better your land, if it will not
grow well or if some harmful thing has been done to it by a sorcerer
[dry] or by a poisoner [lyblace].[2]

Take then at night, before dawn, four sods from four sides of the
land, and mark where they were before.

Then take oil and honey and yeast, and milk of each animal that is
on the land, and a piece of each type of tree that grows on the land,
except hard beams, and a piece of each herb known by name, except

burdock [*glappan*] only,[3] and put then holy water thereon, and drip it three times on the base of the sods, and say then these words:

Crescite, grow, et multiplicamini, and multiply, et replete, and fill, terre, the earth. In nomine patris et filii et spiritus sancti sit benedicti. [In the name of the father and the son and the holy spirit be blessed.] And the Pater noster [Our Father] as often as the other.

And then bear the sods into church, and let a masspriest sing four masses over the sods, and let someone turn the green [sides] to the altar, and after that let someone bring the sods to where they were before, before the sun sets.

And have made for them four signs of Christ [crosses] of quickbeam and write on each end: Matthew and Mark, Luke, and John. Lay that sign of Christ in the bottom of the pit [where each sod had been cut out], saying then: crux Matheus, crux Marcus, crux Lucas, crux sanctus Iohannes.

Take then the sods and set them down there on [the crosses], and say then nine times these words, Crescite [grow], and as often the Pater noster, and turn then to the east, and bow nine times humbly, and speak then these words:

> Eastwards I stand, for mercies I pray,
> I pray the great domine [lord], I pray the powerful lord,
> I pray the holy guardian of heaven-kingdom,
> earth I pray and sky
> and the true sancta [holy] Mary
> and heaven's might and high hall,
> that I may this charm [*galdor*] by the gift of the lord
> open with [my] teeth through firm thought,
> to call forth these plants for our worldly use,
> to fill this land with firm belief,
> to beautify this grassy turf, as the wiseman said
> that he would have riches on earth who alms
> gave with justice by the grace of the lord.

Then turn thrice with the sun's course, stretch then out lengthwise and enumerate there the litanies and say then: Sanctus, sanctus, sanctus to the end. Sing then Benedicite with outstretched arms and Magnificat and Pater noster thrice, and commend it [the land] to Christ and saint Mary and the holy cross for praise and for worship and for the benefit of the one who owns that land and all those who are serving under him.[4] When all that is done, then let a man take unknown seed from beggars and give them twice as much as he took from them, and let him gather all his plough tools together; then let him bore a hole in the beam [of the plough, putting in] incense and fennel and hallowed soap and hallowed salt. Take then that seed, set it on the plough's body, say then:

Erce, Erce, Erce,[5]   earth's mother,
May the all-ruler grant you,   the eternal lord,
fields growing   and flourishing,
propagating   and strengthening,
tall shafts,   bright crops,
and broad   barley crops,
and white   wheat crops,
and all   earth's crops.
May the eternal lord   grant him,
and his holy ones,   who are in heaven,
that his produce be guarded   against any enemies whatsoever,
and that it be safe   against any harm at all,
from poisons [lyblaca]   sown around the land.
Now I bid the Master,   who shaped this world,
that there be no speaking-woman [cwidol wif]   nor artful man
    [cræftig man][6]
that can overturn   these words thus spoken.

Then let a man drive forth the plough and the first furrow cut, say then:

Whole may you be [Be well] earth,   mother of men!
May you be growing   in God's embrace,
with food filled   for the needs of men.

Take then each kind of flour and have someone bake a loaf [the size of] a hand's palm and knead it with milk and with holy water and lay it under the first furrow. Say then:

Field full of food   for mankind,
bright-blooming,   you are blessed
in the holy name   of the one who shaped heaven
and the earth   on which we live;
the God, the one who made the ground,   grant us the gift of
    growing,
that for us each grain   might come to use.

Say then thrice Crescite in nomine patris, sit benedicti [Grow in the name of the father, be blessed]. Amen and Pater noster three times.

How should we read this ceremony for blessing the fields? As pagan or Christian? Demonic or Godly? Manipulative magic or supplicative prayer? By the standards of a later age, this remedy is problematic because it defies the neat categories used to judge what is Christian or rational. The text was the product of the literate clergy who represented the formal church in late Saxon England. Yet it has enough identifiably pre-Christian elements to cause consternation among many later theologians and modern scholars, who see it as evidence of the retention of paganism in the practice of magic and as a failure of the Christianizing effort in the late Saxon church. My argument in this work is that the Christian charms, such as the formulas in the remedy above and the elf charms analyzed in Chapter 5, are not some kind of "Christian magic" demonstrating the weakness of early medieval Christianity but constitute evidence of the religion's success in conversion by accommodating Anglo-Saxon culture. This book proposes a different model for understanding Christian conversion, one that allows us to consider these folk rituals within their own context. This model is popular religion, a modern construct that examines the broader religious experience of a society.

Popular religion, as one facet of a larger, complex culture, consists of those beliefs and practices common to the majority of the believers. This popular religion encompasses the whole of Christianity, including the formal aspects of the religion as well as the general religious experience of daily life. These popular practices include rituals marking the cycles of life (birth, marriage, and death) or combating the mysterious (illness and danger) or assuring spiritual security (the afterlife). Popular belief was reflected in those rituals and in other symbols exhibited in the society, such as paintings, shrines, and relics.

The cultural history approach employed here departs from traditional church history studies that focus on the well-defined area of formal Christianity—the institution of the church with its hierarchy of clergy and its canons, councils, and theological constructs.[7] Representatives of this formal religion, the missionaries, reformers, and church historians, present conversion as a dramatic shift in religious orientation, a radical transformation in belief—a definition that is still common today. Writers such as Gregory of Tours, Bede, Ælfric, and Wulfstan follow a long tradition dating back to Eusebius and Augustine that tends to portray the world in a dualistic fashion, pagan versus Christian, magic versus miracle, Devil versus God. Conversion for them is therefore a dramatic event switching from one side to the other.

This formal religion, however, is only a subset of a larger whole; popular religion encompasses all practicing Christians and all everyday practices and beliefs. Expanding our view to this larger Christian community allows us to see the gradual nature of conversion. Under the influence of recent cultural history, the study of popular religion has begun to elucidate the slower processes of accommodation between culture and religion in everyday life that show how Christianity became an integral part of culture and, vice versa, how emerging European cultures changed Christianity.

In the context of popular religion, then, conversion is both an event and a process whereby an individual or a group changes religious orientation, in both belief and practice. Even though early Christian and medieval narratives frequently emphasize conversion as a dramatic event for a prominent individual and his or her society, these narratives also suggest that it was a dynamic process stretched over time involving a great deal of cultural assimilation between the imported Romano-Christian religion and the native folklife of the various "Germanic" peoples settling in Europe.[8] This acculturation process creates many gray areas, containing practices that do not fit into tidy categories and are subject to differing interpretations, such as the Christian charms against the attack of elves examined at length in Chapter 5.

Late Saxon England, circa 900–1050, was a dynamic period of growth for popular religion, as seen in expanding local churches and in more documents recording folk religious remedies. In order to understand popular religious practices in this period, we need to place them in the context of this gradual process of cultural conversion, in which Germanic folklore and Christian belief bled into each other as much or more than they sought to destroy each other. Instead of focusing, as many histories do, on the traditional dualistic view of oppositions in conversion (magic versus religion, for example), this study examines the middle ground, the gray area of encounter and accommodation between Germanic cultures and the incoming Christian traditions.

The Field Remedy quoted at the outset is an excellent example of a ritual that needs to be seen in the context of a developing popular Christianity.[9] In its invocation of both Father God and Mother Earth (subordinated here to the Allruler) and in its appeal to the combined forces of earth, sky, Mary, and Heaven, it draws on both the Germanic and Christian traditions in an unselfconscious way. The multiple spiritual agencies, mostly chthonic in nature, referenced in this remedy show continuity from Germanic animistic belief, and yet the use of masses and prayers and the ultimate appeal to a supreme divinity demonstrate the overlordship of Christianity. It is more appropriate, then, to see these practices as the retention of Germanic folklore in a popular Christianity rather than as the continuance of paganism as a religious system.

Folk medical remedies, merging across the boundaries into the spiritual cures found in liturgy, are one clear type of evidence illustrating the conversion of Germanic folkways to Christianity or, to put it the other way, the adaptation of Christianity to Germanic ways. Anglo-Saxon charms against the attack of invisible elves, and their demonization in late Saxon remedies, exist in sufficient numbers in the medical manuscripts to show a variety of accommodation techniques that reveal this conversion process. These middle practices, as I term them, symbolize a unique creation, an Anglo-Saxon Christianity. This model of popular religion thus highlights the flash points between the formal religion and the popular, the areas where some kind of negotiation between the two took place. Folklore as an areligious concept is therefore a more appropriate term than paganism or magic to describe the transmission of Germanic practices and beliefs that ultimately lost their pagan context as they were integrated into popular Christianity.

I am arguing here for a more favorable view than that reflected in previous scholarship of this mixture of Germanic folklore and Christian belief: not as evidence of the lowest, degenerate fringe of a dominant Christian orthodoxy (the older view prominent in nineteenth- and early twentieth-century treatment of charms) or even as evidence of the failure of Christianization in the face of a recalcitrant pagan population (the more recent view promulgated especially by Jacques Le Goff), but as evidence of the dynamic interaction that takes place between a native culture and an introduced religion.[10] This is Christianity succeeding by way of acculturation and Germanic culture triumphing in transformation. Neither is the passive victim of the other. Likewise, most ordinary Anglo-Saxon Christians were not suffering from a split personality; rather, they created a wholeness out of their mixed heritages. Whether to refer to this hybridization process as Christianizing the Anglo-Saxons or as Germanicizing Christianity is problematic. The biblical analogy of new wine in old skins shows the dilemma of trying to understand this transformation: Is Christianity the new wine put into old skins? Or is it the new skin into which old wine is poured? These questions about form and substance defy precise answers because they are a matter of perspective.

This first chapter reviews some of the various historiographical perspectives on the issue of Christianization and outlines a model for understanding popular religion and conversion. The second and third chapters explore the context for the development of late Saxon popular religion by examining the tensions between local clergy and reform leaders. Chapter 4 analyzes the specific context for the charms in the intermingling of medicine, liturgy, and folklore. Chapter 5 demonstrates how the elf charms in particular are a hybrid of these diverse, intertwining contexts and constitute middle practices that reveal the negotiated territory between popular and formal religion in the process of cultural conversion in the late Saxon world.

Historiographical Perspectives

Popular religion as a modern construct is part of the cultural history movement toward democratizing and diversifying history. Its broader vision adds new perspectives to the controversy over the Christianization of Europe. The nineteenth-century view of the Middle Ages as "an Age of Faith," dominated by an essentially Catholic worldview, came under attack in the 1970s in a de-Christianizing effort begun in part by Jean Delumeau. As historians interested in popular culture brought to light more and more exceptions to the rule, evidence of magic or paganism, the whole notion of a Christian society was discredited as an idea limited to the minority elite of medieval society. However, the pendulum is now swinging back from this extreme reaction to something between the traditional, "Christian society" view and the un-Christianized view, and a dynamic synthesis between Christianity and folk cultures is being postulated.[11] This middle position works if popular culture is studied as a meeting ground between elite and folk cultures and not as the antithesis of "high" culture. In other words, if popular culture assimilated and internalized Christianity through interaction with the formal religion, then the label of Christian society can be used to describe medieval culture as a whole; however, it will not be the narrow, highly controlled Christianity of the religious elite.

The difficulty with the reactionary view positing an incomplete Christianization is that it depends on an assumed model of pure religion rather than on a complex, diverse, and changing one.[12] The de-Christianizing approach accepts from the traditional view the elite definition of religion, that Christianity in its purest form is represented best in the expressions of theologians and churchmen; deviations from or additions to this pure doctrine and ritual are aberrations and therefore "less Christian" or, worse yet, not Christian at all. This definition gives primacy to abstract concepts and literacy over symbolic rituals and devalues the religious comprehension of those who "mindlessly" participate in religious rituals without being able to articulate the meanings behind them.[13]

If, however, the religion is defined not just by its elite leaders but by the behaviors and norms of all of its adherents, then Christianity becomes a broader and more pervasive phenomenon in society. The approach of cultural history, under the rubric of *mentalités* in the Annales school and through the influence of ethnography, offers a way to read the inarticulate rituals of popular behavior and to view them as just as meaningful as clearly articulated theological statements.[14] Reading rituals as meaningful is more in line with medieval views, which closely linked word and ritual and read material objects allegorically, without the separation between abstract and concrete that the modern era posits. This new, synthetic approach, evident in the work of Aron Gurevich, John Van Engen, Alexander Murray, and Richard Kieckhefer, refuses to regard medieval society from either an exclusively elite or a popular perspective, but examines the interaction between the two perspectives.[15] The advantage of looking at this boundary rather than the polarization between popular and elite is in seeing the tremendous diversity of practices in light of the norms of the times that produced them. That very diversity of traditions and ideas exhibited in the Christian charms was the strength of late Saxon culture and religion, forming the foundation of Christian practice over the coming centuries. Adaptability in culture and religion is a more highly valued trait in cultural history than the homogenization and single-minded purity emphasized in traditional political and ecclesiastical historiography.

However, one of the persistent legacies of the cultural history focus on the non-Christian character of medieval popular religion is this dualism of popular and elite. Because scholars working from a popular religion paradigm, such as Raoul Manselli, Michel Vovelle, and E. Delaruelle, are reacting to the traditional historical model of a dominant church seen institutionally and theologically, they define popular culture or religion in opposition to this dominant elite.[16] Through this adversarial process they developed a dialectical model for religion, using various labels for the two components: *religion savante* and *religion populaire*, official and unofficial religion, great and little tradition, reflective few and unreflective many, intellectuals and the masses, the elite and the nonelite or "the people," literate and illiterate, and clergy and laity.[17] Some of these terms have negative connotations (unofficial, little, nonelite); others are vague (the masses, the people). The synthetic model proposed here sidesteps these dualities by treating both popular and formal religion as overlapping spheres of influence and by situating formal religion as a subset of the larger popular religion. The term *formal* is a more neutral term than *elite* for describing the institution of the church as one part, but by no means the whole, of Christian society.

Scholars of the high and late Middles Ages have productively applied this duality of popular versus formal religion. Raoul Manselli, in his *La religion populaire au moyen âge*, succinctly defines popular religion as concerned with everyday life and emotive and practical values in contrast to *religion savante* or learned religion, which is concerned with logical values. Manselli moves this duality in the right direction by emphasizing the "dialectical rapport" of conflict and mutual influence between the two.[18] Other scholars simply take popular religion as a given and devote their attention to recounting it. E. Delaruelle, in *La piété populaire au moyen âge*, effectively describes popular religious practice as an entity separate from elite religion by establishing specific sources for popular religion, such as saints' lives, pilgrimages, artifacts, and images such as the cross. Rosalind and Christopher Brooke, in *Popular Religion in the Middle Ages*, do not define popular religion other than to focus attention on ordinary lay people and describe the phenomenon by narrating many case histories.[19] This descriptive approach is useful but avoids the issue of definition and the problem of an artificial separation between popular and formal religion.

Only recently have medievalists begun to challenge this duality. For example, Aron Gurevich points out that despite the contradictions (pagan and Christian, popular and elite) in the medieval worldview as expressed in the surviving evidence, these two different, seemingly contradictory cultures were combined in the medieval consciousness.[20] Just as the term *folklore* avoids the pagan-versus-Christian duality, so too the interaction of the popular and formal duality can usefully create a middle ground for study. The concept of a shared consciousness produced in the interchange between popular and formal provides the basis for the model of popular religion described below, which focuses on middle practices.

Conversion and Magic

The study of popular religion using ethnographic models creates new possibilities for understanding conversion and so-called magic. While this approach is becoming common in high and late medieval studies, it has barely touched the early Middle Ages, with Anglo-Saxonists as perhaps the most unmoved by these developments. This book addresses that need, bringing to bear a number of disciplines and sources on the problem of conversion as exhibited in the Christian charms. The relative paucity of work in Anglo-Saxon studies utilizing this more synthetic view of cultural history is partly the product of certain conservative and ultimately deadening forces within the discipline that favor the study of text and language while avoiding the problematic nature of philology's scientific origins, a trend elucidated by Allen Frantzen in his *Desire for Origins*.[21] Most Anglo-

Saxonists, in the picturesque language of Ladurie, are "truffle-hunters," more comfortable in the detailed study of a word, a text, or an artifact, instead of "parachutists," willing to risk looking at the whole picture. Both, as Richard Hodges argues, are essential for the discipline.[22]

The issue of conversion, prominent in the early medieval period, is ripe for this new kind of cultural study. The problem of the Christianization of early medieval Europe is widely debated at various levels, from the big picture of whole societies down to individual poems or even lines of poems: Is Beowulf Christian? Did Guthrum "really" convert? Are Christmas trees evidence of continuing paganism? The ways in which these questions have been addressed, reframed, or rejected have varied with the changes in scholarly currents but have yet to take advantage fully of developments in ethnographic history, as adapted from anthropology. This book pursues such an ethnographic approach with the aim of getting inside the early medieval worldview in a sympathetic way.[23]

A few recent works have begun to apply these new methods to Anglo-Saxon studies. For example, Stephen Glosecki, in *Shamanism and Old English Poetry*, makes the radical suggestion that the great works so beloved by modern literary critics represent something far deeper and older than the aesthetics of poetry; he argues for a strong sense of the power of words over objects, of the concrete objectivity of language as a thing of power. By using the "primitive" concept of the shaman, Glosecki shocks the reader out of the anachronism of reading Anglo-Saxon poetry through the lens of modern aesthetics and reverence for the classic texts canonized in the literature curriculum.

One of the most prominent issues to arise in this shift of ideas about Christianization concerns the definition of magic. Valerie Flint's book, *The Rise of Magic in Early Medieval Europe*, follows the de-Christianizing trend of cultural history described above. She moves the focus away from Christianization as a one-way and dominant force toward an active Germanic culture that is no longer the passive victim of a new religion. Christianity becomes the victim of a Germanicizing process that subverts the Christianizing effort of missionaries and reformers, who succumb to the temptation to mix a little magic into their religion. James C. Russell, in *The Germanization of Early Medieval Christianity*, also employs this reverse model of emphasizing the compromised position of Christianity in relation to paganism, bringing in a modern sociological construct of religion ("BAVB") and fitting the evidence into that mold.[24] The result, in these interpretations, is a syncretic Germanic Christianity that can include the oxymoron "Christian magic," a notion developed by Keith Thomas (in his chapter "The Magic of the Medieval Church" in *Religion and the Decline of Magic*) and carried backward by Flint.

This construct of a European magical religion is anachronistic; it presupposes a distinction between magic and religion (or science) that developed only later. The model of the rise and decline of magic projected in Flint's and Thomas's titles is based on a progressive view in which magic is superseded by superior religion, in turn superseded by the more rational science. This view is increasingly coming under attack by anthropologists such as Stanley Tambiah in his *Magic, Science, Religion, and the Scope of Rationality*. Two other scholars have responded to Flint's model in review articles. Alexander Murray ("Missionaries and Magic") reflects on the simplified two-sidedness of her definitions, questioning the boundary of magic and religion as both inconstant and uncertain. Murray urges instead a softer view, one that allows for both intellectuals and rustics to partake of both modes of rationality, the magical and the religious, without being schizophrenic. Richard Kieckhefer ("The Specific Rationality of Medieval Magic") also critiques Flint's definition of magic as nonrational by exploring the rational principles underlying so-called magical practices. Kieckhefer offers his own definition of magic as a crossroads in his book on the subject (*Magic in the Middle Ages*). What both critiques reject is the negative view of medieval participants in popular religion: the masses as ignorant of what they should have known was magic/not Christian, and the church leaders as knowingly perpetuating a fraud, purposefully demeaning Christianity by compromising it with pagan magic. Both reviewers suggest a different model that can accommodate the mixture of apparent opposites (at least to our minds) without de-Christianizing medieval society.

The construct of popular religion introduced here proposes to take a similarly sympathetic approach to the views in place in the Anglo-Saxon world prior to the magic-religion-science distinctions that became such a prominent feature of Europe's intellectual landscape after the twelfth century. This exploration of Anglo-Saxon worldviews allows for a great deal of blending between so-called magic practices, such as charms, and Christian rituals, such as the mass, simply because so many of these practices shared a common sensibility. The transformative power of words to alter bread and wine or to enchant an herb hint at this shared, overlapping worldview.

Magic, Religion, Science, and Culture

This scholarly debate over definitions of magic in relation to religion or science is at the heart of the conversion issue and the construction of a model for popular religion. Undergirding the notion of popular religion employed in this book are the definitions of *religion, science,* and *magic* as "modes of rationality," as different systems of thought developed in response to life or as human strategies of survival for organizing perceptions and behaviors.[25] The study of Christianity as a religion in some past time is a study of the forms and ideas held by the people participating in the religion, both clergy and laity, and what these forms and ideas meant to them.[26] The Latin-rooted science as a concept represents a particular mode of rationality developed in Euro-American culture that is based on an assumption of the reliability of knowledge produced by human reason. In the medieval view, science worked together with revelatory knowledge. Thus in its medieval origins science and theology were complementary modes of rationality that functioned indistinguishably in the prescholastic period of the early Middle Ages.[27] Magic in European usage is a category of exclusion, used to define an unacceptable way of thinking as either the opposite of religion or of science. Early medieval Christians defined magic as a rejected category of practices based on their religious worldview and associated it with the Devil; to speak of a Christian use of magic in Christian rituals is therefore pointless.[28]

Religion, science, and *magic* are culture- and time-specific terms that have a complex relationship to culture, and therefore popular religion. Complexity and diversity in culture means recognizing the interrelatedness of various phenomena in a culture, and the potential for contested meanings.[29] Religion is one component in culture; likewise, religions do not exist outside of cultures, so religions have cultural aspects. In the study of Anglo-Saxon culture, overlapping, sometimes competing views grow and change in diverse ways geographically and over time, producing a uniquely "Anglo-Saxon" culture different from other areas and times. When the various Germanic groups in Europe, including the Anglo-Saxons, converted to Christianity, they did not abandon their culture with their religion; they ostensibly gave up certain religious beliefs and adopted new ones. Therefore, Germanic cultural traits continued. Christianity as a religion does not exist in a vacuum but in cultural settings, whether Jewish, Roman, or Germanic. When Germanic peoples converted to Roman Christianity, they assimilated some Roman cultural features embedded in their new religion. Similarly, Christianity among the Germanic peoples evolved into Germanic versions.

This complexity of religion and culture manifests itself in the phases of conversion in the early Middle Ages. Because conversion is a process as well as an event, it involves gradual transformations of existing cultural practices at the same time that new definitions of what is Christian or pagan, magic or miracle, are evolving. The question "What is Christian?" has multiple answers in the late Saxon world. The multiplicity of views expressed even among the literate indicates a much greater diversity throughout the general population. From the words of reformers, to poetry, to medical remedies, to popular sermons, to laws, we see a range of attitudes that hints at a much larger popular religious transformation taking place.

The duality of pagan versus Christian, or magic versus religion, is an inadequate model for understanding this transformation because it gives primacy to a literate mentality that was only just beginning to emerge in the late Saxon period. The dualistic thinking of reform-minded clergy making distinctions between Christian and pagan, miracle and magic, exists in a creative tension with the wider and slower processes of accommodation and assimilation that form a larger, if less visible, aspect of Christianization, and more influential in the long run. The tension between these forces, then, and the consequent Germanicizing of Christianity, is not so much a symptom of a failure of the Christianizing effort but evidence of its gradual success.

A Model for Medieval Popular Religion

Popular religion is a modern construct used to examine one facet of a larger, complex culture. This construct has greater breadth and depth than the traditional approach that examines the formal church. Popular religion consists of those beliefs and practices shared by the majority of the believers. Rather than being a separate, opposite phenomenon from elite or formal religion, it embraces the whole of Christianity.[30] Its inclusivity encompasses the formal aspects of the religion as well as the general religious experience of daily life.

These two categories, popular and formal, are overlapping spheres, with the formal nestled almost completely within the popular. (See fig. 1.2.)[31] The popular is the more comprehensive and yet more amorphous sphere, incorporating the widest population and practice. The formal sphere is smaller and tighter, making up a self-defined dominant minority within the total practice of the religion. Since "secret" doctrines or rituals are antithetical to the Christian tradition, it is hard to locate any formal church practices that would fall outside popular religion—perhaps certain abstruse theological constructs.[32] In general, all doctrine and ritual technically belonged to the entire Christian community, whether presented formally in Latin or explained in the vernacular for lay persons. Likewise, the formal church did not exist in isolation from the culture it inhabited; churchmen and scholars were Anglo-Saxons too. A common Christian worldview was shared by both popular religion and the formal religion. For example, the Field Remedy assumed that words have power over natural objects, whether the words were Anglo-Saxon folk charms or Latin masses and prayers.

Popular religion and formal religion thus have a symbiotic relationship within a shared culture, each actively engaged with the other. The dynamism of medieval Christian society lies in this symbiosis. Christian charms, by their combination of popular and formal, are a window into the Anglo-Saxon Christian mentality, into an intriguing holistic worldview that effectively brings together several heritages, Germanic and Roman Christian, to form a new, resilient culture. The strength of this culture only becomes clear when the whole of it is viewed in all of its diversity, with all of its apparent contradictions. The idea of popular religion gives us this view.

Popular versus Formal

Popular religion is the more inclusive category since it is concerned with the general religious beliefs and practices of the whole community, not with select individuals or specific institutions. Its commonality makes it hard to define; the "majority" of believers is relative to time and place and subject to regional variations (as demonstrated in recent and controversial works by Emmanuel Le Roy Ladurie and Carlo Ginzburg).[33] Late Saxon England was a period of tremendous change and regional variation (partly due to the Viking invasions), as explored in Chapter 2; yet the processes at work in England in this period indicate some common trends in popularizing Christianity.

The inclusivity of popular religion means that only a few erudite expressions of doctrine were wholly outside the popular religious experience. For example, the Nicene Creed concept of *homoousios* (Christ as the same essence as God) was probably known only to a few scholars in the early Middle Ages; however, the belief in Christ as God was well known and hence "popular." But all the rest of the formal church apparatus was popular in the sense that the rituals were performed in the context of the larger population. The Latin of the Field Remedy was unintelligible to lay audiences but was nonetheless performed for their benefit and formed part of their consciousness of the power of the Christian religion.

Within this rather amorphous category of Christian popular religion the formal aspects of the religion thus constituted a distinct area that included the institution of the church (its hierarchy, councils, and laws) and its logical system of doctrines and practices. Because the sphere of formal religion is so easily defined and prominent in the surviving evidence, it tends to receive the most attention and the most credit in formulations of what medieval Christianity was. The goal of studying popular religion is to place this narrow, articulate formal religion in a broader, less articulate context. Because the surviving evidence was generated by the formal environment, the most fertile ground for exploring popular religion is at the textual boundary between popular and formal. Through this permeable membrane popular and formal ideas flowed back and forth, and the literate, formal side recorded these ideas in texts. This fluid boundary reveals evidence of a common Christian sensibility in middle practices that contain elements from both the popular and the formal. In this middle ground we find documents by the formal religion aimed at the popular, and evidence of popular ideas working their way into the formal documents. The bilingual, bicultural Field Remedy is a case in point. The vernacular invocations to Mother Earth are combined with the Latin liturgy addressing Father God, but in a subordinate role—it is the Allruler who grants to Mother Earth the power to grow and prosper.

The way the formal acts in relation to the popular is an issue of power. Formal religion consisted of the institution of the church with its clerical hierarchies, its canons, and its councils. Formal religion also included the intellectual aspect: doctrines and practices carefully formulated based on logically derived values.[34] The formal religion was concerned with consistency with doctrinal tradition and the functioning of the church hierarchy. The members operating in this group, mainly churchmen, are the "professionals of culture" who are dominant because they combine knowledge and power.[35] The tremendous power of literacy over orality is exhibited in the Field Remedy. The traditionally oral charms were written down in full and hence codified; the Latin liturgy and prayers, already available in written form and theoretically memorized by the priest, were merely invoked in the instructions ("Say the Pater noster"). The literate priesthood, using their hierarchical authority, took control of this popular event, formalizing it into a standardized ritual. This textualization, however, did not inhibit the continued oral performance of the ritual in variant forms reflecting local communal interests. The text of the Field Remedy we have, existing on that boundary between the popular and the formal, hints at the oral performances now lost to us.

Popular religion is the medium that allows us to look at these communal interests and needs. It is a product of the community as a whole; it is the general, everyday practice of the religion, including the experience of the formal religion. The emotive and practical values of popular religion were expressed in forms that the community viewed as timeless repositories of truth. Such practices were concerned with the alleviation of the mysterious elements of life—death, disease, and disaster. The Field Remedy is a practical preventive cure, used to ward off a bad harvest. The emotive values of popular religion are reflected in this traditional, communal ritual. The kinetic experience of gathering the produce, making the loaves, setting all these items in the church, placing them in the four holes, and blessing the plow before it begins the furrow was tremendously meaningful to the participants, presumably the whole manor or village, from lord and bailiff down to the lowliest peasant, with the priest officiating.

Bridges between Popular and Formal

Thus the dynamism of medieval religious culture occurred in the interaction of the spheres of popular and formal religion.[36] Several bridges link these two spheres, pairs of opposites that have often been mistakenly identified with only popular religion or only formal religion. Formal and popular religion should not be defined exclusively by class (clergy versus laity), type of expression (doctrine versus practice), mode of transmission (literate versus oral), or way of understanding (knowing versus doing). Rather, these dynamics should be seen as part of the connection between popular and formal, not as part of the separation between them.

One of the traditional ways of thinking about formal versus popular religion is according to class boundaries (priests versus laity), a distinction that is misleading because it does not take into consideration the shared culture of both groups.[37] Certainly, the clergy played a larger role in formal religion than did the laity, since priests, bishops, and popes maintained the church structure. Yet since the clergy were the leaders in doctrine and practice, they were responsible for making Christianity intelligible to their congregations, a process that involved popularizing doctrines and practices. This process of mutual assimilation through the activities of the priest was even more fluid during the early Middle Ages, when the clergy were not sharply separated from and elevated above the laity, particularly the priests in small, local churches discussed in Chapter 2. Hence, the clergy as a class stand as one form of mediation between the formal and the popular religion, evident in the priest's role in the communal ritual of the Field Remedy.

Likewise with the type of religious expression, identifying doctrine solely with the formal and practice with the popular is problematic. Doctrine does fall more into the province of formal religion than it does popular because formal religion was concerned with the logical expression of belief and the maintenance of tradition. But practice has a role equal with that of doctrine in formal religion because of the need to have uniform rituals clearly expressing Christian truth. Formal religion sought to insure consistency in Christian doctrine and practice. Popular religion, on the other hand, was less concerned with doctrinal statements and more concerned with the practical expression and implications of those truths as expressed in rituals.[38] Recognizing this overlap of doctrine and practice allows for interchange between popular and formal in a zone that produces rituals such as Christian charms. The Field Remedy example begs the question of doctrine versus practice; the ritual was clearly practical in nature but incorporated doctrinal truths about God, nature, and humankind. Priest and people performed the words and the actions together as an integrated whole expressing communally held truths and values.

In a similar fashion, the dynamic of literate versus oral in the mode of transmission shows the overlap between popular and formal. The formal church was primarily textual since it was oriented toward providing a written tradition that could maintain consistency in doctrine and practice. This concern for logical values was expressed analytically in texts by the literate who lived in their own enclaves, such as cathedral chapters or monasteries. These "textual communities," as Brian Stock calls them, were centers of formal religion, spheres of influence in Christianity.[39] Popular religion, however, functioned mostly through oral transmission and thus is largely lost to us except where the formal religion recorded its practices and beliefs in texts.[40] Other texts that might fall into the popular sphere are those written by representatives of the formal religion and aimed at the populace.[41] Both types of literature are revealing for popular religion: sermons and saints' lives reflect formal concerns about the popular comprehension of Christian truth; oral rituals such as charms become textual/Christian in the hands of the formal religion, carrying folk knowledge into the texts. The Field Remedy falls into this latter category. What is important about the ritual is not just its pagan oral roots but its incorporation into a manuscript so that it becomes a formalized Christian ritual.

These distinctions of class, expression, and transmission conceal a deeper dynamic, that between knowing and doing. As discussed earlier, the literate values of theologians as well as of modern scholars tend to place a premium on knowledge articulated in the written word rather than on belief expressed only through rituals and other oral performances. In general, the formal religion appears to be oriented more toward knowing as a way of being, while the popular is oriented more toward doing as a way of being. The primacy of abstract thought in subsequent intellectual history has led to the assumption that those who "know" are somehow experiencing the religion in a deeper way than those who merely do. But the swing toward studying popular religion has led to a greater respect for the meaningfulness of doing as a way of experiencing and expressing belief.[42]

The relationship of knowing, being, and doing is much more complex than a set of dichotomies. Ritual actions can be read as "texts" with just as much meaning as printed words. The popular mind "thinks with things" (ritual actions, objects, icons) rather than abstract constructs, and this kind of material thinking can lead to just as much internalization of the ideas as being able to explain them in conceptual terms.[43] Illiteracy and its association with a lack of abstract thinking, contrary to the biases of some intellectuals, are not necessarily barriers to religious belief or religious experience; material thinking is simply a different way of thinking that, from the point of view of those with highly developed abstractive abilities, is limited and borders on the "superstitious" through its lack of critical judgment.[44] The Field Remedy was meaningful in different ways to all its participants, the object-oriented laity and the literate clergy, the sod-toting man and the Latin-spouting priest. In a culture steeped in animistic thinking, the physicality of this ritual reflects a deep spirituality in which all things were animated with spiritual presence. The ritual allowed the participants to connect with that spiritual realm through the material reality of crops and animals as well as through the potency of the mysteriously spoken words.

The other aspect of this problem of intellectual bias is that the formal church appears to control the meaning in the rituals, leading to the suspicion that the acts were not meaningful to the popular participants. Part of the problem is the nature of the evidence as literate and hence primarily from the formal point of view. The danger is in separating the literate from the illiterate along the lines of the formal versus the popular, forgetting that both share the same culture. We lose sight of the fact that the authors of literate records were not just using popular folklore as part of some propaganda for the church, but they lived in folk culture just as much as the popular participants did because folkways were part of a shared culture.[45] Behind the written development of the Field Remedy must lie some real events. The players and the setting can be read in the text: an agricultural environment; an Anglo-Saxon priest, not necessarily a well-educated one, who knew both the folk tradition of blessing the fields and the Christian liturgy and who was responding to very real needs among a rural, Christian populace; an opposition between a Christian wiseman reciting Latin and a rival, excluded cunning man or woman; and an attempt on the part of both the priest and the populace to negotiate the boundary between popular and formal by combining both traditions. In this scenario, both the popular and the formal were attempting to adjust to the clash and synthesis of the Germanic and Christian cultures.

Examining the middle ground between popular and formal, pagan and Christian, in these interactions of clergy and laity, doctrine and practice, literacy and orality, creates a neutral space for examining the diversity of religious belief and practice. The middle practices I analyze here lie in between popular and formal. Likewise, the term folklore stands as a neutral concept for the transmission of Germanic beliefs and practices into the Christian era without the necessity of labeling them pagan. Because folklore is a carrier of culture, constantly in motion and endlessly diverse, it provides a bridge between these categories.

Conversion and Popular Religion

These bridges between popular religion and the formal religion demonstrate that there was a necessary dialectical rapport between the two, a dialectic consisting of conflict and assimilation during the initial phase of conversion in the sixth through eighth centuries and the later phase of reaction to the Viking presence and reform in the ninth through eleventh centuries. From the perspective of popular religion, conversion is both an event and a process. The "first contact" events as described in church histories emphasize conflict between the old and the new religions and highlight the radical transformation of belief, usually focusing on the decision of a ruler to convert: Clovis in Gregory of Tours's and other Frankish narratives, and Edwin, Ethelberht, and other rulers in Bede's account. These dramatic stories played a role in fostering conversion and unity in subsequent ages. However, for conversion to a new religion to have a long-lasting impact, it must spread beyond one individual and one moment's decision. In the dissemination of Christianity to larger numbers of ordinary people and into everyday life, we see less conflict and more acculturation taking place as part of a natural process: the placing of stone crosses artfully decorated with Germanic themes, the building of churches on older religious sites, and the development of liturgical remedies for common ailments. In this phase of conversion the mutual interchange, not the conflict, between popular and formal becomes critical.

This symbiotic relationship of popular and formal religion can manifest in several ways and can be observed from different perspectives, from the point of view of the formal church seeking to convert and reform (Christianization) and from the viewpoint of native converts actively adapting Christianity to their own cultural needs (Germanicization). From the formal, and traditional church history, point of view, two types of conversion strategies are visible: conflict/imposition and integration/adaptation.

The first strategy is open conflict between the two, in which the formal rejects certain popular practices as pagan or magical, evident particularly in the initial conversion events and in later reform efforts. Missionaries sought to replace paganism with Christianity, to get rid of unacceptable popular practices and to replace them with acceptable traditions. Likewise the goal of reform-minded clergy was to change the laity, to cause them to conform to the formal religion. This type of imposition or social control produced tension, visible in laws against certain pagan activities, such as divination, and laws regulating Christian participation in rituals, such as church attendance, tithe, and fasts. Zealous clergy condemned customs such as worshiping pagan deities or harming others through sorcery by clearly identifying these practices with the Devil and his malevolent and illusory powers. By invoking the Christian dualism of God and the Devil, these churchmen were effective in demonizing the enemy.

Linked to this formal agenda of extirpating popular/pagan traditions was their replacement with Christian customs. This substitution could be subtle or dramatic. The strategic placement of rood-trees (crosses) took the place of the trees used in pagan worship, which were sometimes forcefully removed (Boniface's famous battle with the Saxon tree, for example). The formal reaction against paganism led to the imposition of rituals and beliefs that originated in the formal structure, most of which the church communicated to the populace in some form, but not always in their full complexity. For example, the literate, formal religion used the Latinate theological language to discuss soteriology, while the vernacular parlance discussed salvation in a much more concrete fashion. Conflict and imposition reflect the formal church's aggressive approach to conversion.

A second strategy used by the formal religion was the integration of popular practices into the structure of the church and its texts. In its attempt to control popular religion, the church as the formal structure of Christianity also adopted some of the methods and practices—preferably the form rather than the content—of Germanic cultures. The most famous example in the Christianization of England is Pope Gregory I's instructions to Bishop Mellitus to adapt pagan buildings, festivals, and sacrifices for Christian use, so that the people might ascend "gradually step by step, and not in one leap."[46] Even in reform the church recognized the practical needs of its constituents and allowed the liturgy and the church to be used to counteract the evils of life, as in the Field Remedy's ritual of bringing the four pieces of sod into the church to have masses said over them. The Field Remedy more than likely had a pre-Christian predecessor now lost to us that utilized the charms addressed to nature. What matters more, however, is that at some point in its oral history a Christian practitioner coopted it, bringing in the liturgy; subsequently it reached that permeable boundary with the formal and was "textualized" and formalized through inclusion in a manuscript whose production the forces of formal religion, literate churchmen in centralized religious foundations, controlled.

The formal church used tradition and reason as the criteria governing this type of accommodation. The literate community evaluated material for incorporation into the textual canon and for promotion based on their reasoned understanding of the tradition—not, however, without conflict and uncertainty, as seen in the reform efforts of Ælfric and Wulfstan treated in Chapter 3. In the surviving late Saxon documents, remnants of these reform efforts reveal a spectrum of practices stretched between the clearly defined categories of magic and miracle. Certain actions, such as the animistic worship at trees, were never acceptable, popular or otherwise, even though worshiping at outdoor crosses appears as its physical counterpart in Christianity. Other folk practices, such as blessing a sick cow, clerical scribes incorporated into liturgical texts and thus gave them a logical foundation within formal Christian practice.[47]

As the intellectual development of Christian doctrine increased in complexity with the advent of scholasticism in the twelfth century, the gap between formal and popular widened, causing some previously acceptable popular practices to appear ridiculous in the eyes of the new rationalists.[48] For example, as scholastics developed the separation of natural and supernatural, healing practices involving ritual actions and words increasingly became identified as unnatural or magical. However, in the early Middle Ages these distinctions were not yet operative, and the line between formal and popular was much more fluid. Any given practice or idea could have moved from the realm of popular religion into formal religion and back.

The two strategies outlined above, conflict and integration, offer the point of view of the formal church, granting it agency in these changes (Christianization).[49] Since ideals and structures emanating from the literate elite do not adequately reflect a complete picture of early medieval Christianity, our perspective on conversion is incomplete unless we can see how Christianity permeated popular culture through language and practice in everyday life. Consequently we ought to look at the process of conversion from the other perspective, that of dynamic Germanic cultures converting to a new religion but adapting it to their worldviews (Germanicization).

From the point of view of popular culture, the mass is a ritualized charm, holy water and herbs are an efficacious mixture, and elves—as invisible agents causing illness and trouble—are properly demonized. Combining these two perspectives helps us see the strength of the folk Christianity in the Field Remedy. Despite its inclusion in a formal manuscript, this remedy demonstrates the power of Christianity in everyday life. It may have been further Christianized during the writing process, but clearly this ritual was at its core produced in a practical context. This ceremony represents communal sentiments about the interrelationship of humankind, nature, and God. Both the Germanic folk elements and the Christian elements were active agents in creating this example of a viable lay Anglo-Saxon Christianity.

Christianizing the Landscape and Germanizing Christianity

Evidence for this dual agency in the formation of Anglo-Saxon religion in the tenth and eleventh centuries is the focus of this book and is examined in depth in Chapters 4 and 5. However, I would like to apply briefly the theory of popular religion developed here to point out several ways in which this two-way transmission process was already at work in the centuries between first contact (circa 600) and the late Saxon church (circa 1000), first through a Christianizing of the landscape in the cult of the saints and second through a Germanicizing of Christian ideas as evidenced in literature and archaeology.

The cult of the saints, as established and fostered by church leaders, consciously or unconsciously made accommodations to the animistic beliefs of Germanic peoples. This accommodation is seen, for example, in the desire for local sites of worship focused on a specific and immediately accessible being such as a saint, and the need for sources of spiritual power to solve life's problems. The concept of saints' relics as a doorway between this world and the next developed in the late antique Roman-Christian synthesis but easily made itself at home in the worldviews of Germanic peoples in the early Middle Ages.[50]

In general the Germanic peoples monastic missionaries contacted were polytheistic with a strong animistic element in their practice. To them, all of nature was alive with spiritual entities, a very holistic view of the world that focused on nature as a source of food and healing, without much distinction between natural and supernatural forces. While the major deities, the Æsir and the Vanir, were honored by the male priests at the temples, they were also memorialized in stories and were part of the fabric of society. For example, their names were, and are, retained in the days of the week (Tyr or Tiw/Tuesday, Woden/Wednesday, Thor/Thursday, and Friga/Friday). Besides these major deities, lesser spiritual entities in trees, wells, and stones, who were propitiated with offerings by local people, inhabited the landscape. Elves, dwarves, and the Norns caused illness or other misfortune, for which cures were handed down in the folk memory.[51] Some of the elements of the belief in these entities were retained in the Field Remedy in the sense of an animate nature addressed as mother, in the use of symbolic elements of trees and other produce, and in the "offerings" planted in the pits in the four corners of the field.

The cult of the saints Christianized this animistic landscape, populating it with loci of Christian power by supplanting the holy trees, wells, and stones of pagan religion and setting up a revised calendar based on saints' festivals. In so doing, Christianity began penetrating everyday life and belief. Church leaders promoted saints by telling their stories as part of a conscious educational effort to spread Christian ideas among the populace and to encourage the laity to patronize saints' holy places. The miracles accomplished by saints at these sites served as validation for the truth of Christianity and a sign of the sanctity of God's chosen messenger, the saint, and by extension the church or monastery for whom the saint was a patron.[52]

This conflation of pagan and Christian holy sites seen in the cult of the saints is increasingly evident in tenth-century textual and archaeological remains. By this time Anglo-Saxon Christianity was emerging as a distinctive entity, different in its local flavor from the Roman Christianity initially imported from the continent. This Germanic-Christian synthesis can be found in the adaptation of the Anglo-Saxon language to Christian concepts, in the writing of texts reflecting a Germanic-Christian worldview, and in changing burial habits.

One example of the effects of this synthesis in the language is in the concept of lordship. The personal and reciprocal relationship between a lord and his vassal in Germanic society became a model for the personal relationship between God and a believer, who was frequently portrayed as a warrior for God. The Anglo-Saxon hlaford, modern lord, literally means "bread-source." This Germanic concept of lord as a giver of life and sustenance to his faithful retainers and the one to whom allegiance was owed was easily transmuted into the Christian concept of Christ as Lord, the source of life, the giver of bread (his body), in whom faith was placed. Likewise, Jesus' disciples were portrayed as thegns, the Anglo-Saxon knightly aristocracy.[53]

This Christian warrior ideal is evident throughout Anglo-Saxon art and literature in the merger or overlap of Germanic heroic and Christian images. The entire modern debate over *Beowulf* as Christian or pagan, both or neither, is evidence of this Anglo-Saxon duality and the difficulty of recapturing what these traditions meant to late Saxon culture. Likewise, the Franks Casket, with its marvelous mixture of Roman, Germanic, and Christian myths, demonstrates a unique and compelling synthesis of traditions.[54] The Franks Casket is a useful corrective to modern explanations of early medieval conversion in two respects. It first reminds us that the origins of a tradition, its earliest formulation, should not obscure or take precedence over the ways that the tradition is adapted. Romulus and Remus, the Adoration of the Magi, and Weland the Smith can coexist (see fig. 1.1). Second, the ivory carvings on the casket demonstrate that assimilation is a creative effort central to conversion. Conversion does not necessarily entail the obliteration of pre-Christian traditions but opens the possibility of cultural transformation.

This two-way transformation is evident in such Christian heroic literature as *Guthlac* and *The Dream of the Rood*. The Anglo-Saxon saint Guthlac (circa 700) was a young warrior who, upon seeing the death and destruction inherent in the warrior lifestyle, converted to a monastic existence, withdrawing into the fens of Lincolnshire. His biography, and the poem of his life in particular, not only followed the pattern of earlier saints' lives but incorporated secular warrior imagery, transforming the pacific monk into a "belligerent miles Christi" (soldier of Christ).[55] Guthlac's contests with spiritual forces in the wilderness resound with images of battles and hillforts.

> Good was Guthlac!   He bore in his spirit
> heavenly hope,   reached the salvation
> of eternal life.   An angel was close to him,
> faithful peace-guardian,   to him, who, as one of a few
> settled the borderland.   There he became to many
> an example in Britain,   when he ascended the mountain,
> blessed warrior,   hardy of battle.
> Geared himself eagerly   with spiritual
> weapons . . .   he blessed the land,
> as a station for himself   he first raised up

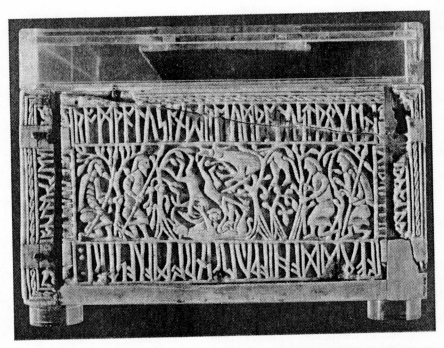

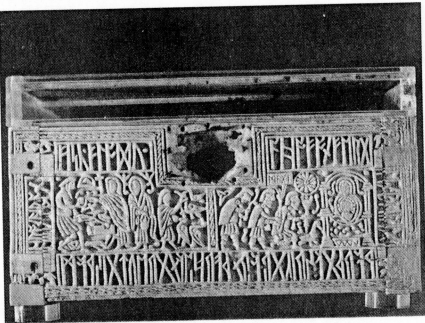

Figure 1.1. Franks Casket. Top: the story of Romulus and Remus on one end panel. Bottom: the story of *Weland* the Smith (left) and the *Adoration of the Magi* (right) on the front panel. (Copyright © British Museum)

Christ's rood,   where the champion overcame
many dangers.[56]

The imagery here is typical of the monastic sense of the wilderness as a place to conquer the Devil and convert the pagan. Guthlac's first act is to Christianize the landscape by setting up a cross, just as a hero might stake a spear or banner on conquered territory.

This mixture of the Germanic warrior ideology and Christian beliefs contained in Anglo-Saxon poetry strikes some modern readers as odd, but to the Anglo-Saxon Christian poet it made sense to idealize and imitate Christ as a heroic figure taking on the cross as a kind of battle. Perhaps the best example of this ideology is in the Anglo-Saxon poem *The Dream of the Rood*. This tenth-century poem personifies the cross, who presents himself to the dreamer as a noble warrior who faithfully stood by his lord (Christ) at his final battle ("There I dared not bow or break against my Lord's command").[57] The cross-narrator describes Christ not as passively submitting to the humiliation of crucifixion as the soldiers nail him to the cross but as actively mounting the cross himself. "Then the young warrior—who was God Almighty—stripped Himself, strong and resolute. He climbed upon the high gallows, brave in the sight of many, when he wished to redeem mankind."[58] This is a radical departure from the usual Christian emphasis on Christ's humility and submission to death. Heroic death in particular was a strong component of the Germanic *comitatus* (warband), and this warrior ethic was part of the pagan cosmology as represented in the Æsir. Thus the poem portrays Christ as aggressively taking on the cross as a battle in which his victory through death heroically saves his people. *Guthlac* and *The Dream of the Rood* contain powerful symbolism for Anglo-Saxon Christians, evidence of a successful acculturation process.

Death and its treatment are among the most revealing aspects of religious beliefs. The establishment of Christian cemeteries and the Christian symbolism used in burial are symptomatic of the Christianization of Germanic culture. Many of these cemeteries, in continuous use from pre-Christian time until long after, show layers of burial practices. Churches were sometimes founded at cemetery sites predating conversion; either the remains were exhumed and the land cleansed or the new place of worship overlaid the old. Pagan burial customs included grave goods such as coins, medallions, and other memorabilia that are subsequently found in Christian burials at churches.[59] For example, a grave could be marked with a cross or be clearly placed in a churchyard yet contain within it a person buried with grave goods. The inclusion of such grave goods in a Christian-marked grave indicates not necessarily the survival of the pagan religion or its structure of beliefs, but the retention through folklore of an important ritual now being subsumed into the Christian framework.[60] These archaeological layers reveal a gradual transition in burial practice, with the Christian progressively overlaying the pagan. This evidence displays graphically how religious practices were gradually converted and how ideas about life and death were transformed.

Churchmen such as Ælfric and Wulfstan greeted this popular synthesis between Christian and Germanic with ambivalence. Confronted with a practice that was a mixture of Christianity and folklore, a Christian leader might have responded to it in one of two ways, depending on which direction he thought the transmission was going. If he perceived a successful Christianization of the Germanic folk practice, then he viewed such an amalgamation as a praiseworthy attempt at getting people into church (as in the case of the pagan temples being renovated as churches). If, however, it appeared to him that "paganism" obscured (lowered, degenerated) Christian belief, then such a leader might call for reform and issue laws against practices such as observing special days for certain actions or leaving offerings at trees, stones, or wells. In either case the churchman was reacting to a synthesis already going on, initiated at a grassroots level.

The existence of a reformer's complaint about such syncretic activities has too often been taken at face value by modern scholars who conclude that Christianity was failing to penetrate popular culture. On the contrary, reformer reactions indicate that Christianization *was* taking place among a laity actively seeking to incorporate Christianity into their everyday lives. Reform movements such as those found in the tenth and eleventh centuries were not just a sign of degeneracy in Christian culture but of an awareness of how this new synthesis was functioning. The issue for these reformers was one of control over the rapid diversification of Christian practice and belief. Unlike conversion aimed at making pagans into Christians, reform was an effort by churchmen to improve a society already Christian in some general sense. In the tenth and eleventh centuries, simultaneous calls for the exclusion of paganism and for Christian reform indicate the transitional nature of this period, in part due to the influx of pagan Scandinavians in eastern England (taken up in the next chapter). By the tenth century a number of different, sometimes competing processes were at work in the development of Anglo-Saxon Christianity, initiated from both the popular and formal spheres; taken as a whole they indicate a vibrancy in the religious experience of late Anglo-Saxon England.

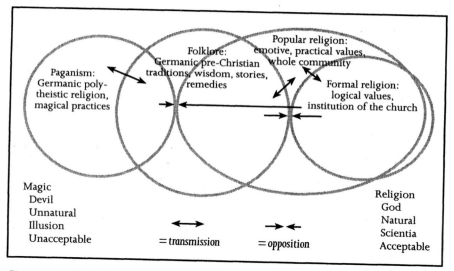

Figure 1.2. *Medieval religious worldview*

Conclusions: Popular Religion at the Center

By focusing on the symbiotic interchange between the popular and the formal, we can rebalance the excessive emphasis on the formal religion's dominant position in measuring the success or failure of the Christianizing effort. Ultimately Christianization and Germanicization are inseparable, each describing the conversion process from different vantage points. By using both concepts we can understand middle practices, such as elf charms, from different perspectives and get a well-rounded view of the developing Anglo-Saxon Christian culture.

This dynamic interaction between the formal and the popular at their mutual boundary makes the process of the formation of Christianity visible to us, especially the largely oral popular traditions. Figure 1.2 is a composite picture of the overlapping spheres of popular and formal religion in relationship to folklore and paganism, on a spectrum stretched between magic and religion. Folklore is a more generic and neutral term to describe the pre-Christian Germanic heritage; it encompasses pagan religious practices but can also transcend them. In this illustration popular religion is not magic or paganism; rather, it is the larger whole of Christianity. Both conflict and assimilation occur between these spheres. Formal religion conflicts with both folklore and paganism, sometimes confusing the two because folklore transmits the older paganism into the Christian era. Popular religion interacts with both the formal religion and folklore and thus acts as a mediating force.

Because the formal religion was verbally objecting to the "pagan" in some cases or absorbing folklore into formal documents on other occasions and trying openly to influence popular practice, we have evidence of these processes left in surviving texts. It is at the point of contact between the popular and the formal that we can learn the most about the daily Christian experience. However, this textual evidence, because of its source in the formal church, is biased, highly copied, and fragmentary. For this reason, quantification methods are inappropriate; counting the instances of a particular popular practice tells us nothing. But if we stand back from the isolated bits of evidence given us, we can form a general picture of what these practices meant. Looking not only at the point of contact but also at the incidents that are hardest to understand provides a means of access into the very different worldviews of the early Middle Ages. While this type of approach appears to be selective in its use of evidence, it offers a way to enter another worldview, to work from the strange, isolated instance in the text to its context and back again.

2

THE
LATE SAXON
RELIGIOUS
ENVIRONMENT
THE GROWTH OF LOCAL CHURCHES

The following oft-quoted story from Asser describes the baptismal treaty of Alfred and Guthrum resulting from the Wessex king's remarkable victory over the Vikings at Edington in 878, after his hard winter in the retreat of Athelney. The story illustrates well the issues surrounding conversion in late Saxon England.

> When he [Alfred] had been there for fourteen days the Vikings, thoroughly terrified by hunger, cold and fear, and in the end by despair, sought peace on this condition: the king should take as many chosen hostages as he wanted from them and give none to them; never before, indeed, had they made peace with anyone on such terms. When he had heard their embassy, the king (as is his wont) was moved to compassion and took as many chosen hostages from them as he wanted. When they

had been handed over, the Vikings swore in addition that they would leave his kingdom immediately, and Guthrum, their king, promised to accept Christianity and to receive baptism at King Alfred's hand; all of which he and his men fulfilled as they had promised. For three weeks later Guthrum, the king of the Vikings, with thirty of the best men from his army, came to King Alfred at a place called Aller, near Athelney. King Alfred raised him from the holy font of baptism, receiving him as his adoptive son; the unbinding of the chrisom on the eighth day took place at a royal estate called Wedmore. Guthrum remained with the king for twelve nights after he had been baptized, and the king freely bestowed many excellent treasures on him and all his men.[1]

The context for Christian charms is found in the unique cultural and religious conditions illustrated in this story, as Anglo-Saxon Christians reacted to the cultural dislocation of the Viking presence and the Viking settlers made themselves at home, partly through becoming Christian. The arrival of large numbers of Vikings in Anglo-Saxon England in the ninth century and after reintroduced paganism to the over-200-year-old Anglo-Saxon church and thus instigated a new conversion need in the midst of the Christianization process already in progress. The Viking invasions of England produced a confrontation between nascent Anglo-Saxon Christian societies, only recently migrated, settled, and Christianized themselves, and groups of Scandinavian sea raiders moving from their homelands and turning themselves into settlers. The time lag between the Anglo-Saxon process of settlement and conversion and that of the Scandinavians created a unique intersection at their meeting, symbolized in the treaty between Alfred and Guthrum. Map 2.1 shows the Norse and Danish settlements in the ninth century, indicating the Danelaw boundary partly defined in the Treaty of Alfred and Guthrum (who controlled East Anglia).

This conversion-by-treaty situation, by no means uncommon in the early Middle Ages, highlights the issue concerning the nature of conversion to Christianity. What are we to make of Guthrum's baptism and adoption by Alfred? What kind of conversion was this, and was it meaningful? Guthrum's settlement with Alfred as told by Asser is a typical conversion story designed to emphasize the radical transformation of an enemy of God and of the good Christian king into a child of God and a child of the king. Despite the seeming superficiality of this dramatic conversion, the event was part of a process of cultural conversion and accommodation in which, apparently, the Scandinavian settlers in England really did become Christian in some sense of the word. The Viking incursions clearly disrupted the Anglo-

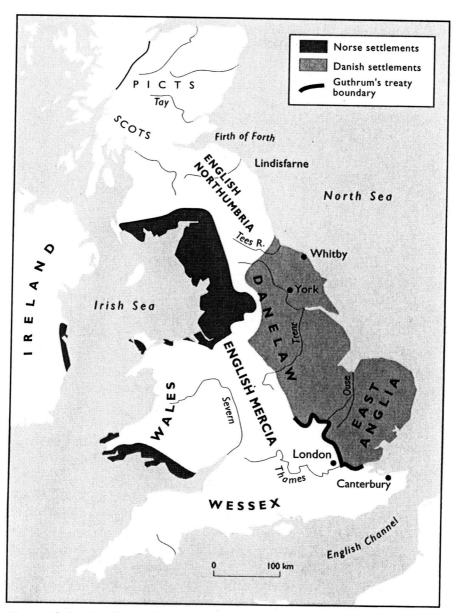

Map 2.1. *The Danelaw. (Cartography by Nancy Hulbirt, University of Hawai'i at Mānoa)*

Saxon Christianization process but also, in a curious way, reinitialized it. Whether because of the invasions or in spite of them, the period 900–1050 witnessed an intense rise in popular religion, as seen in the growth of local, lay-owned churches. In fact, the Viking presence may have actually accelerated the popularizing process by breaking up the centralizing system of dioceses in the eastern regions and subsequently encouraging the grassroots movement toward lay-founded churches.

The traditional way of conceptualizing the ninth-century invasions, inherited from Anglo-Saxon chroniclers, is in terms of opposition, the same tendency toward duality observed in the distinction between popular and formal religion discussed in Chapter 1. In this case the good Christian forces are the centralizing, "civilized" monarchies versus the evil pagan forces of disruption represented by these "uncivilized" raiders. This progressive view of civilization is the same as the progressivist view of magic-religion-science observed in Chapter 1. In this view the steady advance of development (settlement, centralization, and Christianization) that leads to the kind of civilization idealized by church historians was rudely interrupted by another wave of aggressive migrants. For progressivists the arrival of these raiders-turned-settlers breaks the steady march of Anglo-Saxon culture toward civilization into two parts: settlement and conversion, the beginning formations of kingdoms, circa 600–800, and the period of recovery, reconquest, consolidation, and reform after the Viking invasions, circa 900–1050. This linear progress model assumes an inevitable directionality for history toward some higher form of human society known as civilization; hence history is seen as the struggle between those peoples moving toward civilized life (Anglo-Saxons) and those who seem to impede it (Vikings).[2]

More recently, however, Anglo-Saxon scholars have placed the Viking invasions in the wider context of European migration and cultural synthesis, questioning the picture of demonized, pagan Vikings versus saintly, Christianized Anglo-Saxons. This is not to deny the horrific social impact of the ninth-century invasions on settled peoples or ignore the religious dimensions of the conflict. Yet these new studies have pointed out the shared characteristics of Viking, Anglo-Saxon, and Celtic cultures as migratory peoples and the ways in which these similarities were used in negotiating accommodations to one another. Donald Logan, in The Vikings in History, places the Vikings as central rather than peripheral to the development of Europe, in opposition to the Francocentric and Anglocentric approaches; he highlights the Vikings' striking assimilative abilities. In regard to the treaty of Alfred and Guthrum, Richard Abels has argued for the common cultural strategies used in the negotiations ("King Alfred's Peace-Making Strategies"). Cyril Hart, in The Danelaw, speaks of the "enrichment" Viking settlements brought to England, which goes along with their "taming"; he attributes the contrasting portraits of Vikings as terrorizing pagans versus resourceful settlers to the vagaries of human nature.[3] Pauline Stafford, in Unification and Conquest, equates Cnut's conquests with William the Conqueror's in the unification of England. The former conquest culminated in a Scandinavian king of England ruling in the Christian model. The reign of Cnut (1016–35) is, in many ways, symbolic of the cultural and religious synthesis accomplished in late Saxon England. Between Guthrum and Cnut the disparate strands of Anglo-Saxon and Scandinavian, Christian and pagan, were woven together into something new.

Seen in this broader context of cultural conflict and accommodation, the period of reconquest and consolidation in the tenth and eleventh centuries becomes a dynamic phase for popular religion as an acculturating process. The simultaneous calls for fighting paganism and for reform of the Christian church and people, evident in the sermons and laws of Ælfric and Wulfstan, indicate the cultural diversity of this period. The evidence from the Danelaw indicates that Christian Anglo-Saxons lived side by side with newcomer pagans who were in the process of converting. Archaeology, Domesday Book, and related documentary sources show that a new kind of local, "proprietary" church grew throughout England and in the disrupted dioceses, while relatively stable Anglo-Saxon minsters (large, centrally located churches) continued to dominate in dioceses outside the Danelaw. Thus, conversion of the pagan newcomers and reform of Christian society merged, as churchmen simultaneously castigated pagan practices and called for renewal among Christians. This religious ferment is clearly evident in the tenth and eleventh centuries in the growth of local churches, particularly in the Danelaw. Typically, a lone priest served in these new, lay-founded churches, usually a man of relatively low origin who had a rudimentary education, was isolated from the church hierarchy and the large collegiate minsters, and was called upon to meet the daily, practical needs of an agricultural population. In this environment, and through this kind of clerical agency interacting with local folk culture and domestic life, popular religion formed.

Late Saxon England was thus caught up in a creative tension between the diversifying, acculturating popular religion that was rapidly expanding and the centralizing, reform-minded formal church that was struggling with these diverse forces. These two perspectives represent two opposing tendencies, a centrifugal force of diversification in the grassroots growth of local religious practices versus a centripetal force implemented by churchmen in their attempts to centralize and homogenize religious practice. Monastic chroniclers and reformers, main sources for modern histories, portrayed the former, diversifying element as impeding progress toward Christianization, and the latter, centralizing effort as the progressive element impelling

Christian society forward. Using the model for popular religion established in Chapter 1, I argue that both the centrifugal and the centripetal forces were necessary for Christianization and that they existed in a creative dialectical rapport to foster a new religious paradigm, a Christianity peculiar to England, an Anglo-Saxon Christianity, or even more appropriately for the Danelaw, an Anglo-Scandinavian Christianity. Critical to an understanding of this Christianization is the recognition of the conversion processes at work in the domestic sphere that balance and fulfill the dramatic conversion events so commonly portrayed in church histories. When Christian practice reached into the home and into daily life, then conversion was succeeding. At the intersection of the local and central forces, where the formal church met the laity in the rural church, stood the local priest as mediator between folk culture and Christian teaching, as an agent in creating a popular Christianity.

The first part of this chapter examines Anglo-Saxon Christianity using the model of conversion as both an event and a process. This section argues for the significance of conversion processes as essential in the formulation of a Christian society, particularly the acculturation that took place on the local homefront. The remainder of the chapter examines the dynamic interaction between the centripetal and centrifugal forces in the late Saxon church in the growth of local churches, their conflict with the older minster system, and the role of the local priest in the development of popular Christianity. This chapter establishes the "ground view" of popular religion, examining local conditions and the formal church's response to them. The next chapter looks at popular religion from within the ideology of the formal church, by examining how reformers such as Ælfric and Wulfstan molded the Augustinian worldview to both control and accommodate local practice. Between these two perspectives, that of local diversity and centralized control, emerges a landscape capable of producing Christian charms, the focus of Chapters 4 and 5.

The Process of Conversion

Conversion is both an event and a process whereby an individual or group changes religious orientation, in both belief and practice. Both event and process are essential for conversion to take place and tend to work in tandem, with event initiating process. A typical example of this dialectic is the dramatic conversion of a pagan king followed by the spread of Christian ideas throughout his kingdom. The event as recorded for posterity emphasized the drama of the moment—a revelatory insight, a miraculous victory in battle, or a ceremonious baptism; the processes that surrounded the event are not as clearly documented but are evident in remains of church buildings and other religious artifacts, the establishment of religious laws, and the propagation of religious literature. This socialization process that produced a "Christianized society" involved a domestication of Christianity in the sphere of the home and everyday life through family networks. This local, domestic side of conversion both accompanies and completes conversion events such as a baptism as part of a treaty.

Direct evidence of an individual's internal process of conversion is, of course, unobtainable. Consequently we are dealing with layers of representation and sometimes contradictory models of what conversion was. Autobiographical accounts (rare), biographies, histories, letters, and homilies all had varying didactic goals and consequently different perspectives on conversion. Yet since all of this written evidence was obviously Christian, it was consciously shaped by a shared Christian framework, a sense of "Christian history" that developed over the early centuries of Christianity's spread and was handed down and imitated, as evident from Eusebius, Augustine, and Orosius, on through the Germanic histories of Gregory of Tours, Bede, Einhard, Asser, and many others. In examining conversion as an event and a process, therefore, we are looking at both conversion as manifested in external markers (events, rituals, statements of belief, physical objects, and places of worship) and conversion as a consciously formulated construct of the church still in its formative stages.[4]

The conversion of the Anglo-Saxon tribal groups in England began in A.D. 597 with the arrival of papally supported monastic missionaries, events narrated by Bede in a church history designed to establish the Christian heritage for English posterity. Four hundred years later, about 1000, the Anglo-Saxons were still wrestling with the process these events initiated in their culture, interrupted in the middle years by the arrival of the Vikings, whose presence in the Danelaw sparked a whole new wave of accommodations.

With the addition of these un-Christianized Scandinavians, conversion event and process collided. Anglo-Saxon-held territories themselves were in the process of Christianization, as churches, ceremonies, and ideas began spreading outward from the central minsters; suddenly these nascent Christian kingdoms had to contend with pagans, either by beating them off or converting them (or both). The latter strategy worked better, as marked in such symbolic events as the baptism of Guthrum and his thirty men at Aller in 878. Such events are problematic because the processes of conversion that should accompany them are invisible; we do not have a Bede for the Danelaw chronicling and shaping the progression of conversion. Nonetheless the processes are there, albeit hidden in more obscure evidence—archaeological remains, polemical laws, and sermons. Guthrum's emblematic baptism becomes intelligible only if we see it in light of this event-process dynamic.

"Becoming Christian" means not only converting from an old belief to a new, but also living as a Christian in some meaningful way after that point of decision. Thus, for every event there is a parallel and consequent process; for every baptism there must be, ideally, a catechism. The representations of these events and processes vary tremendously in the histories and chronicles. Some of the medieval ways of signifying conversion in national histories, chronicles, and saints' lives may appear strange or go unrecognized unless the symbolism and rituals are understood. For conversions such as Guthrum's to be comprehensible, they need to be placed in the iconographic context of early medieval conversion events and processes.

Representations of conversion events are easier to identify than processes, for the same reasons that conflicts between popular and formal religion, or magic and religion, appear more prominent than the accommodations—the inherent western Christian tendency toward binary oppositions is highlighted in the drama of the narrative. Baptisms, divine revelations, and miracles dominate the accounts of conversions from the New Testament through the writings of Gregory of Tours and Bede as well as other early medieval church histories and saints' lives. The predominant theme in most of these accounts is the perception of the conversion event as a spiritual battle, a reflection of the dialectical mode of Christian thought (good versus evil, pagan versus Christian). Conversion as a dramatic shift in religious orientation was frequently portrayed as an actual battle of some kind, as seen in Constantine's miraculous victory at Milvian Bridge, St. Benedict's monkish battles with temptation and miraculous victories in his wilderness retreat, and Clovis's challenge-victory ("I want to believe in you, but I must first be saved from my enemies").[5] In all of these stories the baptismal idea of death and rebirth was acted out in very physical ways.

The accounts of the conversion of Anglo-Saxon rulers also contain this dual layer of meaning as military victory and spiritual victory, treaty and baptism, go hand in hand. Bede's *Ecclesiastical History*, widely read in late Saxon England in both Latin and the vernacular, recounts dramatic victories of Christian kings over pagan kings, either in battle or in subsequent sainthood (for example, the struggles in life and after death of the saint-king Oswald).[6] Likewise, Alfred's victory over Guthrum is typecast by Asser as a near-miraculous triumph of the good forces of the Christian king over the pagan forces of disorder, the Vikings. The treaty, with its baptism and adoption, is an event marker that signals the conversion. In a similar story Rollo, Viking victor over the Franks, founded Normandy in a legendary treaty with the French king that used baptism, marriage, and fealty as rituals of peacemaking.[7] The negotiations involved in such Germanic and Scandinavian conversion events are sometimes problematic for modern readers, who fail to see how homage, fealty, marriage, baptism, and adoption were all strategies used by medieval rulers, Celt, Frank, Saxon, or Viking, to make peace between men and peace with God. All of these conversion events were meaningful because they were symbolic rituals indicative of long-term processes of accommodation. These rituals worked, when they worked, because they meant something to the participants, evident in subsequent social and religious changes.

The processes that followed these conversion events and brought meaning to them are harder to locate in the narratives but are essential to an understanding of the accommodation strategies that form the basis of popular religion. These processes are inherent in Christian theology concerning conversion. Baptism initiated the believer; confession and penance maintained the soul. Miracles of instantaneous healings attributed to saints' relics find their spiritual meaning in the context of pilgrimage, a journey-image that emphasized moving toward God as a lifelong spiritual progress. Late tenth-century Anglo-Saxon poems such as *Exodus*, *The Wanderer*, and *The Seafarer* project the Germanic theme of exile into a spiritual allegory of conversion.[8] Beside the stories of kings converting through miracles and treaties stand the stories of kings such as Cædwalla, Ina, and Ceolwulf, who gave up their kingdoms to go on pilgrimage or join a monastery; they serve in Bede's narrative as examples of sincere conversion to the heavenly kingdom.[9] After the marvelous came the mundane in the conversion of kings and kingdoms: the building of churches, the establishment of Christian rituals, and the passing of religious laws. As a counterpoint to the idea of conversion as a spiritual battle focused on a miraculous moment of triumph stood the various peace-weaving strategies of conversion involving cultural assimilation.

Perhaps the most significant sphere for conversion process that counterbalanced the public rituals of baptism, adoption, or marriage was the private life of the family, particularly of women and the home. Marriage between a non-Christian ruler and a Christian was not an incidental event in treaty negotiations, but central to the Christianizing effort. Parallel to the mysterious baptisms and adoptions in treaties, kinship ties became part of the subsequent conversion process. For every monk, fiery preacher, or zealous priest we need also to imagine women in their domain, which included the family and daily religious practice. The influence of women in the spiritual life of the home has been overshadowed by the public conversion events emphasized in the narratives, but in fact the transformation of everyday rituals was probably accomplished largely by women.

Communal and domestic life and the horizontal and reciprocal bonds of that environment were much more powerful in the maintenance of the society than has usually been acknowledged in traditional institutional histories.[10] The interchanges between politics and religion, king and priest, are widely studied patriarchal models of government and religion typical of urban societies. But the daily practice of religion centered in the social and domestic environment of the local community deserves equal attention. If a new religion were truly to convert a people, it would have to penetrate to the level of the village and home, the locus of the most common religious practices.

Marriage of a Christian woman to a non-Christian was a conversion strategy in late Antiquity and the early Middle Ages, often associated with treaties. Thus examples of prominent Christian women as effective missionaries to their husbands or children abound: St. Augustine's mother, Monica, as recorded in his own conversion account; Emperor Constantine's mother, Helena, finder of the "true cross" in the Holy Land; and Clovis's patient and clever wife, Clotild, as chronicled by Gregory of Tours. In Bede's account of the conversion of King Ethelbert of Kent after the arrival of the monk-missionaries, the king was already married to a Christian, Bertha, to whom he had promised freedom of religion.[11] Bede also records the sanguine advice of Pope Boniface to another of these long-suffering queens, the Northumbrian King Edwin's wife, Ethelberga. The pontiff explained to her how God had placed her there for the very purpose of converting this man and his people and that she must persevere with patience.[12] He goes on to praise her devotion and obedience to Christian truth, remarking on her husband's continuing paganism and its deleterious effect on her marriage, thus unequally yoked.[13] In the pope's view the coldness of the king's heart would be melted by the fire of devotion she established in the home. Thus the warmth of hearth and home were one way of persuading a man of the truth of Christianity. Confirming this religious significance of women is the prominence of abbesses (many times princesses or former queens) in dual-house monasteries and later in the missions of Boniface to the continent (Abbess Leoba, for example).[14] These queens and abbesses functioned as missionaries and as partners with the monks, endeavoring to teach, set an example, and persuade or, in the case of the queens, "soften their husband's hearts." Similar processes undoubtedly occurred in the homes of the less socially prominent, as evidenced in the increasingly Christian landscape of England described below and in the development of folk remedies using Christian symbols discussed in Chapters 4 and 5.

Thus, the traditional picture of England's conversion as a series of political events needs to be supplemented with an examination of the process of converting daily practice. The pagan hierarchical structure disintegrated rapidly in the seventh century in the face of Christianity's systematic organization. But folk practices were all-pervasive in everyday life. The animistic character of Germanic belief prior to Christianization, with its emphasis on nature, holistic cures, and worship at wells, trees, and stones, meant that it was hard to counteract on an institutional level of organized religion. Small religious sites were everywhere; people carried amulets to ward off misfortune and relied on the belief in spiritual agents as explanations for many life experiences. The synthesis of Christian and Germanic ideas gradually transformed these practices, undoubtedly at the local level. The mixture of traditional herbs and Christian symbols (the cross, holy water, and prayers) found in the charm remedies indicates a collaboration between the domestic and the religious spheres, between the laity and the local priests. In this way Christianity ultimately penetrated the homes and daily lives of the various Germanic peoples in the centuries after the arrival of the first missionaries.

These same processes of acculturation at the domestic level, although virtually impossible to document, undoubtedly occurred after the baptism of Guthrum in East Anglia and throughout the Danelaw during the reconquest of the tenth century. The Viking settlers displaced the existing English landholders and brought with them their own customs and laws; yet these newcomers also made new relationships with the English Christian population, as new owners, as neighbors, and as in-laws. While we may question the depth of Guthrum's conviction at the moment of baptism, there is no denying the evidence of Scandinavian Christianization over the next century at the grassroots level of popular culture, as seen, for example, in the rise of Danish churchmen in the tenth century and the popularity in the Danelaw of the cult of St. Edmund, martyred by Danes themselves.[15] Most of all, the growth of Christianity following the Danish settlement is visible in the spread of local, lay-owned churches, both inside and outside the Danelaw. It is to this local environment that we need to turn in order to understand the context in which popular religion developed. On manors and in vills, priests hired by lay proprietors served their congregations by combining their spiritual expertise, such as it was, with their knowledge of local practice. Within these everyday domestic and agricultural conditions, Christian charms were born.

Local Churches

The tenth and eleventh centuries produced more intensively than before, and in greater quantity, evidence of assimilation between Christian ideas and popular culture, as the church grew and spread in the century after the Viking invasions. Lay piety increased rapidly, evidenced especially in the building of privately owned churches, a decentralizing force. On the other hand, the church hierarchy pushed a program of reform to homogenize Christian belief among the laity and centralize control over this growing body of disparate clergy. Inevitably conflicts emerged between the centrifugal forces expanding in the rural areas and the centripetal forces attempting to control them from the church hierarchy. This tension engendered a new synthesis, popular Christianity.

By looking at the expansion and diversification of Christianity evident in the growth of local churches, we can see how the religion was getting into people's homes and lives to such a degree that popular ideas were flowing back in the other direction, into the formal religion. Popular practices that incorporated both local custom and Christian tradition developed primarily in the environment of the local church, specifically in the relationship between priest and laity. The development of small, local churches in the tenth and eleventh centuries, privately owned by lords or villagers and only loosely connected with the church hierarchy, allowed for a closer interaction between the individual priest and his congregation distinctly different from the collegiate environment of the older, more remote large churches (minsters), centrally staffed by a group of clergy. The local priest, isolated from other clergy, became a mediator between Christian ideas and local needs. His position as a tenant of the manorial proprietor and as a spiritual elder gave him an ambivalent social standing between aristocracy and peasantry. In the social and economic environment of the local church, the priest's involvement in the daily life of his congregation put him in a position to apply Christian ideas to their domestic problems.

The conflicts between the local churches and the older minster system indicate the tension generated by the interplay of centrifugal and centripetal forces in the growth of local churches. The local priest, by virtue of his environment, stood in the middle of a network of competing relationships—with the bishop, the proprietor, and the laity. The local connections were undoubtedly stronger, although most of the written sources we have come from the bishops and other leaders attempting to gain control over this burgeoning church population. Before exploring these dynamics, the nature of these sources requires some explanation.

Sources

Diverse sources—documentary, legal, religious, statistical, and archaeological—help establish the social and economic environment and conditions under which the local priests were operating. The laws of Æthelred and Cnut reveal how churches were defined in late Anglo-Saxon England according to their rights, revenues, and conflicts of interest. Sermons and letters from the reformers Ælfric and Wulfstan address the hierarchy's standards for priestly conduct. Domesday Book and other documentary sources, along with archaeological remains, attest to the rapid growth of local churches. This combination of sources reveals the priest's social relations with the church hierarchy, the church proprietor, and his own congregation. These three competing roles put the local priest in a unique position as a catalyst for cultural change (conversion) in the development of popular religious practices.

The written sources for late Anglo-Saxon church organization offer us the point of view of those in authority, primarily monastically oriented reformers from the reign of Edgar (959–75) through Cnut (1016–35), and reveal their goals and some of the problems faced by the late Anglo-Saxon church. These sources all emanate from the literate church hierarchy, closely associated with the governance of the king. A select group of men—such as Ælfric, abbot of Eynsham (ca. 955–1010), and Wulfstan II, Archbishop of York (1002–23)—worked assiduously to unify English society under the banner of Christianity, supporting the centralizing efforts of the king as part of their agenda. Consequently they wrote laws, sermons, and letters on behalf of the church and on behalf of the royal government seeking to reform English society. These canons, homilies, and letters contain a mixture of secular and spiritual, royal and ecclesiastical, concerns. They legislated church organization, income, and rights alongside moral injunctions for priests and the laity; most of all, they emphasized the role of education in promoting Christian society. These sources provide a view of late Saxon popular religion and society "from the top looking down."

Domesday Book, the massive land survey ordered by William the Conqueror in 1086, along with recently excavated church sites, adds invaluably to the study of local churches by giving us another perspective—from the ground, as it were.[16] These singular sources reveal a substantial church building effort in the late Saxon period.

Documentary and statistical sources such as Domesday Book, however, have just as many limitations as other written sources. Domesday Book and its satellite surveys covering 36 counties and recording 13,418 locations was a fiscal account of land tenure and hence interpreted everything, from acreage to pigs to mills and churches, in terms of value. Because of its orientation toward land rights and values, it recorded church organization only incidentally.[17] Domesday Book's statistical record of churches is therefore incomplete, not only because priests and churches were not recorded at all in many counties, but also because even in counties where they routinely were registered, many churches known from unrelated sources (such as other surveys and archaeological evidence) are missing.[18] Moreover, as both Richard Morris and John Blair have pointed out, the uncertainty of Domesday's records is partly the product of the incredible flux in church building and landholding in this time period.[19] Manors and villages were not static entities, and the period 900–1050 was a dynamic era in church growth and change.

Likewise, the recent archaeological work on local churches is rich but also difficult to interpret. On the one hand, the Council for British Archaeology, along with other agencies concerned with British churches, has done excellent work in studying all layers of church buildings, including the early levels of Anglo-Saxon stone and timber churches.[20] Even amid continuing disputes over the dating of late Anglo-Saxon and early Norman churches, the archaeological evidence shows that the building of local churches was carried on uninterrupted regardless of the Conquest. Still, much of what has been found and reported by archaeologists has yet to be interpreted and is controversial, especially with respect to dating.[21]

All of these sources lead to a fairly typical historical ambivalence. On the one hand, Domesday Book and archaeology are treasure troves of information not readily available through other sources, and yet the problems of their usage are daunting. However, combined together, the literary, statistical, and archaeological information of these sources does show a fairly clear pattern of small church building on a rapid and massive scale in the last century before the Conquest and continuing beyond it. Moreover, the ecclesiastical reaction to this explosion in growth seen in the reform literature of Ælfric and Wulfstan shows a recognition of the inherent problems of these privately owned churches and these churchmen's awareness of the opportunity for reforming society through these new churches and priests.

Centripetal and Centrifugal Forces

Royal-ecclesiastical reformers attempting to centralize and homogenize the late Anglo-Saxon church were faced with a disparate, rural, kinship-linked population with diverse interests and tremendous regional variety. Despite the demise of the regional kingdoms and the gradual rise of a single king of the English, local ties still played a dominant role in the identities and affiliations of most people.[22] The two major centrifugal forces in the tenth century rivaling any attempts to centralize some aspects of governance were the lay aristocracy, as representative of local, nonroyal interests, and the Viking presence in the Danelaw creating regional distortions.

Local aristocratic interests in the church became evident in the reactions to the monastic reform movement begun under King Edgar (959–75) through the churchmen Dunstan (abbot of Glastonbury and then archbishop of Canterbury, 960–88), Oswald of Worcester (961–92), and Æthelwold of Winchester (963–84). These monks worked under royal patronage to reestablish the Benedictine rule in the major ecclesiastical centers, including the restoration of monasteries in the Danelaw, most notably the fenland monasteries of Ramsey, Ely, Peterborough, Thorney, and Crowland.[23] Many members of the local aristocracy opposed this effort to "monasticize" the secular collegiate churches not because they were anti-Christian but because they objected to the changes in landholding entailed in these endowments and the subsequent encroachment on their traditional rights and privileges. Operating within a set of local, communal bonds, the lay aristocracy sought to preserve their right both to support and to control minsters in their territory in the face of these royally supported and endowed monasteries now dominating the landscape.

The role of the ealdormen in this tenth-century turmoil is significant, revealing the tensions between royal and local control, centralized reform and aristocratic piety. The ealdormen of Mercia and Essex, trading off dominance at the court during the tenth century, are good examples of this aristocratic tradition and its religious ideals; clearly the ealdormen as leading magnates strongly supported religious foundations within their own landholding system and under the influence of their families, with or without royal support.[24] Ealdorman Æthelred of Mercia (880–912) and his wife, Æthelflæd, lady of the Mercians and daughter of Alfred, were fairly autonomous in their control of their ancient kingdom; they were also instrumental in the extension of authority into the Danelaw. Likewise, Ealdorman Athelstan "Half-King" of East Anglia (dominant 943–57) was a major force in the church building and founding in the Eastern Danelaw and on a national level. Ealdorman Ælfgar of Essex (d. after 946) left a majority of his possessions to ecclesiastical foundations, a trend carried on by his descendants. After the death of King Edgar in 975, Ealdorman Ælfhere of Mercia led a group of lay aristocrats to dissolve some Mercian monasteries established under Edgar because they objected to the monastic reform's intrusion on Mercian autonomy. On the other hand, Ealdorman Byrhtnoth of Essex (d. 991 at the Battle of Maldon) supported the reformed monasteries during this antimonastic reaction, especially patronizing the foundation of Ely. Both royal and aristocratic support for religious institutions is evident within these political dynamics of competition between ealdormanric families and between royal and local interests.[25]

The other major factor impeding an easy homogenization of the kingdom was the tremendous regional diversity, most notably the Danelaw, which was composed of distinct regions separately governed, and the persistence of Danish institutions in these areas.[26] The ninth-century invasions and establishment of Viking settlements were followed in the tenth century by English reconquest and consolidation, as well as repeated uprisings and negotiations into the eleventh century. The reigns of Æthelred and Cnut are prime examples of the negative and positive aspects of the resulting cultural tensions.

Æthelred "Unræd" (978–1016) not only had to face the conflicts created by the monastic reform efforts (in which he was caught between the ire of Dunstan and the ire of his aristocratic opponents) but also was confronted with a divided aristocracy of Anglo-Saxons and Anglo-Scandinavians as well as renewed invasions. Æthelred's laws (authored after 1008 by the reformer Wulfstan) show an increasing desperation couched in religious terms. Calls for moral reform cite the disasters across England as judgments from God, soluble only if all the people of England collectively unite under one belief. In this, Æthelred recognized the need for cultural unity to create a stable political order.[27]

Cnut (1016–35) accomplished what Æthelred was unable to do, perhaps because of more fortunate circumstances but also because Cnut as an Anglo-Scandinavian embodied the cultural synthesis necessary to bring the English kingdom together. In content, Cnut's laws were not that different from Æthelred's (because they were authored by the same reformer, Wulfstan), but Cnut was more successful in gaining consensus. The Oxford council of 1018 brought peace; in it both English and Danish agreed to unite under Christianity, Cnut, and the Anglo-Saxon laws formulated under Edgar.[28]

Churchmen played a dramatic role in this long process of political and cultural consolidation, especially the archbishops of Canterbury and York who wielded formidable political power at the court. Prominent churchmen emerging from the reformed fenland monasteries often filled the archbishopric of York as well as the see of Dorchester in the Danelaw.[29] Under Æthelred and Cnut, Wulfstan, Archbishop of York, had a clear reform agenda that was colored by his knowledge of conditions in the Danelaw. Together with Ælfric, Wulfstan sought to take the monastic reform ideals of their mentors, Dunstan, Æthelwold, and Oswald, to the lower clergy.

Nonetheless, this organizational effort extended down only so far into the structure of the English landscape. The majority of England, predominantly rural, was still dominated by a relatively independent aristocracy ruling a subject peasantry on their manorial estates. Outside the main centers of the church controlled by the bishops a vast array of churches grew up under local patronage.

The Growth of Local Churches

The rapid growth of local churches in the last century before the Conquest was part of a phenomenon throughout early medieval Europe known as the privatization of the church. Increasing lay interest in the church manifested itself in the building of private chapels and churches and the hiring of priests by their lay owners. These churches in many ways arose outside the church hierarchy, instigating a conflict between leadership and ownership. Late Anglo-Saxon church organization was thus in a state of transition. The older, established system of large, centralized churches or minsters was now challenged by the foundation of small, locally owned or proprietary churches, established independently in vills or on manors by lords or sometimes by a group of free laymen.[30] The motivations for the founding of these churches reflect both material and spiritual perceptions and interests.

Economic, social, and political factors governed the material conditions of churches. In the history of church foundations both on the continent and in England, secular boundaries and ideas of property and lordship, Roman or Germanic, determined ecclesiastical structure. The reason for the competing structures of governance in the early Middle Ages had to do with the twin roots of European societies, Roman Christianity and Germanic tribal groups, and the tension between centralized forms of governance based on an urban structure and regionalized forms located in a rural environment.[31]

The late Saxon church structure, dating back to the eighth century, was based on a Roman, centralized, and monastically oriented model adapted to the early English kingdoms. Royal *tun* or *villa regis* were logical centers for church foundations. The monastic impulse toward founding monasteries in remote locations led to the establishment of outlying mission stations in areas distant from royal centers.[32] As collegiate foundations these minsters were staffed by a group of clergy, sometimes monastic (especially under the reform effort), who could collectively carry out a full panoply of divine services. They also frequently had relics of saints, drawing the rural population in for festivals and on pilgrimages.[33]

These minsters ideally functioned as centers of a network, overseeing and serving wider territories in which there were several vills (or a town), a jurisdiction that was probably five to fifteen times larger than a normal parish of a later period.[34] They often served as mother churches sponsoring smaller, daughter churches and chapels within their territory. Thus English church organization relied more on monastic centers founded on political boundaries than it did on any attempt to form coherent dioceses.[35] This system of large churches was originally well suited to the Roman Mediterranean regions of urbanization but was ill suited to reaching the rural population of nonurbanized areas.

The predominantly rural population of tenth- and eleventh-century England, living in self-sufficient village communities (vills), was relatively isolated from these ecclesiastical centers. For example, in the Anglo-Saxon version of Bede's *Ecclesiastical History* (translated under King Alfred's educational program), the Latin description of Aidan's journeys through urban and rustic areas is rendered in Anglo-Saxon as through mynsterstowe (minster-places) and folcstowe (folk-places).[36] This distinction recognized that minsters as ecclesiastical centers represented a rare type of urban establishment that formed an island in the midst of the rest of the population. It also indicated the physical and psychological distance between collegiate clergy in their corporate and church-dominated environment and the majority of the laity living outside that environment. The minster was a place the laity visited that was distinctively different from their homes and villages. The church as represented in the minster was separate from their daily existence.

Local, privately owned churches developed in part as a response to this distant church. The local church was a single church with a single priest serving an area appropriately small, be it manor or vill. The term *parish church* is anachronistic because a network of parishes developed only later in medieval England, partly as a product of these nascent proprietary churches.[37] These small, local churches were not founded primarily by the church hierarchy or as part of the minster system. Rather, they reflect the pious desires of the laity, framed within the context of the manorial structure of landholding.

Piety was the motivation and proprietary interest was the means for the establishment of local churches. While the minster offered relics, many priests, elaborate festivals, and prestigious burials, the small, local church provided a familiar and nearby place for worship and intimate contact with the priest who often was hired to pray for the soul of the proprietor. For example, the Norfolk Domesday contains two cases of a priest being retained specifically for the purpose of saying masses for the lord of a manor.[38] Nonetheless, this pious desire to have a church found expression in contemporary secular forms, with the result that lay lords who founded churches saw them as property and the priests as tenants. These new local churches were an outgrowth of Germanic law and uniquely Germanic proprietary attitudes.[39] Thus the material circumstances of Germanic life shaped the spiritual conditions of churches.

All ranks of lay and ecclesiastical landholders, from earls to thegns and even groups of freedmen, founded and "owned" these churches.[40] The king, earls, bishops, and abbeys all appear in Domesday Book as proprietors of churches, but thegns, the pre-Conquest warrior aristocracy, seem to have been the largest group founding local churches in late Anglo-Saxon England.[41] Increasingly these local churches became an expected part of the religious and social landscape. Several eleventh-century documents indicate thegns were expected to have a church; both the laws of Æthelred and the Preamble to the Ely Inquest make the assumption that every vill had a priest.[42]

In the tenth and eleventh centuries the sheer number and diversity of these local churches clearly offset the church hierarchy's ability to centralize control under the minster system. Evidence from both archaeological records and documentary sources such as Domesday Book indicates the rapid growth of lay church building, particularly in the Danelaw, which reflects the strong growth in popular belief and practice. Using combined evidence, scholars estimate that a minimum of 3,000–4,500 village churches existed in late eleventh-century England.[43] Domesday Book records over 2,000 churches and over 1,000 priests; thus the survey lists approximately 2,700 places as having a church or a priest out of the over 13,000 places the surveyors recorded.[44] It is obvious that this is only a fraction of the churches in England at this time. Other surveys and archaeological evidence reveal many churches unrecorded by Domesday Book; many counties in the survey's circuits silently included them under other property or tenants. Even excluding instances of minster churches or of priests as landholders, the vast majority of churches and priests listed in Domesday Book represent local, proprietary churches serving a single manor or vill.[45] Map 2.4 shows the distribution of local churches and minsters, confirming and adding to this picture given by Domesday Book.

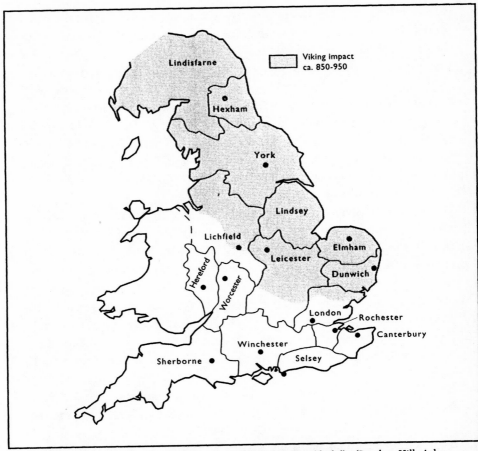

Map 2.2. Diocesan boundaries, ca. 850, prior to Viking incursion (shaded). (Based on Hill, Atlas, p. 148; cartography by Nancy Hulbirt, University of Hawai'i at Mānoa)

Differences in the Danelaw

The large number of these local churches evident in Domesday Book and archaeological remains might easily be attributed to the gradual progress of the Anglo-Saxon Christianization effort, finally reaching out into rural areas, if it were not for two factors. First, these churches were founded not so much by the formal church itself but by lay people, lords or groups of villagers who wanted their own church nearby. Second, the incidence of small church building is greatest in eastern England, where the Vikings severely disrupted the dioceses and minster system. In some ways, then, the catalyst for the development of popularized religion on the local level can be linked to grassroots efforts, partly in response to conditions created by the invasions.

Map 2.3. Reorganized diocesan boundaries, mid-tenth century. (Based on Hill, Atlas, p. 148; cartography by Nancy Hulbirt, University of Hawai'i at Mānoa)

The impact of the Viking invasions in general and on the church structure in particular is a subject of great debate among scholars (particularly Peter Sawyer and Nicholas Brooks).[46] The decentralizing effect of Viking settlement on landholding and political structures is evident in the development of different patterns of landownership and new terminology (for example, soke land), and yet the relatively rapid recovery and rebuilding of churches indicates considerable continuity. The most recent, detailed treatment of the Danelaw, by Cyril Hart, conveys the striking diversity within the Danelaw itself in the patterns of adaptation in landholding. Hart notes in particular the uniqueness of East Anglia, Guthrum's territory.[47]

Historians concerned with the growth of *eigenkirchen* likewise take different positions on the cause and effect relationship between Viking-induced decentralization, the decline of minsters, and the increase in privately owned churches. Colin Platt argues that the decline of the minsters led to the rise of the smaller churches, while M. J. Franklin argues that pressure from the smaller churches and the weakness of the bishops led to the minsters' decline. J. Campbell suggests that the decline of the minsters after the invasion was not that great and that many new minsters and refoundations occurred under the same impetus as the building of smaller churches, the growth of lay piety. Hart, who has the weight of detailed onomastic, archaeological, and Domesday Book evidence behind his arguments, asserts that the survival of churches was greater outside East Anglia than within it; consequently, East Anglia was more likely to have an abundance of lay-owned churches.[48]

Thus the Viking invasions and the creation of the Danelaw had a curious effect on church growth and organization. Clearly these Scandinavians had an initial damaging impact on the traditional church structure, but in the long run the rebuilding effort may have strengthened local church organization.

From a central, hierarchical point of view, the Viking invasions were devastating for the church, as seen in the disruption of the dioceses displayed in Maps 2.2 and 2.3 (after David Hill).[49] Map 2.2, circa 850, shows the original dioceses; the shading indicates the area taken by the invaders. Map 2.3 shows the reorganization of dioceses circa 950. These enlarged dioceses indicate, taken purely on their own, a severely weakened church system. Certainly the church reformers responded to this disruption by seeking to reestablish centralized control with what resources they had, using the traditional pattern of collegiate churches (preferably monasteries). The reformer Æthelwold made a concerted effort to rebuild and to build anew reformed monasteries in the Danelaw, making sure they had sufficient property to survive. Despite the efforts of the formidable East Anglian ealdormen, Athelstan "Half-King" and his son Æthelwine, however, East Anglia seemed particularly resistant to the establishment of reformed monasteries.[50] Scandinavian reaction against the church, for its lands or its beliefs, was characteristic throughout the Danelaw in the ninth and tenth centuries. Wulfstan as archbishop of York clearly felt the burden of his huge task, as demonstrated in his sermons and law codes.

On the other hand, this diocesan weakness and antimonastic reaction seemed to allow for more proprietary church building independent of minster control, as evidenced in both archaeological remains and Domesday

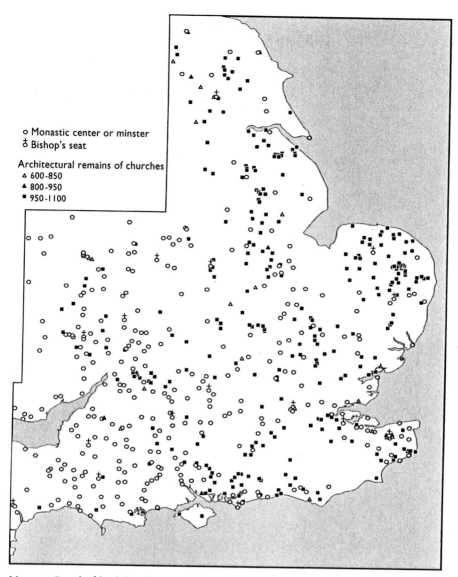

Map 2.4. Growth of local churches. (Based on Hill, Atlas, pp. 157–64; cartography by Nancy Hulbirt, University of Hawai'i at Mānoa)

Book. Map 2.4 (based on David Hill) shows the differences in regional distribution of small churches relative to larger churches in the Anglo-Saxon landscape.[51] The darkened triangles and squares indicate churches built after 850. The hollow markers indicate cathedrals (with crosses), minsters, and monasteries. The distribution differences between the Danelaw and other areas is dramatic: a proliferation of newly built churches relative to collegiate foundations in the Danelaw; a number of such newly built churches in other areas, but nowhere near the numbers found in eastern England; and the continued dominance of minsters in the landscape outside the Danelaw.

Domesday Book also indicates significant regional variations between the Danelaw and elsewhere in the types of property holders of manors with churches. The Danelaw had less ecclesiastically held property with churches and more lay-held property with churches. Outside the Danelaw, in Wessex especially, minsters and local churches were linked in a mother-daughter church relationship. The *Domesday Monachorum*, *Textus Roffensis*, and *White Book of St. Augustine*, for example, have chrism lists showing the dependence of daughter churches on Kentish minsters.[52] A similar dependent relationship is visible in sokes in the Northern Danelaw and Five Boroughs, in which central manors, possibly with a minster church, had control over a network of sokes and field churches.[53] However, East Anglia (Norfolk and Suffolk), where disruption was greater, had an abundance of lay-owned local churches with little evidence of connection to the ecclesiastical hierarchy.[54] Throughout the Danelaw, most local churches were on lay-held property, many times founded by a group of ordinary freedmen.

Thus the relationship of the local church with the church hierarchy—the episcopal centers and other minsters—varied depending on the nature of its proprietorship and the strength of ecclesiastical authority in the area. In the Danelaw, lay piety manifested in church building far exceeded the ecclesiastical organization of minsters destroyed by the settlers' Viking ancestors. In the rest of England, the minsters still had a strong hold in competition with the new local churches. Overall, Christianity expanded at the local level, not necessarily from a top-down effort but from a grassroots movement of lay piety and, hence, popular religion. This situation produced tension between the old system of minsters centrally controlled and the newer, privately owned local churches.

Conflicts and Relationships

Pre-Conquest England was a confusion of various types of churches developing through different means and conflicting in their interests and ties. On the one hand were collegiate churches over which the archbishops and bishops attempted to exercise a certain degree of control, as evidenced in the monastic reform movement. On the other hand, by the eleventh century, all local churches were seen as somebody's property, whether an ecclesiastical or a lay landowner, and hence relatively independent of episcopal control.

The laws of late Saxon kings clearly tried to create order out of this disorder. They attempted to impose a logical hierarchy onto a range of churches that grew organically and were established without any reference to a central model or system. For example, the laws of Æthelred and Cnut (written by the churchman and reformer Wulfstan) describe four sizes of churches (although all are of course equal in sanctity) and accord them different payments for breach of their peace.[55]

1. *Heafod-mynstres*, literally, head minsters or principal churches, were probably cathedrals, the seat of the bishop and the diocesan center.
2. *Medemram mynstres*, or medium-rank churches, were minsters with a collegiate or monastic group of clergy but were probably differentiated from the first group in not being cathedrals. Nonetheless, as minsters they had a wide parochial jurisdiction and possibly daughter churches under them.
3. *Git læssan*, literally, "yet lesser," had a graveyard but "little divine service," evidence of insufficient clergy to carry out liturgical services on a regular basis. The term is more a description than a name, indicating churches smaller than the minsters.
4. *Feld-circan*, or field churches, were country chapels without a graveyard. This may refer to small chapels or even mission waystations marked with a cross. More than likely such a church did not have its own priest.

The third category undoubtedly refers to the local churches founded primarily by lay owners.[56] The lack of a clearly identifiable name for this category indicates its organic origins. These were neither churches founded from a central organization nor temporary waystations or private chapels. The ability of this type of church to bury people but not offer regular divine services indicates its problematic status; what it can offer in the way of services was linked to both its income and its relationship to ecclesiastical authority.

Conflicts thus arose between bishops and lay lords and between minsters and local churches over jurisdiction, and the temporal and spiritual rights of these churches, especially concerning the control of the church's endowment represented in land (glebe) and revenues (tithe). The local church itself was caught in the middle, with its land and its priest enmeshed in a web of conflicting jurisdiction, between the *dominium* of the seigneur and the *gubernatio* of the bishop.[57]

The legal differences between minsters and local churches indicate the tension between episcopal and proprietary control, a jurisdictional as well as an economic issue. At stake was where the five customary revenues—tithe, church-scot, plough-alms, light-dues, and soul-scot—should go and who should receive the benefit of the church lands.[58] For example, the presence of a consecrated graveyard diverted soul-scot (payment at burial) to that church. The laws furthered this by linking the distribution of tithe to burial. If a thegn's church had a graveyard, one-third of his tithe went to it; but if it did not, he had to pay the priest on his own while the church dues of all the free households went to the old church—the minster.[59] Thus the presence of a graveyard was crucial in the dispute over tithe and soul-scot between local and minster churches. Recent archaeological work indicates not only that early churches might have been built on or near an older (pagan) graveyard but that new graveyards could have been established around or even moved to an existing church.[60]

Laws and canons also linked other rights and revenues. The right to baptize required not only a baptismal font but also chrism, which the church had to obtain yearly from the bishop and for which it paid a fee. The minsters maintained the right to distribute the chrism, a source of revenue, as seen in the chrism lists of Kent discussed above. The Roman ritual of baptism requiring a bishop was difficult in an area such as England, where bishops were few and centralized; hence the custom developed whereby the priest would baptize the infants and the bishop would confirm all these children on his yearly visits.[61] The minsters by law also received church-scot.[62] Plough-alms and light dues, however, more directly related to the daily manorial existence, may have gone to the local church, although there is no clear evidence one way or the other.[63]

This legal tension between local churches with their proprietors and minsters with their ecclesiastical authority is also manifested in the foundation and consecration of the church building and the appointment, ordination, and investiture of its priest, rights that were divided between the lay proprietor and the bishop.[64] The lay proprietor might build the church, but the bishop had the spiritual authority to consecrate it, and the bishop might use this liturgical ceremony as a means of exerting his authority.

Likewise, while the lay church patron assumed the right to appoint the priest, a bishop must have ordained him.[65] The lord's investiture of the priest with some symbol (key or bellrope), for which he paid the lord, was an expression of the lay patron's lordship over the priest. However, the patron must somehow acquire an ordained priest approved by the bishop, since ordination involved an interview by the bishop testing the priest on his knowledge of liturgy and the computation of festivals.[66]

The laws indicate that both bishops and proprietors preferred that the priest be someone well known to them. The canons prohibit uncuth (unknown) priests from serving in churches without the consent of the bishop, who would want to investigate their background. The bishops understandably favored, however, priests trained and ordained under their own authority. On the whole, bishops did not like the idea of priests wandering about, so they required them to stay where they were ordained and hence under the authority of the bishop who ordained them.[67] Similarly, a church proprietor would rather have a priest who was brought up locally, even a serf off his manor, than a stranger.[68] Frequently, then, the incumbent priest would train promising boys (sometimes a son) to help him and follow in his place, a practice canon law encouraged (not with regard to the son).

This preference for priests who were known to both the bishop and the proprietor worked only insofar as these two authorities agreed on such a person. But the reform canons indicate that conflicts of interest did arise. For example, Ælfric prohibited laymen from exerting authority over clergy, advising proprietors to seek the advice of wise teachers in the appointment of their priests. Likewise, the laws did not allow proprietors to dismiss clergy. The layman's support, in Ælfric's opinion, was limited to worldly concerns.[69]

Given the proprietary nature of churches, the jurisdictional aspects of hiring a priest were nightmarish, as indicated in the canons discussed above. A proprietor could hire one of his own tenants or bring someone in from another diocese. In the latter instance, the priest so hired was ordained by some other bishop or with ties to a minster outside the diocese in which he now resided, so that the bishop who now had authority over him was not certain of the priest's credentials or abilities. Even more disconcerting was a situation known as a peculiar, in which a priest hired and serving on a property owned by a minster or churchman in another diocese had two bishops over him, one the proprietor of the land and church, the other the ecclesiastical authority.[70] These conflicts mirror the secular landholding patterns of late Saxon England but are compounded by the overlap of spiritual and temporal affairs. While a situation in which a bishop's two roles as landowner and spiritual leader conflicted did not happen frequently, the tension between two hierarchies, material and spiritual, was a constant problem for local priests.

In this struggle between bishop and lay proprietor, more than in any other, we see how the local priest and his church were pulled in two directions. These temporal conditions influenced the type of ministry the priest had as a clergyman. His relationships with the bishop, with the proprietor of the church, and with his congregation of fellow villeins were all factors affecting his training, physical livelihood, church facilities, and status with his congregation.

The Priest and the Bishop

The relationship of the local priest to higher ecclesiastical authority is difficult to establish, in part because of the regional variation visible in Domesday Book and the haphazard, proprietary nature of church organization, but mostly because of lack of evidence. Reading between the lines of the laws and canons of tenth- and eleventh-century reformers such as Ælfric and Wulfstan, we can gain a partial picture of a rural priesthood relatively isolated from ecclesiastical connections, struggling to carry out the simplest duties of their calling.

A wide geographic and social gap separated the local priest from the bishop. According to the canons of the church, the priest had initial contact with his bishop at ordination, potentially at a church consecration, yearly to acquire the chrism and perhaps to attend a diocesan synod at the same time, and also on those occasions when the bishop visited, presumably at least annually to confirm baptized children. Although we have no records of ordinations, consecrations, synods, or episcopal visitations, references to them in canons, homilies, and saints' lives demonstrate at least an awareness of this function of the bishop.[71]

In an ideal world a bishop would travel extensively in his diocese. For example, hagiographers praise saints such as Wulfstan and Swithun for their active visitation schedules and numerous church foundations and consecrations, but the writers extol these practices as exemplary, not ordinary.[72] Both Ælfric and Wulfstan emphasized synods as an integral part of the reform of the clergy, and Joseph Ayer has argued, despite the lack of evidence for them, that diocesan synods were more likely to have occurred through necessity than provincial synods, which declined through decentralization and the merger with the king's Witenagemot.[73] In the case of ecclesiastically held properties with churches, discussed above, it could be argued that minsters sent out priests from the minster household to serve local churches and hence maintained a closer link with them through such a mother-daughter relationship.[74] On the whole, it is difficult to know how much these laws and canons reflect the expectations of reformers and the copying of continental canons as opposed to what was done in reality.

Regarding the selection and training of the typical local priest, there is even less information. References in canons and other ecclesiastical literature, cited above, indicate that both proprietors and bishops preferred local candidates as opposed to outsiders, and this reform literature encourages lone priests to take on boys to train and to assist at the mass. The reforming canons do place special emphasis on education, showing a deep concern for inadequately trained priests, an indication that the education of priests was a problem. For example, eleventh-century ordination instructions speci-fied that a priest may show evidence of his education by bringing some token from his teacher attesting to his abilities; these same instructions also allowed a "half-educated" [samlæredne] priest to be ordained.

These eleventh-century ordination instructions, probably authored by Wulfstan, give some insight on the basic training a priest should acquire from his teacher before presenting himself to the bishop for ordination. The examination of the prospective priest by the bishop specifies that the candi-date should be able to explain to other people the true faith, including what God has done in the past and what he will do; he should know his duties and the symbolic meaning [getacnunge] of the rituals he performs, baptism and the mass in particular; he must explain how much of the canons he knows; and then he must demonstrate how to compute the annual calendar for festivals. Failure in these essentials delays ordination, with the excep-tion allowed for "great need."[75] The implication of these instructions is that candidates would arrive at the minster, present themselves to the bishop with a token from their teacher, take the exam, and remain some time to receive further instruction through participating in the collegiate life of the minster. Ælfric also urged priests to teach one another—presumably this was possible only in the collegiate setting of the minsters.[76] Both Ælfric and Wulfstan clearly favored the corporate environment of the minster for educating priests.

However, local priests' connections with collegiate clergy varied, but must have been minimal in many cases. Minsters were well enough staffed to have an assortment of the various ranks of clergy listed in canon law, per-haps all seven, to carry out the various clerical duties. At the other extreme, the local priest, lacking even a deacon to assist him, faced the problem of having to celebrate mass alone, strictly prohibited in canon law.[77] It was possible for a minster to send out some of its duly ordained priests to serve in churches on properties it owned or at the request of a local lay church proprietor. But given the power and pressure of lay proprietorship on these churches, especially in the Danelaw, and the proprietor's right to select his own priest, it is more likely that most clergy serving in local churches rarely saw the inside of a minster. The proprietor would appoint a young man from the ranks of his tenants or as the son of the previous priest and then have him ordained by a bishop, who would rarely be in a position to refuse such a request even if he did, following the canons, require some evidence of the candidate's fitness.[78]

Given these conditions, it is doubtful that these priests even came close to meeting the standards of training, books, liturgical utensils, or learning set by canon law, standards especially prominent in the reforming work of Ælfric and Wulfstan. The Canons of Edgar by Wulfstan specify that priests have the book in front of them while performing the mass, which raises many questions: Were they incapable of performing the liturgy properly without such an aid? Did they have the books? Could they read them? Despite the increase in books in minster libraries after the tenth-century reform, few local priests themselves would own any of the books so many minsters now proudly listed in their charters.[79]

The reformers Ælfric and Wulfstan, following the monastic impulses of their training, focused on two aspects of the clergy to improve: character, which was directly related to their learning and influenced their ability to teach the laity, and status in relationship to the church hierarchy and their congregation. These aspects were linked in the reformers' minds, as they sought to elevate the clergy by bringing them under tighter episcopal control (through teaching and synods) and by setting them apart from the laity in lifestyle and behavior.

The priest's character should set him apart from the laity, making him a respected teacher. In Wulfstan's favorite words (also used by Ælfric), priests were to bodnian and bysnian the laity, teach and set an example.[80] Ælfric even went so far as to tell priests that if they could not teach (and he is trying to tell them how), then at least they should set a good example.[81] Half-learned priests ordained as exceptions in the eleventh-century ordination ritual were to rely on more learned priests to teach them.[82]

Priestly differentiation from the laity was a crucial issue to Ælfric and Wulfstan, linked to a sense of social cleanliness and spiritual separation.[83] Priests were not to be merchants or gleemen (minstrels), engage in drinking sprees, or otherwise act like laymen.[84] Central to these ideas of cleanliness and separation was the issue of celibacy. The marriage of priests, common at this time, hindered the priest's abilities, according to reformers, in several ways. The earthly wife took away from the priest's devotion to his spiritual wife, the church; his married state put him at the same level as the laity, whereas celibacy set the priest apart from the laity in sanctity; and, although the reformers do not stress this as much as the other reasons, marriage allowed for a hereditary priesthood that bypassed episcopal authority.[85]

The reward the reformers offered to the celibate priest was the rank of thegn, an aristocratic status above his economic station as a villein and equal to the lay proprietor in many cases. However, celibacy of the rural priesthood as an aim of the reformers did not have any real effect until after 1100. The reformers' failure, as evidenced in the celibacy issue, is in part the result of the proprietary character of the church and the churchmen's consequent lack of effective control over the rural priesthood.

The Priest and the Proprietor

If, then, the local priest's connections with the church hierarchy were tenuous, his relations with the church proprietor were more solid. The owner was much more directly involved in sustaining the existence of the church and the priest and had a greater voice in how the church was run, in terms of both his responsibilities for it and his rights over it.

The proprietor had certain responsibilities in the care of his church. Ælfric and Wulfstan, in the laws he authored, expected lay proprietors to take an interest in the promotion of Christian beliefs in their area. Ælfric wrote to prominent thegns explaining Christian doctrine, while the laws emphasized the need to support Christianity in order to promote a unified Christian kingdom.[86] The proprietor was also expected to protect the church and its land from any incursions and to maintain its property.[87] The laws and canons further specified the distribution of tithes in three parts, one for the priest, one for church maintenance, and one for the poor — perhaps an attempt to protect the tithe from personal use by the proprietor.[88] A charter of 955 indicated that a prudent landowner made himself responsible for church dues, burial fees, and tithes.[89]

For bearing these burdens, however, the proprietor also assumed rights of lordship over the church's property and its priest. The priest was obliged to serve the lord who appointed him in more ways than as a priest. Since the lord invested the priest with the church and its lands, the priest had a dependent relationship with that lord just like any other tenant.[90] Despite the wide variety in the size of the manor having a church as seen in Domesday Book, the property of the church itself, where Domesday Book recorded it, was more uniform. The glebe of local churches tended to average 1 hide, about the size of a typical villein's property.[91] Thus a priest's obligations in rents and services to the lord were approximately the same as a villein's.[92] The proprietor's expectations added these secular duties to the priestly burdens of keeping up the church and carrying out liturgical duties.

This duality of the priest's life, secular and spiritual, had several implications. Small wonder that most of these priests were married; they would need helpmates to assist them in caring for the church and household. One also wonders what kind of pressure this dual relationship placed on the priest, as a loyal villein and yet a spiritual teacher. Late Anglo-Saxon laws stressed that laymen were to obey their spiritual teachers.[93] The Canons of Edgar indicates some conflict when it instructs priests to report at the synod any laymen too powerful for the priest to rebuke.[94] The priest also served alongside the reeve as an arbiter between lord and villeins, urging both to cooperate with each other.[95] Certainly the local priest's ambivalent economic and social status benefited from any spiritual enhancements to his rank he could claim. These spiritual powers also put him in a position as social mediator and catalyst for cultural change.

The Priest and the Folk

The local priest's economic status as a villein placed him in intimate contact with a large proportion of his congregation, the villeins and other tenants of the manor or vill. Frequently the Domesday Book entries lump priests with the villeins and indicate that the priests had a share in the ploughteams.[96]

While he was their equal in economic terms, however, the priest had the advantage of the ecclesiastical power vested in him, especially evident in the mass. Performing the mass was the central duty of a priest and was a symbol of his role as mediator; in his person and actions he brought together the divine and the earthly, uniting the community spiritually and physically as the congregation came together for the celebration.[97] The local priest's abilities to perform the mass correctly made little difference, for despite his inadequacies, the power remained in the office.[98] Cnut's laws ordered the kingdom to honor all clergy because of their power in the mass.[99] Because of this theoretical power, the priest, no matter what his physical age, maintained the position of *ealdwita*, "old one who knows," Ælfric's translation of the Latin *seniorem*.[100] Thus the priest was ideally a respected leader in his community.

The Local Church as a Locus of Spiritual and Communal Strength

Through the priest's relationships with the various ranks of early medieval society (ecclesiastical authority, aristocracy, peasantry), he played a pivotal role in the development of popular Christianity. The local church became the center of the manorial community, linking spiritual, social, and political interests. As Susan Reynolds has admirably shown, communal bonds were as important as, if not more important than, hierarchical connections.[101] Thus the local church with its priest was a vital locus of communal activity.

Physically the church may have been in the center of the vill and used for a wide variety of functions other than liturgical. While many early private chapels were attached to lords' halls, gradually they moved out, becoming separate buildings serving more than just the lord's household.[102] Many early churches were timber—some so flimsy that Dunstan could realign one by leaning against it.[103] But recent archaeological studies show that many wooden churches were rebuilt of stone in the tenth and eleventh centuries, indicating a commitment to the church as a permanent part of the rural landscape.[104]

The shape of these early churches also reveals their function. Early churches were of the simple cellular type—a single room serving as both nave and chancel (see fig. 2.1). Most were wooden and have since disappeared, unless their remains are preserved under a stone church. Rebuilt churches of stone were usually of the two-celled or cellular linear type (a separate yet connected nave and chancel) with space for the priest to perform the liturgy and space for the congregation. The altar was often at the meeting of the two areas (fig. 2.2).[105] Hence, in both these styles the priest and the congregation were much closer during the mass than in a large, complex minster.

The interior of the church reflected the clergy's educational concerns and the illiteracy of the congregation. The walls were frequently plastered and decorated with paintings that communicated various biblical stories.[106] Churches were usually dedicated to a saint, although local churches did not have relics.[107] This saint served as an exemplar of piety for the inhabitants but also filled the need for a local cult, perhaps replacing the animistic worship at springs, wells, and trees. Some holy wells, for example, may predate Christianity but were renamed after a Christian saint; presumably the water from such wells continued to have curative properties now enhanced by the saint's heavenly position.[108]

The church and the priest had secular roles as well. Although the canons prohibited unseemly things—anything not related to the liturgy—to be brought inside the church, other evidence suggests that nevertheless congregations used churches for secular meetings such as parish feasts and church ales as well as the adjudication of legal disputes and possibly healing rituals.[109] Likewise, the priest had secular duties, particularly in law enforce-

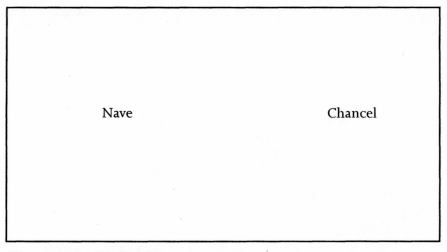

Nave   Chancel

Figure 2.1. Single-celled church plan

ment and as an arbiter, but also in the care of the poor by distributing the alms.[110]

The priest's duties were many and his rewards scanty. He heard the confession of sinners, took the Eucharist to the sick, insured the baptism of the newborn, cared for the poor, and enforced the keeping of the Sabbath and festivals, as well as taught the laity basic Christian truths. Throughout their writings Ælfric and Wulfstan demonstrate a strong concern that priests be able and willing to carry out all of these duties.[111] Ælfric prohibited priests from taking payment for performing these rites, an indication not only of greedy priests but also of the narrow straits they could be in if the proprietor and the minster absorbed the church revenues.[112]

Care of the sick is a good example of the complex duties of the priest. The priest used the chrism "purchased" from a minster not only for baptism but also to anoint the sick, to whom he also gave the Eucharist.[113] Two problems occurred in taking the Eucharist to the sick. Ælfric and Wulfstan condemned the practice of saving the elements consecrated at Easter for distribution to the sick over the next year (they could spoil)—an indication that the priest was attempting to avoid having to say mass whenever someone was ill, especially since he was prohibited from saying mass either alone or in anyone's house.[114] Second, many sick people were afraid to receive the Eucharist for fear that, if healed, they would have to live some sort of holy life.[115] This introduces some popular notions about the power of the mass, and consequently of the priest, that the charms also indicate.

The intimacy of the priest's relationship with his congregation is evident

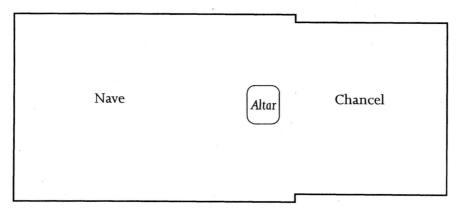

Figure 2.2. *Two-celled church plan, showing possible location of the altar*

in the hearing of confession and administering penance. The proliferation of vernacular penitentials in the late Saxon period indicates two things. The increased need for instruction on this matter means confession and penance were becoming common practices, and the vernacular indicates more widespread usage of these texts, reaching to the large body of illiterate (that is, non-Latin-reading) priests, which included the local clergy.[116] This penitential role for clergy involved a judicial as well as an educational angle; the priest must judge the behavior and character of his parishioners as well as teach them Christian morality.

For the reformers this teaching was fundamental to the role of the priest in making a Christian society. Ælfric wrote his collections of homilies precisely for that purpose, to give priests some basic sermon examples.[117] According to both Ælfric and Wulfstan, priests should teach the gospel in English on Sundays and massdays.[118] As a result of the priest's instruction, the laity should at least know the Pater noster and Creed as well as confess and receive the Eucharist no less than once a year.[119]

His duties as priest to teach, baptize, anoint the sick, celebrate mass, hear confession, and administer last rites, however, probably extended beyond mere duty to include care and concern for the ignorant, the newborn, the ill, the dying, and the sinful. Sharing the concerns for land and productivity gave him ample opportunity to apply the power of Christian ritual in appeals to the Almighty for aid. It is doubtful, then, that the priest would have used his liturgical training, however scanty, only in regular, perfunctory ways. Rather, it is likely he adapted his knowledge of Christian ideas, however inadequate, to meet local needs, frequently using local customs. Thus the local priest as a mediator between the ecclesiastical hierarchy and the laity became a catalyst for the development of popular religion. The

Field Remedy cited at the beginning of Chapter 1 is a literate representation of the kinds of ceremonies that a local priest might have created to provide spiritual help for material concerns in an agricultural setting.

Conclusions: Popular Religion in the Local Church Environment

The development of local churches in large numbers throughout England in the tenth and eleventh centuries created an entirely new environment in which priests and the laity interacted on a level different from that in the minsters. Due to the differences in proprietorship, the economic, social, and religious position of a local priest was distinctly different from that of a minster priest. The environment of the manor or vill allowed for a closer interaction between clergy and laity in a small church, in which common needs could be met by the spiritual power of the priest.

Popular religion was a product of this local environment, in the meeting between everyday domestic and agricultural concerns reflecting Germanic folk customs and the rudimentary Christian expertise of a local priest. Conversion by acculturation was the logical outcome, evident in the transformation of folk remedies and practices in their combination with basic Christian ideas and rituals, both giving assurance of good health and prosperity. This local picture of the process of conversion gives a broader view of the Christianization of late Saxon England than just a survey of the major events of conversion and helps make sense of those events. Guthrum's baptism under Alfred's fatherly hand is an event symbolic of this cultural transformation, an event whose deeper meaning developed in the next generation as both Anglo-Saxons and Scandinavians found common ground in the local church.

3

MAGIC AND MIRACLE
THE AUGUSTINIAN WORLDVIEW
AND THE REFORM OF POPULAR
CHRISTIANITY

Seen from above, from the perspective of the formal hierarchy, the mushrooming church structure of the late tenth and early eleventh centuries appeared chaotic and out of control, in need of reform. The new generation of reformers, faced with this localized church structure, burgeoning lay piety, and newly or un-Christianized Scandinavians, endeavored by laws, homilies, and letters to take the moral value system they inherited from the earlier monastic reformers to the level of common priests now serving independently in churches throughout rural England. The efforts of these reformers reveal a cosmological shift, as these churchmen attempted to reorient popular belief within a Christian framework of meaning.

If local priests stood on one side of the boundary between popular and formal religion, mediating folk culture, then literate reformers such as Ælfric and Wulfstan stood on the other, popularizing Christian doctrine. These two churchmen applied principles from their own training in the monastic reform movement to the growth of local churches and the renewed threat of paganism from the Viking presence. Ælfric and Wulfstan took positive action to accommodate Christianity to popular needs, if only to counteract other popularizations they perceived as dangerously erroneous. The result was the implementation and spread by these reformers of a Germanic-Christian worldview that scholars often refer to as Augustinian. This worldview integrated a wide variety of native ideas with classical Christian concepts, on a spectrum ranging from what some might call magic to religion, with a lot in between.[1]

This chapter first explicates this generic Augustinian worldview by examining homilies, and those of Ælfric in particular, as sources for a Germanic-Christian view of nature and knowledge that did not separate natural from supernatural. Second, this chapter explores the categories of miracle, magic, and things "in-between," from a late Saxon view, using healing as an example. This category of middle practices, accommodations made to meet the needs of daily life with Christian truth, is the foundation for the analysis of the charms carried out in Chapters 4 and 5. This chapter argues that despite the obvious conflicts between paganism and Christianity, and magic and miracle, in popular homiletic sources, the accommodations in ritual allowed in between these extremes reveal the most about how Christianity came to be established popularly in late Anglo-Saxon England.

The Augustinian Worldview

Worldview is a convenient category for understanding on a comparative basis how an individual or a group of people perceived their reality, specifically their relationships to the environment, one another, and the divine or supernatural. Especially in examining the early Middle Ages, when social patterns were in flux, it is best to speak of worldviews, plural, to indicate that beliefs were diverse and in transition. The predominant view in the surviving texts represents a literate and therefore highly classical-Christian view usually called Augustinian. On the other hand, evidence even in these texts indicates the existence of a surviving Germanic folk worldview that was not always necessarily in conflict with the Christian attitude dominating the texts. The Augustinian worldview so evident in the majority of Anglo-Saxon religious texts was mainly the product of medieval interpretation and popularization of the ideas of the great fourth-century church father Augustine.[2]

The homilies of the late Anglo-Saxon reformers are good examples of this tradition of interpretation and popularization in Anglo-Saxon style. They shaped the basic ideas of the Augustinian worldview to make them comprehensible to an Anglo-Saxon audience; this shaping involved both rejecting paganism and understanding Anglo-Saxon popular folk belief. The significant similarities between Germanic and early Christian beliefs described below meant that such accommodation occurred quite easily.

However, from a modern or even post-twelfth-century view of Christian theology, some of these accommodations appear untenable. The rationalism developed by scholasticism from the twelfth century on operated from a framework of knowledge, an understanding of nature, and definitions of magic and religion different from their early medieval predecessors. The modern bias toward scientific thought and rationality is especially strong in the treatment of magic and religion. Magic became in the early modern era anything viewed as nonscientific, while religion came to encompass purely spiritual considerations that fell outside the realm of science. An understanding of the early medieval view of knowledge and nature, magic and religion, helps explain the accommodations made and prevents us from mistakenly calling something magic which late Saxons would not have so designated.

The Augustinian worldview did not make a distinction in the same way that later ages did between knowledge gained through human observation and reason, and knowledge acquired directly or indirectly through revelation from God (Scripture, tradition, miracles, or visions). Consequently, early medieval thinkers made little attempt to separate natural from supernatural phenomena. Nature was itself a revelation from God, and extraordinary occurrences such as miracles were simply God "raising His voice."[3] What distinguished magic as the opposite of miracle (parallel to the pagan-versus-Christian dichotomy) was not its methods but its source. Magic was illusory, a deception of the Devil to entrap souls. Miracles, on the other hand, were wonder-provoking, unusual events in the physical realm that led a person to give glory to God and usually contained a moral message from him; frequently they verified the sanctity of a holy person. Because of this definition by source, medicinal and other practices evolved in the early Middle Ages that in their method appear to us to be magic (that is, unscientific) but that were at the time considered Christian because they invoked God. Such practices were not exactly miracles by strict definition either, however, but fell somewhere between magic and miracle.

Early medieval ways of dealing with the mysterious elements of life—death, disease, and disaster—thus fall into two extremes as propounded by the Augustinian worldview, magic and miracles, but with a wide spectrum of practices, such as charms, that lie in between. These three modes of interaction—magic, miracle, and the various middle practices—can be seen in the writings of the reformers Ælfric and Wulfstan as they attempted to bring about popular reform. Homilies in particular are excellent sources for the popularizing efforts of these reformers as they grappled with Anglo-Saxon folk culture in relation to Christian belief.

Homilies

The surviving collections of sermons in the Anglo-Saxon language, despite their heavy reliance on traditional sources, reveal a good deal about the mentality of Christian leaders in the tenth and eleventh centuries. The authors of these sermons copied in whole or in part from earlier, renowned Christian writers, most notably Augustine, Pope Gregory I, Isidore of Seville, Caesarius of Arles, and Bede. The age and prominence of the sources increased the authority of the sermon in a society that valued tradition as highly as Scripture; homilists thus built their sermons on traditional, and therefore accurate, interpretations of God's revelation. However, this copying was not mindless. The way in which these authors assembled, restated, and interpreted their sources in the vernacular can reveal a tremendous amount about the authors and their perceptions of culture.

Anglo-Saxon homilies fall into two groups in modern scholarly analysis: (1) the popular sermon collections, such as the Blickling and Vercelli Homilies; and (2) the collections of the reformers Ælfric and Wulfstan, who framed their sermons consciously in contrast to the first type, which they felt had distorted Christian truth in their popularization of Christian ideas.[4] It is in this second group, the sermons of Ælfric and Wulfstan, that we find a clear presentation of an Augustinian worldview adapted to an Anglo-Saxon audience. In a queer twist of irony, we find out more about the accommodations of Germanic beliefs in the sermons of these reformers, because they were trying so self-consciously to manipulate these beliefs, than we do in the so-called popular sermons, which essentially translated continental sources without much manipulation or sophistication.

Hence the *Blickling* and *Vercelli* collections of homilies reveal a mishmash of Christian ideas without a clear agenda. Both collections predated Ælfric and Wulfstan and their authors tended to copy continental sources much more uncritically and therefore with some contradictions.[5] Neither collection has an overarching purpose or reform agenda; rather, the homilists attempted to present basic moral Christian truths and the most necessary information about Christian living.

The *Blickling Homilies* (circa 971) represent late tenth-century popular concerns.[6] The most common theme motivating the exhortations to Christian living was eschatology, the coming end of the world. For example, Sermon X urged penitence based on this truth contained in its title, "The End of the World Is Near."[7] The nearness of this end was evident in natural calamities, human crimes, and warfare. The homilists read these events as signs that the world was evil and getting more so; doing good deeds was getting harder. The lesson was to work harder at good through charity, peace, right teaching, humility, and confession. This emphasis on doomsday is found throughout the Blickling collection.[8]

The *Blickling Homilies* used this eschatological theme to expound lessons on the dichotomies of Christian truth: soul versus body, eternity versus temporality, heaven versus hell, God versus devils. Death, Judgment Day, and Christ's harrowing of hell were favorite subjects for communicating the message of repentance. The homilies examined the life of Christ more as example than as theology. The soteriology was very practical and simple, focused on the dual nature of Christ (divine and human), while the deeds of Christ formed the basis of the lesson. The homilies presented Christ's miracles and his teachings as specific revelations from God, models to emulate: "The Lord came into the world among the people of Israel, and set for them the example of eternal life, and invited them to heaven's kingdom, through his miracles [*wundor-geweorc*, 'wonder-works'] and evangelical lore."[9]

Such homilies represented magic and miracles at opposite poles, in the same way the Devil opposes God. The stories of miracles and magic were all traditional tales: Christ's resistance to temptation after his baptism, his miracles of healing, the magic of Simon Magus versus the miracles of the apostle Peter, and the miracles of saints such as Andrew. The only occasion where the Anglo-Saxon word for charm, *galdor*, appears in these homilies is in the context of evil deeds, taught to men by the Devil. The people in hell include thieves, the covetous, the proud, and "sorcerers [*scinlæcan*] who practice enchantments [*galdor-cræftas*] and deceptions, and with them deceive and seduce unwary men, and wean them from the contemplation of

God with their sorceries [*scinlacum*] and deceptions [*gedwolcraeftum*]."[10] Thus the *Blickling Homilies* presented a simple, dualistic picture of the world in which evil works through illusion and deception.

The *Vercelli Homilies*, found in the *Vercelli* manuscript containing such famous poems as *The Dream of the Rood* and *Soul and Body*, present another series of popular homilies, produced in the generation before Ælfric and Wulfstan. Like the *Blickling*, they contain a strong eschatological emphasis. For example, Sermon 9 focuses on a comparative description of heaven and hell, emphasizing the separation of body and soul.[11] Again, traditional dichotomies or oppositions played a central role, presenting a polarized worldview.

The *Blickling* in particular and the *Vercelli* to a certain degree relied exclusively on their traditional sources and, other than in the process of translation, made no interpretive efforts to relate these ideas to the local scene. Consequently, ideas in them are very simple, black and white. Ironically, this means that these more popular sermons reveal less of the accommodations made in the formation of a consistent worldview encompassing Germanic and Christian ideas, other than to show the simplification of Christian doctrine into something comprehensible.

On the other hand, the attempts of Ælfric and Wulfstan to bring about a reformed popular Christianity (or, as they would have said, to educate the laity in basic Christian doctrine) reveal a more systematized worldview that is worth examining to see how these two reformers set the parameters on magic and religion according to a certain system of knowledge and the kinds of in-between practices that were acceptable, and those that were not.

Ælfric and Wulfstan

Ælfric and Wulfstan represent two distinctive personalities in the world of reform in the late tenth and early eleventh centuries. Both men were involved in the same mission and were part of a similar homiletic tradition, but they exhibited very different characteristics in their homilies.[12] In general Wulfstan reveals more of the dichotomies of the Augustinian worldview (pagan versus Christian), and Ælfric displays more of the accommodations used to bridge the gap between reformed clergy and illiterate clergy and laity.

Their goal was to extend the reform movement begun in the previous generation under Dunstan, Oswald, and Æthelwold.[13] The difference was that Ælfric and Wulfstan did not aim their reforms primarily at monasteries, as their predecessors did, but at the secular clergy through laws, canons, and homilies.[14] Moreover, the political circumstances had changed drastically. The relatively peaceful rule of Edgar had been replaced by the upheaval brought about by renewed Danish raids under King Æthelred Unræd. Ælfric and Wulfstan wrote explicitly to counteract false teaching in the face of difficult circumstances that seemed to indicate the coming end of the world.[15]

The Augustinian worldview as it operated in late Anglo-Saxon England is clearly evident in the homilies of Abbot Ælfric of Eynsham (ca. 955–ca. 1010), who relied on Augustine as his source in his discussions of magic, miracles, and natural medicine. His vernacular homilies, in the two sets of *Catholic Homilies* (989 and 992) and the *Saints' Lives* (1002), were works of popular religion in the sense that they attempted to adapt and communicate Christian theology in Anglo-Saxon terms to a lay audience.[16]

Ælfric wrote his *Homilies* and *Lives* for clergy to preach to lay congregations. He demonstrated his concern for lay congregations in proprietary churches in his correspondence with prominent laymen. In his letters to the rural landowners Wulfgeat, Sigeweard, and Sigefyrth he instructed them in basic Christian doctrine similar to that expounded in his homilies.[17] Thus the homilies may also have been read by literate lay persons who were considered "unlearned" or "lewed" in its original sense because they could not read Latin.[18] Consequently, Ælfric's homilies had wide circulation, as is evident in the number of surviving manuscripts.[19]

Ælfric was aware that in adapting theological material for a less learned audience there was a certain loss in the transmission. For example, he apologizes for his simplicity to any learned person reading his books: "If any learned man [*gelæred man*] read over this account, or hear it read, then I bid him not to blame this shortening: to him can his own understanding speak fully about these things; and for you laymen [*læwedum mannum*] this is enough, though you know not the deep secret [*digelnysse*] therein."[20] His concern in writing was for the ignorant who might be led astray by false teaching, and so he adapted his material to that level: "One must speak to laymen [*læwedum mannum*] according to the measure of their understanding, so that they be not dismayed [*æmode*; lit., 'out of mind,' 'mad'] by the deepness, nor bored by the length."[21]

On the other hand, Ælfric's prolific writing of sermons was motivated by his disdain for other sermon collections that did not reflect his reformed ideas. He wrote "not through the boldness of great lore, but because I have seen and heard of much error in many English books, which unlearned men [*ungelærede menn*], through their simpleness, have held as great wisdom;

and I grieved that they neither knew nor had the gospel lore in their writings, except those men only who knew Latin."[22] So Ælfric balanced very carefully the need to communicate in a language people could understand and that priests could transmit, and the need to maintain the integrity of the doctrines and practices he knew he understood more deeply than they could.[23]

Ælfric's colleague Wulfstan, Archbishop of York from 1002 to 1023, had a different disposition. His most prominent works are the law codes he promulgated under both Æthelred and Cnut and his now famous Sermo Lupi; but he also produced a series of homilies, though not as extensive as Ælfric's. More so than Ælfric, Wulfstan battled with the forces of heathenism, perhaps because of his direct experience with Vikings in the north. His De Falsis Diis, for example, even if reliant on Ælfric's work, demonstrates an overt concern over the continuation of paganism.[24] The tone in the law codes of Æthelred is particularly desperate, attributing all present difficulties to heathenism, revealing the basic assumption in early medieval worldviews that physical circumstances (political, social, or environmental) are reflections of a spiritual reality. If the kingdom was in trouble or natural disasters abounded, then there was need for repentance, as reflected, for example, in the edict issued by King Æthelred in 1009 but probably authored by Wulfstan.

> This was decreed when the great army came to the land. All of us need eagerly to merit that we might have God's mercy and his mild-heartedness and that we through his help may be able to withstand enemies. Now it is our will that all the people fast as a general penance [*dædbote*, or "deed-remedy"] for three days on bread and vegetables and water . . . and that every man come barefoot to church without gold and ornaments, and go to confession.[25]

The greatest statement of this call to reform comes from Wulfstan's Sermo Lupi, written in response to the deteriorating conditions late in Æthelred's reign.

> For it is clear and visible in all of us that we have before this broken [commands] more often than we have bettered [ourselves], and therefore many things assail this people. Things have not been good now for a long time within [our land] or without, but there has been war and hunger, burning and bloodshed on every side time and again; and theft and murder, plague and pestilence, murrain and disease, slander and hate and plundering of robbers have harmed us very severely.

And excessive levies [for tribute] have greatly oppressed us, and bad weather has very often caused bad harvests; because in this land there has been, as it may seem, now for many years many injustices and unstable loyalties everywhere among men.[26]

Wulfstan's words reinforce the notion that spiritual ills lie behind the material problems of life, a view consonant with native Germanic views of spiritual agency and causation. Homilists blame bad harvests on moral failure and divine retribution, just as the charms link physical illness to spiritual attacks by elves and demons. Wulfstan's aim here is to put a moral twist on this causation, to locate the troubles in the sinful behavior and disunity of the community (partly attributed to the Danelaw troubles). Even in Cnut's reign, where things were significantly calmer, Wulfstan carried on his battle against heathenism, although without the same desperation. More as a warning and as a show of Cnut's God-favored status, the king's new codes repeat laws against heathenism from earlier law codes.[27]

Wulfstan's writings therefore emphasized the adversarial role played by reform in society. More so than Ælfric, Wulfstan stated things as black and white, us versus them, good versus evil, and Christian versus pagan. This antipathy to the slightest taint of evil or compromise may have been not only a function of his personality but a reaction to the impact of the Vikings in the Danelaw and his consequent efforts as archbishop of York to rebuild the Christian church in that territory. Therefore his castigations of paganism may reflect his personal experience with such practices in his own territory. His exhortations in law and sermon aim to make a change by force of word through the king.

Ælfric, on the other hand, worked more with the mediators of Christianity to the people, the priests, and so he was more concerned with reaching across the gap, finding ways of accommodating reform ideas to daily reality. His goal was to upgrade the priests in their behavior and knowledge so that they could properly lead the lay people into a right understanding of Christian truth. While Wulfstan also had these same goals, he accomplished them mostly by commanding; Ælfric provided the means, in his sermon collections. Therefore, much more of the detailed workings of the Augustinian worldview were revealed in his writings, which can be analyzed in terms of his understanding of knowledge and nature as well as his views on miracles, magic, and things in between miracle and magic.

Knowledge and Nature

Although Ælfric's worldview was not unique, his use of the medieval Augustinian system was peculiarly Anglo-Saxon, if only because he was translating these ideas into the Anglo-Saxon language and thought patterns; this translation process gave a different tone to the concepts.[28] For example, typical of the Augustinian approach to nature, Ælfric asserted that it was not for man to investigate how God, for whom all things are equally easy, could create Adam out of dirt.

> Now we cannot examine how out of that dirt he made flesh and blood, bones and skin, hair and nails. Men see often that out of one little kernel comes a great tree, but we can see in that kernel neither root, nor rind, nor boughs, nor leaves; but the same God who draws forth from the kernel tree, and fruits, and leaves, likewise may from dust raise flesh and bones, sinews and hair.[29]

In this passage Ælfric endeavored to explain a theological mystery in terms familiar to his Anglo-Saxon readers.[30] Unlike in modern science, the emphasis was not on how the universe works, except by analogy, but on the God who made it.

This same emphasis on the deity colors the Augustinian view of knowledge. The distinction between scientific and religious knowledge so important in later ages did not exist; all *scientia* was from God.[31] Likewise the modern distinction between natural and supernatural was unclear. All phenomena, all of nature, visible and invisible, miracles or natural healing, were seen as an expression of God, part of the created natural order. Thus Ælfric did not readily distinguish between supernatural and natural things in the way that post-twelfth-century thought did. Rather, he recognized two realms using sense observation (sight and touch): visible versus invisible, body versus spirit, "within and without." Christ and man participated in both the unseen (*ungesewenlice*) and seen (*gesewenlice*), having both body (*lichaman*) and soul (*gastas*). When the good man dies, "the body turns to earth and awaits the resurrection, and in that space-time [*fyrste*] senses nothing."[32]

Ælfric also explained how in a Christian worldview divinity relates to the natural and human world, making difficult theology explicable through the use of vernacular terminology. In this view God is everywhere, not spatially but by the presence of his majesty; thus God's spirit fills the circumference of the earth, and he holds and maintains all things.[33] This view would appear comfortingly similar to pre-Christian belief about the presence of spiritual agencies inhabiting the natural world. However, in the Christian cosmology, Ælfric makes clear that God is distinct from creation. Every substance that is not God is a creature and that which is not creature is God. While creation has measure (*gemete*), number (*getele*), and weight (*hefe*), God does not.[34] God's omnipresence permeates nature because he is the Creator who yet stands outside his creation as well as within it. How well that distinction of an immanent and yet separate God was comprehensible to the late Saxon lay mind is hard to assess, particularly when Germanic entities such as elves and dwarves are blended into the picture.

Early medieval iconography displays this spiritual worldview by picturing angels and demons as divinely appointed actors on a God-directed stage. Many illuminated manuscript illustrations, such as those in the *Canterbury Psalter* discussed in Chapter 5, represent the heavenly realm as a cloud-bordered section impinging on the human world at the top of the picture, sometimes with the hand of God extending out of that realm into the action of the scene depicted in the psalm.[35] Some of Æthelred's coins display an image of the hand of God coming down from the sky, a significant reminder of divine judgment. While these vernacular writings and artwork all expressed traditional Christian doctrine, the explanation in particularly Anglo-Saxon terms emphasized the greatness and yet nearness of God in relation to his creation, a view of God's immanence that resonated well with earlier Germanic folk belief. Thus the peopling of the atmosphere and nature with spiritual agencies is a shared characteristic of Christianity and Germanic religions.

Nonetheless this Christian cosmology altered the relationship between humanity and the rest of creation. Within Ælfric's Augustinian worldview humans are different from other creations because each person has a soul, and each has something of all the other creatures. In this essentially Neoplatonic view humans stand in the middle of creation since they have existence (*wunigende*) like stones, life (*lybbe*) like trees, sense (*gefrede*) like beasts, and understanding (*understande*) like angels.[36] Humankind is thus placed in a unique position within this world that God has created and inhabits. Humans live within nature and yet have, by virtue of their soul, a connection with the divine. Therefore a person can relate to nature by relating to God, and vice versa. It was in this context that Ælfric asserted that God is the true "leech" or doctor, the one who controls all sickness and health; ultimately one must appeal to God or use God's creation properly to achieve any well-being.[37]

Categories: Miracles, Magic, and Middle Practices

Ælfric's insistence on a monotheistic deity inhabiting all knowledge and all nature was an attempt to shift a polytheistic and animistic cosmology toward a Christian worldview. Everything is alive, yes, but with the presence of one God. This effort to Christianize the Anglo-Saxon cosmology and establish an orthodox popular religion becomes clearer in Ælfric's treatment of miracles, magic, and the things left in-between. He defined miracle and magic in terms of their source, God or the Devil, and allowed other, middle practices insofar as they partook of something divine and not something demonic.

Miracles

Miracles fit into the context of Ælfric's view of nature and health. God acts in the world in a way consistent with nature as a natural means of communication with people. The world and all that happens in it he therefore reads allegorically. Miracles were an extension of this same principle of communication, that God creates miracles in order to speak to human beings, to reveal himself and his purposes.

Regarding the relationship of miracles to creation, Augustine presupposed that the possibility of miracles was inherent in nature. A miracle was in this view a drawing out of the virtues hidden by God within a cosmos that was all potentially miraculous.[38] A shift in this view takes place in the twelfth century, when a miracle becomes something unnatural or contrary to the normal way that we reasonably perceive nature to work, although it may fulfill some higher reasoning. For example, Caesarius of Heisterbach asserted that "we call a miracle that which happens against the usual course of nature, hence we wonder. Nothing about a miracle is contrary to higher reasons."[39] However, in the early medieval period the rationality of miracles on a supernatural versus natural scale was not an issue. The question asked of miracles was never how something could happen but whether it was of God and if so what it expressed about humanity's relationship to God. The Augustinian view put miracles and nature on an equal footing as a sign from God to humanity.[40] Homilies and saints' lives presented miracles as the shining example of Christian truth. Miracles were of God and stood in opposition to the evil, corrupt influence of magicians. Ælfric's sermons reflect this Augustinian definition of miracles.

The two Anglo-Saxon words most commonly translated as "miracle" are *wundor* (wonder) and *tacn* (sign). Ælfric used these two words extensively, but in very particular ways. The terms could be used interchangeably, but generally when Ælfric used *tacn* he was stressing the meaning of miracles. *Wundor*, which implies the wonder of men and women in response to some phenomenon, was a more general term that could also describe wonders done by the Devil, although in a Christian context it meant the same thing as *tacn*.[41] *Tacn* was more specifically a miracle as Ælfric viewed it, for the word indicates the purpose of miracles as a sign (*tacn*) from God to his people.

The major purpose of miracles, then, was to reveal God to humanity, to disclose his might and his glory, and thus to promote faith in people.[42] Miracles could also teach specific lessons: "It is not enough that we wonder [*wundrian*] at the *tacnes*, or through it praise God, unless we also understand its spiritual sense [*gastlice andgit*]."[43] In the saints' lives in particular, certain miracles communicated a specific truth. For example, the *wundra* of the Anglo-Saxon saint Æthelthryth made known her sacred relics and her virginity; moreover, the miracle of her uncorrupted body showed God's power to raise up corruptible bodies, giving each individual hope for the resurrection. Another Anglo-Saxon saint, Swithun, performed many *wundra* that manifested to the people that they might merit the kingdom by good works even as the saint now shines through his *wundra*.[44]

Ælfric saw miracles as part of God's ever-continuing communication with humanity, as evidenced in his sermon for Midlent Sunday on Christ's miracle multiplying the loaves of bread. He used this story to explain his hermeneutics but also to relate God's revelation to his agricultural audience.

God has made and makes daily many *wundra*; but those *wundra* are much weakened in men's sight, because they are very usual [*gewunelic*]. It is a greater *wundor* that God Almighty each day feeds all the world, and directs the good, than that *wundor* was, that he filled five thousand men with five loaves; but at this men wondered [*wundredon*], not because it was a greater *wundor*, but because it was unusual [*ungewunelic*]. Who gives now fruit to our fields, and multiplies the harvest from a few grains, except that one who multiplied the five loaves? The might was then in Christ's hands, and the five loaves were, as it were, seed, not sown in earth, but multiplied by the one who created the earth.

This *wundor* is very great, and deep in its significations [*getacnungum*]. Often someone sees fair letters written, then praises he the writer and the letters, but knows not what they mean. He who knows the distinctions of the letters praises their fairness, and reads the letters, and understands what they mean. In one way we look at a picture, and in another way at letters. No more happens for a picture except that you see and praise it; it is not enough that you look at letters, unless you also read them and understand their meaning [*andgit*]. So it is also with the *wundre* which God did with the five loaves: it is not enough that we wonder [*wundrian*] at the *tacnes*, or through it praise God, unless we also understand its spiritual sense [*gastlice andgit*].[45]

Ælfric clearly placed miracles in the Augustinian context of nature as a continuing revelation of God. As he shows in this passage, the miracle of the harvest each year, upon which everyone's very existence depended, was as much a miracle as Christ multiplying the loaves; Christ, as creator, performed the miracle in a way just as "natural" as the miracle of seeds growing. In this meaningful way, through analogies familiar to his audience, Ælfric communicated that miracles constituted a spiritual message.[46] Moreover, he pointed his audience in the direction of looking at their everyday life as a miraculous message from God, in the same way that the Field Remedy quoted at the beginning of Chapter 1 does; in both, the natural world is a wonder explicated by the power of God.

The Christian sense of duality between spiritual and material in the world permeates Ælfric's discussion of miracles, as he tried to emphasize the spiritual meaning while not denying or ignoring the material realities. At one point Ælfric implied that miracles were no longer God's way of speaking, a subject of theological debate. He argued that *wundra* were more necessary at the beginning of Christianity just as a person waters a tree or herb until it takes root, but the church now worked spiritual *wundra* as the apostles did material ones. Yet despite this emphasis on the spiritual aspect of miracles, Ælfric definitely affirmed the possibility of contemporary physical miracles, associated with saints, as support for orthodoxy.

> We have the belief that Christ himself taught to his apostles, and they to all mankind; and that belief God has with many *wundrum* confirmed and strengthened. First Christ by himself healed dumb and deaf, halt and blind, mad and leprous, and raised the dead to life. After, through his apostles and other holy men, he worked the same *wundra*. Now also in our time, wherever holy men rest, at their dead bones God works many *wundra*, because he wishes to confirm folks' belief with those *wundrum*. God works not these *wundra* at any Jewish man's tomb, nor at any other heretic's, but at right-believing men's tombs who believed in the Holy Trinity, and in the true Oneness of one Godhead.[47]

Moreover, God has also blessed England with such saintly miracles, supporting the link between the nation's divine destiny and the maintenance of orthodoxy. For example, Ælfric's view of St. Edmund, venerated in the Danelaw among the Scandinavians who martyred him, highlights Edmund's role as a local saint who represents English Christian values.

Worthy is the place for the sake of the worth-full saint [Edmund] that men should honor [wurthige] it, and well provide it with God's pure servants, to Christ's service, because the saint is greater than men may consider. The English race [Angelcynn] is not deprived of the Lord's saints, since in English land [Engla-landa] lie such saints as this holy king, and the blessed Cuthbert, and saint Æthelthryth in Ely, and also her sister, incorrupt in body, for strengthening belief. There are also many other saints among the English race [Angelcynn], who work many wundra, as is widely known, to the praise of the Almighty in whom they believed.[48]

Miracles were a sign that God had chosen the nation, as Ælfric quotes from Gregory's letter to Augustine of Canterbury concerning the miracles done by the missionary.

My dearest brother, I know that the Almighty God declares many wundra through you to the people whom he chose, for which you may rejoice and also dread. You may certainly rejoice that the people's souls through those outward wundra are drawn to inward grace; yet fear lest your mind be not lifted up with arrogance by the tacnum which God through you accomplishes, and you then fall into vain-glory within, when without you are raised in worthiness.[49]

Contained within this message as recorded by Ælfric are several layers of meaning: a warning that the power to do wonders can lead to the sin of pride, an affirmation that miracles are an outward sign of inward grace, and an assurance that the memory of such miracles and their continuation into their own day was a sign for Ælfric's readers that God was with them, giving a sense of divine destiny and some comfort in perilous times. The telling of miracle stories continually reinforced the Augustinian notion that God was active within the world he had created and that humanity could tap this divine source.

It is no wonder, then, that Anglo-Saxons who imbibed this message began to turn to the church, its relics, and its sites for ingredients to use in healing remedies, in the hopes of drawing out this miraculous potentiality in the God-created natural order. Later ages might call this manipulative use of the miraculous "Christian magic." It was not deemed so in the early Middle Ages.

Magic

The modern mind, steeped in the scientific worldview, tends to see the similarities between miracle and magic: both are scientifically unverifiable. In the duels between Christian saints/missionaries and heathens the methods of both could appear identical.[50] However, the Augustinian system of thought, focused on God as the source of things, perceived magic as the antithesis of miracles because demons wrought these magical wonders. For medieval Christian leaders and writers miracles were always a sign of God's presence, his love, and truth; the Devil could not exhibit that kind of love and truth. Early medieval writers condemned magic as of the Devil and usually associated it with heathen activities; it involved magicians, sorcerers, witches, and the like. These people might manipulate natural objects, but the basis of their activities was deception in order to trap souls for the Devil.[51]

Ælfric thoroughly defined the category of magic, relying heavily on Augustinian sources for material.[52] As a consequence, the practices he condemned were continental as much as they were Anglo-Saxon. The material on the subject of magic and the Devil in Ælfric's homilies was mainstream theology for its time; nonetheless, his forceful presentation of this theology in the vernacular gives a very clear sense of how the early medieval mind adapted Christian cosmology to Germanic worldviews through Anglo-Saxon language and concepts.[53]

The source of magic, and the basis of its condemnation, is found in the development in Christian cosmology of the Devil as the representation of evil. In this view, the Devil had the ability to work visibly or invisibly, just as God and his angels could.[54] However, since God controlled all nature, it would be theologically untenable to assert the reality of the Devil's works, so stories portrayed the wonders the Devil produced as delusions, a view that emphasized the spiritual element over the material. The Devil could heal only diseases he himself inflicted on people; he would do this, of course, so that when he cured them at their request they would believe in him and he would thus obtain their souls.[55]

The oppositional nature of magic's definition is evident in saints' lives in which miracles battle against magic. These stories frequently portrayed the miraculous power of the saint as undoing magical delusions. For example, Ælfric repeats a popular story of St. Macarius in which the saint "heals" a girl who, according to her family and all who saw her, was turned into a mare. Macarius tells them, "But it [the transformation] is nevertheless a delusion, by the Devil's art; and if anyone makes the sign of the cross over it, then the delusion ceases."[56] The cross in any form was a powerful weapon against such delusions by the Devil, because its inherent meaning caused a reorientation in an individual's perspective, refocusing attention on the true reality found in Christ.

Magic as associated with the Devil was therefore always evil in its purpose. Authors such as Ælfric expressed their condemnation of practices associated with the Devil not in a single word (magic) but in a list: magic (drycræft), sorcery (wiglung), enchantments (galdras), witchcraft (wiccecræft), and the use of pagan sites (trees, stones, and wellsprings). Ælfric demonstrated how such practices were inconsistent with a Christian view of nature by asserting that they had to be deceptions because their evil purpose did not contain God's truths as revealed in Scripture and nature. Therefore he declares their unreality as contrary to the way God made nature. In a passage condemning witchcraft, Ælfric uses the tried-and-true Christian argument against the pagan practice of taking offerings to idols, in this case earth-fast stones, trees, or wellsprings: how, he asks, can the dead stone or dumb tree help or give health when it cannot even move?[57]

Ælfric was clear on the difference between right and wrong practice and sought to categorize the practices of his own day accordingly. In his sermon "The Octaves and Circumcision of Our Lord" he goes off on a tangent concerning the first day of the year, condemning people who celebrate it with improper rituals, and reveals much about his views on magic.

> Now foolish men practice [wigliath] manifold sorceries [wigelunga] on this day, with great error [gedwylde], after heathen custom, against their Christianity, as if they might lengthen their life, or their health, when [thus] they provoke the Almighty Creator. Also many are taken with as great an error, that they order their lives by the moon, and their deeds according to days, and will not weaken their things on Monday [monan-dæg], because [it is] the beginning of the week; but that Monday is not the first day of the week, but is the second. Sunday is the first in creation, and in order, and in worthiness. Some heretics [gedwæsmen] also say that a certain kind of animal a man may not bless, and say that through blessing they fare badly, and through curses [wyrigunge] they perform; and then [they] enjoy God's grace to their harm, without blessing, with the Devil's cursing. Every blessing is of God, and cursing of the Devil. God shaped all created things, and the Devil cannot make any created things, but he is an exhorter of evil, and worker of lies, the origin of sins, and seducer of souls. . . .
>
> Woe to the man who enjoys God's creation, without his blessing, with devilish sorcery [wiglungum], when the teacher of the people

[apostle of the Gentiles], Paul, said, "Whatsoever you do in word or in work, do always in the Lord's name, thanking the Almighty Father through his Son." That man's Christianity is naught who with devilish sorcery [wiglungum] directs his life; he appears as a Christian man, and is a wretched heathen-worshiper, just as the same apostle about such said: "I believe that I labored in vain, when I turned you to God; now you keep days and months with vain sorcery [wiglungum]."

It is, however, according to nature in the created order that each bodily created thing which the earth brings forth is fuller and stronger in the full moon than in the waning. As also trees, if they be hewed in a full moon, are harder and longer-lasting for building, and strongest if they are worked on when sapless. This is no sorcery [wiglung], but is a natural thing through the created order. So also the sea wonderfully agrees with the moon's circuit, they are always companions in growing and waning. And just as the moon arises daily four points [an hour?][58] later, so also the sea always flows four points later.

Let us set our hope and our happiness in the Almighty Creator's providence, he who set all creation in three things, that is in measure, and in number, and in weight. Be to him glory and praise ever in eternity.[59]

This passage reveals a significant part of Ælfric's worldview and his attempt to shape a Christian cosmology for Anglo-Saxon society. Much of what he tries to do here shifts popular practice into clearly definable categories. For example, his contrast between licit and illicit uses of nature aligns these practices with their source, either the Devil's magic or God's power, either curses or blessings, illusory things or true God-created things. His insistence on the basic goodness of all creation accomplishes two things: it means that God is the only source for material prosperity and that nature has an orderliness to it. Thus certain practices that in our age would be condemned as magic were reasonable to Ælfric, as proper uses of nature within the Christian cosmology. He based his defense of cutting down trees at the full moon on his understanding of nature as God made it.[60]

Based on the same kind of reasoning, he condemned magic as an illusion or distortion of that godly order in nature, a denial of God's omnipotence. For example, in another sermon he challenged astrology by putting man in his proper place in relation to the heavens. Man was not created for the stars, but the stars were created as a light by night for men.[61]

Ælfric placed Christian power against illusory magic. He offered as a substitute and antidote for magical practices the use of the sign of the cross

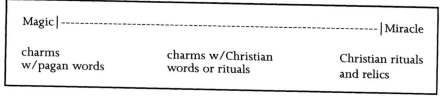

Magic | -- | Miracle

charms   charms w/Christian   Christian rituals
w/pagan words   words or rituals   and relics

Figure 3.1. Spectrum of middle practices between magic and miracle

and Christian prayers in order to put the demons to flight.[62] Thus Ælfric argued from a Christian view of nature against practices that denied God's role in nature or that were animistic, and yet he accepted other practices that were consistent with the way God made the world. It is in this context that certain middle practices emerge as legitimate uses of Christian power in the natural world.

Middle Practices

As the first two categories, magic and miracles, are relatively well defined, the problem becomes how to fit other types of healing and uses of natural objects into this cosmology. They tend to fall in between magic and miracles without any clear designation; hence the term *middle practices*.[63] This intermediate area represents an application of medieval ideas about causation. The popular notion, found in Germanic societies prior to the advent of Christianity, of occult virtues in natural objects found a close parallel in the idea of hidden virtues present in Augustine's discussion of miracles. Practitioners of natural medicine then applied the Augustinian principles to the Germanic ideas of occult virtues. Thus these ideas of power in nature merged, with a variety of results.

The spectrum of these middle practices ranges between the extremes of magic and miracle, from charms to relics and Christian ritual, as figure 3.1 shows.

Closest to condemned magic are remedies known as charms, words and actions spoken or performed in a ritual manner with herbs. Although Christian authors condemned pagan charms as magic, they allowed those remedies using Christian words and rituals with herbs. Medical remedies using only herbs or other natural elements are natural and nonmagical by modern definitions, but it is wise to remember that they are in the same manuscripts with remedies using charms. Medical texts recorded the remedies with charms and those without as both part of medicine.

Saints' lives usually presented healing through the relics of saints as miracles, as evidence of God's power being manifested through his servant, revealing God's character through the saint. But in some ways the use of relics for healing is not that different from the use of herbs in medical remedies. For example, in a story about the church on Mount Olivet, mold taken from the sacred footsteps healed diseases, and yet the footsteps wonderfully never changed.[64] The use of similar organic matter in medieval medicine was common, and the specification of a special location was not unusual. What Christianity added to this practice was not an entirely different remedy or practice but a new cosmology to explain it, and specific meanings associated with the new locations of power.

The use of Christian ritual as a means of cure also comes close to miracles, but the idea of using the mass, the cross, and Christian prayers to effect cures or bless fields was distinct from the medieval concept of miracles as a direct communication from God to man. Rather, remedies used Christian ritual like charms and herbs as a way of tapping the God-given potential of nature. The rituals for exorcism, for example, slide into medieval medical texts as easily as cures for various mind-altering illnesses, as discussed in Chapters 4 and 5.

Thus charms, other medical remedies, and Christian ritual all form an intermediate noncategory and exist in a spectrum between, but different from, magic and miracles. These legitimate uses of medicine or Christian ritual to activate the potential of nature were not magic and should not be designated as magic because such a use of the term radically distorts the cultural context in which these things were practiced.

If Ælfric represents one of the strongest, most reform-minded Christian leaders of his time, then his views, at the very least, must be accepted as Christian views. To call "magic" things that he condoned as legitimate would be to distort everything he said about magic as evil and of the Devil. In several passages Ælfric discussed phenomena such as charms, herbs, and Christian ritual and clearly gave them a place in his cosmology. Ælfric himself never treated them as a separate category in themselves, as he did magic and miracles, but they crop up throughout his writings in places where he was trying to establish the dominance of the Christian cosmology over popular practice—as, for example, in the sermon quoted above discussing the moon, where he allowed for the God-ordered natural effects of the moon.

Healing as an Example

One way to focus on these diffuse middle practices, in comparison with the categories of magic and miracle, is to examine the subject of healing. Illness was a prevalent phenomenon that invoked the use of magic, miracles, charms, herbs, and Christian ritual. The healing of illness by these means was by far the most common usage, but other uses included blessing fields, controlling the weather, seeking protection from the elements, and warding off evil. However, healing provides a good focus for discussion because of its spiritual analogy, "divine medicine." Physical and spiritual medicine many times became indistinguishable. Saints sometimes imitated the example of Jesus, who told a man his sins were forgiven but also healed him of his physical infirmity to prove to his critics that he had the power to do both.[65]

The context for understanding Ælfric's views on sickness and healing is his understanding of creation, as outlined above. Essentially he portrayed the Creator God as the true Leech, who controlled life, death, sickness, and health.[66] Ælfric's picture of leeches (doctors) was not necessarily positive. He associated their work with surgery and suffering and drew the spiritual lesson that pain was necessary for physical healing, just as penance was necessary for the cure of the soul. The spiritual context for physical illness was therefore complex, with a number of factors contributing to an explanation for disease.[67] Illness could be the result of sin; on the other hand, Ælfric also reasons (based on Augustine) that the Devil may cause illness in a strong Christian who resists him. Nonetheless, any affliction, even one of demonic origin, required the permission of God, who has reasons for afflicting a Christian; God might demonstrate his power through the affliction suffered by a saint, for example.[68] Thus whatever the immediate cause, illness should prompt an individual to turn to God: "We ought to seek, if we be afflicted, remedy from God, not from the cruel witches, and with all our hearts please our Saviour, because nothing can withstand His might."[69]

This reliance on God for healing did not mean that Ælfric rejected all doctors or medicine. His primary aim was to establish that ultimately all good things, like healing from illness, come from God, and that the spiritual dimension has primacy. He did, however, specify the appropriate means of gaining health, defining the boundary between magic and medicine. "Medicine [lǣcedom] is permitted for bodily weakness, and holy prayers, with God's blessing; and all other treatments are hateful to God."[70] The heart of medicine in the Augustinian-Christian view of nature was a recognition of God as ultimately responsible for all phenomena within nature and affecting humankind. Any person desiring healing should first and foremost acknowledge God as the source and continue to acknowledge him while seeking cures through the things he has made, all the while invoking his power. Picking an herb, blessing it with holy prayers, and preparing it according to a recipe was perfectly acceptable.

There were, though, different types of medicinal practices contained within the medical manuscripts circulating in late Anglo-Saxon England (see Chapter 4). They included charms or *galdor*, verbal formulas used in a remedy that usually included ritual actions performed either during the collection of herbs or in the presence of the patient.

How would Ælfric have viewed these texts and remedies? Although we have no direct references to such manuscripts in his writings, several features emerge in his attitude toward healing. He favored spiritual solutions — prayer, the sign of the cross, miracles through saints, and divine medicine for the soul. He condemned heathen practices calling on devils. But he accepted herbal remedies, with some ambivalence about their preparation. He would undoubtedly question whether they were Christian or heathen, natural or unnatural, of God or of the Devil.

In his clearest passage on the subject of medicine and magic, one that relies heavily on Augustine, Ælfric recognized the validity of herbs as a cure, though still condemning magical uses of herbs.

> The Christian man who is afflicted in any way like this [example of bodily weakness], and then wishes to seek his health from unlawful cures, or from cursing charms [*wyrigedum galdrum*], or from any witchcraft, then will be like those heathen men who offered to devil-worship [*deofolgylde*] for their bodies' health, and so destroyed their souls. Let him who is unhealthy pray for his health from his Lord, and patiently endure the strokes; look how long the true Leech provides it [health?], and let him not buy the body's health through any Devil's craft with his soul; let him ask also good men's blessing, and seek his health at holy relics. No Christian man is allowed to fetch his health from any stone, nor from any tree, unless it is the holy cross-sign [*rode-tacen*], nor from any place, unless it is the holy house of God. The one who does otherwise undoubtedly falls into heathenworship [*hæthengild*]. We have, however, examples in holy books, that he who wishes may cure [*getemprian*] his body with true leechcraft, as did the prophet Isaiah, who made for the king Hezekiah a salve for his sore, and healed him.
>
> The wise Augustine said that it is not dangerous if any one eat a medicinal herb [*læce-wyrte*]; but he censures it as unlawful sorcery [*wiglung*] if any one ties those herbs on himself, unless he lays them on a sore. Nevertheless we must not set our hope in medicinal herbs, but in

the Almighty Creator who gave that virtue [cræft] to those herbs. Nor must any man shall enchant [besingan] an herb with charms [galdre], but with God's words must bless [gebletsian] it, and so eat.[71]

Ælfric thus substituted the cross and relics for pagan sites, Christian blessings for witchcraft and enchantment, and prayer over herbs for their enchantment by magical words. Cræft functions as a neutral concept here, signifying power, art, science, knowledge, or skill; witches and the Devil have their own evil craft whose purpose is to enslave the soul, as opposed to God's health-giving craft, placed in nature, that redeems body and soul. Thus Ælfric's condemnation of paganism through its association with the Devil is clear; he sets it against Christian practices that point to the one God. Herbal medicine for the body is good because it is from God. Consequently it is to the God who made the herbs that the sick person should appeal in the preparation of the medicine. Any herbal remedy—wearing the herbs as an amulet or to cure an invisible ailment—that does not call upon the virtue placed by God in the herb is suspect, as is any remedy that seeks to bring out the power of the herb through an appeal not directed to God the creator. Ælfric's recommendation to seek health at the church is amply fulfilled in the medical remedies specifying masses over herbs placed under the altar, as discussed in Chapters 4 and 5.

The difficulty in interpretation is with words said over herbs, charms or galdra. Although some extremists forbid all galdor except prayer itself, this rule from the Penitential of Egbert exemplifies a common attitude.

It is not allowed for any Christian to observe empty divination, as heathens do (that is, they believe in the sun and moon and the course of the stars, and seek to divine the time to begin their things), nor gather herbs with any charms, except with the Pater noster and with the Creed, or with some prayer which pertains to God.[72]

The last part of this rule reflects the tendency to Christianize charms through the use of Christian prayers, evident in the charms themselves. Ælfric in his homilies was condemning galdra with pagan, magic connections; the context was always a discussion of witches, enchanters, and sorcerers.[73] However, he recommends that Christian words be said over the herbs. In fact, the "charms" as isolated in the Anglo-Saxon medical manuscripts by modern scholars contain surprisingly few pagan elements (that is, few recognizable ones—folklorists have pointed out numerous elements that have a pagan past). Instead, Christian elements predominate.

Conclusions: The Power of Ritual

It is misleading to designate all charms as "pagan," because pagan and Christian elements cannot easily be distinguished in their use. It is anachronistic to call them "Christian magic" because the idea of such a thing would have been an oxymoron for a Christian of that time. Assuming that "Christian" things are whatever things Christian people at a given time thought were Christian, then we should look at the charms as found in the existing texts through the eyes of the kind of person who wrote and read them, that is a Christian Anglo-Saxon.

Taking this perspective enables us to see the continuity of thought between Germanic folklore and Christianity as the charms gradually evolved. Both Germanic religion/folklore and Christianity expressed themselves in ritual. Ritual was a form of imitation, a dramatic expression of belief in certain principles of order in the universe, clearly evident in Ælfric's cosmology. Ritual in the charms reflects the people's belief in the possibility of intervention from an invisible power, a Germanic as well as a Christian concept. This blending of Germanic folklore and Christianity is evident in the charms, both in their wording and in their actions.

Christian ritual—the sign of the cross, the mass, holy water, holy oil, and other elements—appear frequently in charm remedies. As Chapter 5 argues, remedies against invisible ailments—those which have an unseen cause, in Ælfric's view—also use the most Christian elements to cure the ailment. This high degree of Christian substitution indicates a conscious effort to Christianize the charms in line with the cosmology fostered by reformers such as Ælfric. The use of Christian ritual as a means of cure was on the borderline between this intermediate category and miracle, for these rituals themselves Ælfric classified as a type of miracle. The apostles worked bodily miracles, but the priest worked a spiritual miracle when he christened an infant, a ceremony that cast out the Devil.[74]

In the early medieval Augustinian worldview, Christian ritual fused nature and the divine, invisible became visible, and man experienced the divine in his body as well as in his soul. The mass was thus seen as a mystery, the how of which could not be understood.[75] In a "Hortatory Sermon on the Efficacy of the Holy Mass" Ælfric repeats stories from Bede and Gregory to show how powerful the mass could be. In one account, whenever a priest said mass for his deceased (as he presumed) brother, the bonds would fall off the brother who was actually alive and being held prisoner.[76] In "A Sermon on the Sacrifice on Easter-Day" Ælfric explains how his audience should understand Christian ritual, after trying to explain Christ's presence in the Eucharist through the duality of signification [getacnunge] and literal meaning, things understood within and things without.

In like manner holy font-water, which is called life's wellspring, is like in appearance to other water, and is subject to corruption; but the Holy Ghost's might draws near to the corruptible water through the priests' blessing, and it can then cleanse body and soul from all sins through spiritual might. Lo now we see two things in this one created thing: according to true nature that water is a corruptible liquid, and according to a spiritual mystery [gerynu] it has healing/saving [halwende] might. Likewise, if we behold the holy housel according to bodily understanding, then we see that it is a created thing, corruptible and changeable. But if we discern the spiritual might therein, then we understand that there is life in it, and that it gives immortality to those who eat it with belief. Great is the difference between the unseen might of the holy housel and the visible appearance of its own nature.[77]

Thus the visible and invisible aspects of nature helped explain this Christian truth employing an orthodox cosmology that nonetheless was congruent with Germanic folk belief in spiritual presence in natural things. The use of the mass and holy water in charm remedies is consistent with Ælfric's view of the place of these rituals within nature, that invisible virtues in all things could be tapped and used against invisible forces such as demons and elves. Ælfric sought to define the limits of approaches to healing, and other uses of natural objects, within the boundaries of a Christian, Augustinian view of nature in which God was the source of all virtues and the only proper avenue of direct appeal was Christian ritual; all other means were condemned as magic.

Ælfric shows us this Augustinian view of the created order in a clearly articulated effort to reshape Anglo-Saxon cosmology according to Christian principles. He insists on the opposition between magic and miracle, heathenism and true Christianity, and yet he allows room for this Christian view of God and nature to control popular practices regarding healing. This view can be seen operating in a less articulate fashion in everyday life as well, through the mediation of local priests. Some of the results of this interaction are visible in the medical manuscripts. The charms examined in the next two chapters are prime examples of the practical applications of this Germanic-Christian worldview, if on a less theologically correct level than Ælfric or Wulfstan would have desired.

LOCATING THE CHARMS
MEDICINE, LITURGY, AND FOLKLORE

The charm remedies found in late Anglo-Saxon medical manuscripts provide a rare glimpse into the intermingling of a Christian worldview and Germanic folklore. Through assimilation and accommodation in both directions, the early medieval Christian (or Augustinian) worldview and the surviving pre-Christian beliefs of the Germanic peoples merged, in part because they shared some fundamental assumptions about the nature of the cosmos. This process is visible particularly in the convergence of liturgy and folklore in a number of medical remedies.

In the context of this overlap the charms become one of the best examples of middle practices because they cross the boundary between popular and formal religion, and they show the interaction between clergy and laity, doctrine and practice, written and oral, and doing and knowing — the polarities suggested in the first chapter. In the charms we find elements of Christianity and survivals of paganism, miracle and magic, and liturgy and folklore, all united through a holistic view of the world in which physical and spiritual realities were intertwined and interdependent. The manuscripts contain both medical and liturgical elements, from both Roman Christian and Germanic traditions. What appears to the modern eye to be a confusion of sources was actually a coherent synthesis drawing on common ideas about the relationship between the microcosm and the macrocosm.

The charms form a nexus where these diverse aspects converged, allowing us a better view of late Anglo-Saxon popular practice in light of the various traditions that were amalgamating to form this culture. Unfortunately, earlier treatments of these texts by nineteenth- and early twentieth-century scholars interested in Germanic origins have suffered from a number of biases that have led to problems in the definition of the charm remedies, most notably the imposition of a modern system of values found in the meaning of words such as *magic* and *superstition*.[1] The cure for this tendency toward valuing modern notions of rationality is to place the texts that contain charms in their own cultural contexts, specifically early medieval views of medicine, the use of liturgy, and the surviving ideas of Germanic folklore. Charms as medicine were part of a Germanicized classical scientific system with specific beliefs about the cosmos, nature, and the way humans relate to both. But charm remedies as found in the surviving late Anglo-Saxon manuscripts also fit into the world of liturgical evolution because their Christianization entailed the extensive use of masses and other liturgical elements, such as holy oil. Nonetheless the charm form itself retained its folkloric roots, even though it took on, in the textualizing process, elements of the Christian liturgy and classical medicine. The mixture or overlap of these three — medicine, liturgy, and folklore — completely alters our perspective on what is Christian and what is magic, evident most dramatically in the liturgical cures for illness caused by an ancient Germanic affliction, the elf, taken up in the next chapter.

After addressing the problem of defining the charms (*galdra*), this chapter examines them in the context of medicine, liturgy, and folklore and shows how they represent the early medieval synthesis of classical, Christian, and native folklore views of nature, evil, and good. The aim of this chapter is to separate the different strands found in the medical sources by using various categories, such as different types of medical practice and beliefs, for the purpose of seeing how they were interwoven in the elf charms studied in Chapter 5. These categories, "sympathetic magic" for example, are modern and hence false to the historical context of the manuscripts themselves; that is, nowhere in these manuscripts is there a section entitled "sympathetic magic" or even a section with remedies of that type collected together. As with magic and miracle in the previous chapter, identifying the strands first helps us understand how they are interwoven.

In examining these strands evident in late Saxon medicinal practice, I use remedies selected out of their manuscript context in order to illustrate the "type." Nonetheless, my overall argument is that we can best understand the remedies by taking into account the early medieval context of beliefs about medicine, magic, and religion, rather than categorizing these beliefs according to post-twelfth-century or modern definitions of these concepts. Therefore, in this chapter I use more contextually sensitive, neutral categories—liturgy, folklore, and medicine—rather than the problematic terms *pagan*, *magic*, and *science* that carry the weight of later values.

Chapter 5 then examines one type of remedy identified by modern scholars, elf charms, to show how they fit into this medical context and how they interweave Christian and Germanic beliefs. Previous scholarly studies separated these strands, isolating the "original" Germanic from the "pure" Christian material that, in their eyes, have sullied or compromised each other. This study argues instead that the combinations of traditions found in these remedies represent a coherent synthesis in the development of a popular Christianity.

Galdra

One major obstacle to understanding the charms in their proper cultural and textual context is the problem of definition. Anglo-Saxon and modern notions about charms differ considerably, as can be seen in the way early twentieth-century scholars assembled editions of charms. The predominant mistake hindering a clear understanding of what a charm was in the Anglo-Saxon period is the tendency to take out of the original medical manuscript that part that seems most odd or unmedical and set it aside with all the other similarly curious bits and study them together. This not only fragments the text but leads to a false categorization and a loss of context. The key to understanding the charms, I argue, is to see them in the intertwining contexts in which they are found: medicine, folklore, and liturgy.

Definitions

The Anglo-Saxon word *galdor* (rooted in the verb *galan*, "to sing or chant") translators have variously rendered as song, charm, or incantation, but to what vocal production this refers is unclear in the texts we have. Whether the performer sang it with some kind of melody or chanted it or both, the texts do not state, although the existence of such compounds as *galdor-leoth* (-song) and *galdor-word* would indicate that different forms of vocalizing existed side by side. When the term appears parallel to a Latin text, it can be *carmen, cantio* (song), or *incantatio*. In many cases the recipe specifies sing (*singan* or *besingan*, "enchant") this *galdor*, in the same way that it might direct the healer to sing a psalm or prayer, which implies that the performer chanted it in a fashion similar to the Gregorian. In other contexts, such as law codes prohibiting sorcery and witchcraft, *galdor* seems to refer to something akin to an incantation. However, the essence of the word in all these contexts points to verbal or written formulas used to effect a change in natural objects. Words were channels of power; chanting or singing words added a special element of rhythm and controlled tone that gave even more power to the words. A related concept is *rune* and its compounds; in Anglo-Saxon folklore and Scandinavian religion, runes were symbols or characters whose secret was a form of power over the forces of the world.[2]

So these verbal formulas were performance pieces as well; a trained person acted them out before an audience both visible and invisible, both the patient with friends and family and the spiritual forces addressed in the charm. These "speech acts" as found in Anglo-Saxon medical manuscripts inextricably intertwined with certain physical actions to create a whole remedy. Only together could these charms and rituals cure whatever ailments the texts specified. The assumption behind this performance was that actions and words combined have the power to change things. Therefore the verbal formula itself should not be extracted from the manuscript as a literary text in isolation from the actions that accompanied it. Even though we have very little textual evidence on the performance aspect, we still must visualize these as integrated productions, meant to be performed, not read.[3]

Historiography

Part of the problem in defining charms emerges from the way modern scholars have chosen and labeled remedies in edited and translated texts of charms extracted from the manuscripts. Charm prescriptions for the most part occur in medical manuscripts mixed with other, noncharm remedies; some charm remedies modern editors found scattered throughout other, nonmedical manuscripts, sometimes as marginalia. Yet editions of Anglo-Saxon charms produced in the early and mid-twentieth century have extracted from these manuscripts those remedies the editors saw as charms, using definitions based on their own sensibilities about magic, science, and religion. Consequently their editions present a picture of charms and medicine very different from what the Anglo-Saxons would have understood.

For example, Felix Grendon in his 1909 edition selected 146 charms defined to "include incantations properly so called, as well as numerous remedies depending for efficacy on the superstitious beliefs of the sufferers."[4] The organization of his edition of charms according to five types of magic likewise uses modern categories of how magic works, subtly altering how the charms are read. Anglo-Saxons did not necessarily perceive these distinctions; rather, the compilers organized the remedies according to herb usage or part of the body, or randomly as they wrote. When a modern editor places together all the remedies with, for instance, "transferential magic," the magic stands out prominently against the background of the medical remedy, as if the magical part were the distinguishing feature of the cure.

While acknowledging the unsatisfactory nature of any organizing scheme, including the Anglo-Saxon methods, Godfrid Storms nonetheless chose to organize his 1948 edition of Anglo-Saxon charms according to the amount of untouched Germanic material present in them, as opposed to the "foreign" (that is, classical, Christian) elements that allegedly intruded later in their development. His organization emphasizes the continuity of magic against the influence of Christianity, relying on that progressivist approach discussed in Chapter 1, in which magic gives way to Christianity and then, later, to science.[5] This approach is also the result of the nineteenth-century romantic view that sought the pure, Germanic roots of Anglo-Saxon culture by dissecting texts dating from a later period. This view values origins more highly than the texts we possess and ignores what these texts tell us about the time in which they were produced. Scholars since the 1970s have challenged and effectively destroyed this romanticizing approach, particularly E. G. Stanley in his series of articles (later a monograph) *The Search for Anglo-Saxon Paganism*. However, the charms and the medical texts still suffer from the ill effects of the definitions used in these editions. For example, M. L. Cameron in his recent text sympathetically surveying Anglo-Saxon medicine is cautious about classifying certain medicinal practices as magic that the users would not have perceived so. He also makes a careful distinction between *pagan* magic as objectionable to the church and magic in some general, yet undefined, sense. Despite this qualification, he nonetheless subscribes to the progressivist view of rationality when he asserts that practitioners and patients resorted to magic only when rational remedies failed.[6]

In almost every case the operative word in defining charms for these scholars was *magic* (or *superstition*), used in a modern sense as anything non-material or nonscientific. They judged charms by modern medical standards as to whether the remedy "worked," discounting as ineffective elements of religion or belief that formerly played a role in medicine. Because of this bias toward a modern scientific worldview, editors such as Grendon, Storms, or Grattan and Singer defined charms as any remedy that involved special wording or actions to accomplish the cure, since these were inconsistent with modern scientific views and medical practice. They were "superstitious," that is, obviously wrong from any rational standpoint.

However, superstition is a relative term; it is an act or belief inconsistent with the prevailing worldview. For example, if someone today holding to the scientific worldview was afraid to step on a crack in the sidewalk for fear of breaking his or her mother's back, that would be a superstition because of its inconsistency with a modern scientific understanding of reality.[7] While the Anglo-Saxon charms are inconsistent with later western worldviews, they are consistent in their own context and hence we should not subject them to such artificial designations as magic or superstition.

Recent scholarship in cultural history derived from the Annales school, from religious studies, and from cultural anthropology offers more neutral categories such as "mentalities" and "modes of rationality" and is cautionary about the word *magic*. The influences of ethnography and world history contribute to an increased crosscultural awareness of diversity and interdisciplinary points of view.[8] These new approaches encourage us to see the relationship of *galdra* to magic in the Anglo-Saxon mind as more complex and less clear than the modern perception of charms as representative of a kind of magic left behind in our progress toward rationalism.

The notion of magic, in particular, underwent a profound shift from the early Middle Ages to the modern period. The modern view evident in Grendon, Storms, and Grattan and Singer classifies charms or *galdra* as efforts at magic in opposition to science. However, when early medieval legal or homiletic texts placed *galdra* with other "magic" practices, such as sorcery (*wiglung* and *drycræft*), they were placing them in opposition to the religious truth of Christianity, since scientific knowledge was not a separate category from revelatory knowledge. These texts banned *galdra* because of their association with demonic and evil practices; in other contexts, such as the medical texts, the word lacks these prohibited associations, implying acceptance of the practice.

The early medieval worldview, described in Chapter 3, included the perception of magic and miracles as two extremes, with other folklore practices utilizing the potential of nature, such as charms, falling in between. Paganism as a religious belief system was objectionable to Christianity as "magic." However, folklore can exist as distinct from religion (pagan or Christian), even though it may carry animistic elements within it. The belief in spirits in nature can be separated from a religious context and passed from one religious tradition to another, as is clear in the case of the medical charms. Likewise, *galdor* can exist conceptually in a neutral sense and be colored by its associations or modifiers, as prohibited pagan magic if associated with evil activities or as good and acceptable medicine if associated with Christian names, rituals, and prayers.

If we only try to see the texts with charms as either pagan magic or Christian, we are left with a puzzle as to why they continued to exist in Christian manuscripts: were these people still pagan? or ignorant? However, if we see these practices as folklore, shading sometimes into paganism or Christian liturgy, then we do not have to either accept or reject them.

Charms as Middle Practices

The ambivalence of the charms' position in this intermediate category is evident in the Anglo-Saxon laws and penitentials, which, like many of the remedies, were based on continental precedents. Laws list the word *galdra* in sections condemning evil and pagan practices such as witchcraft, sorcery, deadly spells, and worship at trees and stones. The concern was with practices whose aim was evil or that gave honor to pagan gods; neither trait was a predominant characteristic in the *galdra* in the medical manuscripts. In fact the overwhelming number of "words of power" in these texts come from the liturgy, and the few pre-Christian *galdra* are relatively free of direct references to pagan deities, as distinct from Germanic folklore.[9]

The concern of the reformers Ælfric and Wulfstan was to cleanse the land of all heathen religion, and, as was shown in Chapter 3, Ælfric supported the use of herbs with prayers and Christian ritual, as did the *Penitential of Egbert*. Contemporary Christian leaders, both clerical and secular, clearly condemned *galdra*, but not because of their inconsistency with scientific laws—a modern objection—but because of their unnatural, hence evil, use of God's creation.[10]

If, however, the remedies replaced the objectionable elements—pagan names and worship and evil acts—with holy Christian names and rites, then this pulled the charms away from the magic end of the spectrum toward the miracle end, in the early medieval view of such things. Hence, while medical remedies that utilized special wording and rites as part of the cure are magic in the modern sense of outside of rational limits, they fell well within the reasonable bounds of an Anglo-Saxon view of nature. The critical question for a good Christian Anglo-Saxon was whether or not the remedy in question was of God.

There was obviously a difference between remedies that contained no such words and rites and those that did, but the early practitioners' perception of the difference was unlike our own. We see a line between the rational and the irrational, the natural and the supernatural, supplication and manipulation; they saw a line between the divine and the demonic, the different sources of power exhibited in nature. Those remedies with special words and rites were usually for ailments associated with the Devil or other unseen evils requiring a special appeal to those good powers that can give strength to the herbs. The convergence of liturgy and folklore in medical practice was a consequence of the nature of the evil being fought— whether that evil be a demon of classical origin or an elf of Germanic origin. The charms, then, make sense in the context of the medical, liturgical, and folkloric traditions in which they developed.

Medicine

Charms are found primarily in late Saxon medical manuscripts; therefore we should first treat them in the context of those manuscripts and medical practice, not just in isolation. The medical context for all remedies, charms and others, scholarly and popular, reveals a worldview in which all things were interconnected, physical and spiritual, microcosm and macrocosm. Charms were a logical part of that system of medicine.

Medical practice in late Saxon England is obscure to us in many ways. References in surviving Anglo-Saxon texts reveal the existence of eight known physicians; accounts of cures or attempted cures scattered throughout Anglo-Saxon literature are mainly of cases involving famous people or unusual circumstances. The scanty pictorial evidence we have relating to professional doctors, or leeches, suggests that this term referred to laymen. We have little evidence of rural practitioners of medicine, whether they were local clergy, hermits, or lay healers, male or female. The idea of women as healers arises out of the problematic evidence of condemnation of women's magic and witchcraft; nonetheless it is highly likely that lay healers were in many cases women. The manuscript evidence indicates also the practice of medicine in monasteries or minsters, since the medical texts we have were produced in these literate communities. This evidence suggests a shift in the possession of healing power from lay wisemen or women to clerical wisemen (a trend reversed in the late eleventh century with a ban on monastic medicine and in the twelfth, with a separation of spiritual and physical medicine).[11]

Medical remedies survive in a few manuscripts that show us not just the ways of the literate minority who followed a Latin tradition but also local, native practice as recorded in the vernacular. Besides actual medical treatises, a few remedies are scattered throughout other manuscripts, particularly as marginalia. All of these manuscripts reveal, at first glance, a barbarism incomprehensible to modern medical practitioners (superstition, sympathetic magic, and a lack of empirical observation). On reflection, however, and seen in context, they show a good grasp of then current knowledge of medicine, anatomy, and herbs, as recent research in these areas has demonstrated.[12]

Manuscripts

Modern scholars tend to divide the medical manuscripts of the early medieval period into two types: scholarly medical texts that are based on classical medicine and thus contain some medical theory, and more "popular" texts with "magical" remedies that appear to have no rational foundation except degraded forms of classical medicine.[13] The problem with this distinction is that its classical bias leads scholars to give greater weight to the small group of monks who had access to classical texts and Christian liturgical practice, as representatives of the greatest intellectual vigor, than to the texts that are a reflection of common practice in the entire culture. The more widespread popular medical practices — native remedies and beliefs about disease and their integration with Christian ideas — are not evident at all in the more scholarly texts and only partially in the so-called popular texts.

The distinctions between popular and formal along the lines of literate versus oral, clergy versus laity, and doctrine versus practice do not work here; they obscure rather than clarify the nature of these texts and the contexts in which they were produced and used. Instead I use here a wider concept of popular religion and culture as evident in the interaction between popular ideas and the formal texts.

In a sense all medical texts were products of an elite because the reading and writing of texts was limited to that select, largely clerical, minority located in major centers (monastery, minster, or cathedral) with a scriptorium or library. However, while these circumstances circumscribed the circulation of the texts themselves, a wider influence and impact was possible through the compilers and readers of these texts. The people involved in the production of these texts were not isolated within their libraries and scriptoria; rather, they interacted with their own culture, reflecting its needs and ideas in what they chose to read, copy, or write down, thus influencing popular practices by transmitting literate ideas.

By weighing these medical texts on a scale of intellectual worth within the elite literate realm, earlier scholars such as Grattan and Singer have neglected the wider sphere of cultural transformation represented by the less classical texts that were trying to integrate book learning with local experience and reality. Moreover, this distinction between classical and Germanic obscures the essential similarity of worldviews shared by all these texts. Despite the apparent differences in intellectual standards between these two types of text, the general medical worldview of both was similar in that both presupposed certain basic beliefs about the natural world that lay the foundation for charm remedies.

The so-called elite or intellectual manuscripts are scientific treatises translated directly from continental or classical sources. Examples include the *Anglo-Saxon Herbal* or *Herbarium Apuleius*, the *Medicina de Quadrupedibus*, the *Peri Didaxaeon*, and the *Handbook of Byrhtferth*. These can show us something of the scholarly medical worldview of the times, but they were not practical guides for the everyday treatment of disease. The *Anglo-Saxon Herbal* and the *Medicina de Quadrupedibus* are arranged by herb or animal, listing the various ills against which they were effective and how to use them.[14] The *Peri Didaxaeon* is a simpler text of Greek and Latin origins (eleventh or twelfth century) with an Anglo-Saxon translation of Greek words, probably more for intellectual interest than for practical use.[15] The *Handbook of Byrhtferth* (1011), Latin with Anglo-Saxon glosses, explains the classical four humors and the view of the world as macrocosm and microcosm as the basis of medicine (accompanied by elaborate diagrams; see fig. 4.1). Grattan treats this Anglo-Saxon text as a last remnant of classical philosophy surviving in a dark age, but as "too abstract for the baldly practical Anglo-Saxon leech."[16]

A literate reader could study these manuscripts to learn about specific ingredients, but a practicing healer would have difficulty looking up a particular disease because of the organization by ingredients. These texts cannot reflect much common practice in England because they were transmissions from outside England.[17] The compilers and copiers of these manuscripts, while demonstrating an appreciation of the scholarly worth of classical learning, rarely sullied these texts they were copying with native medical knowledge. While these texts are of interest to modern scholars who value the preservation of classical learning, they are not as interesting to those who want to study actual medical practice or popular culture in late Saxon England.

On the other hand, there are texts that contain remedies that can be traced to Anglo-Saxon or Germanic culture. These manuscripts are more eclectic in compiling remedies, not just copying remedies from continental manuscripts but including others that percolated up from native medical practice and were put into writing. Two manuscripts in particular fall into this category of popular medicine and formed the basis of M. L. Cameron's recent study of the rationality of Anglo-Saxon medical practice (*Anglo-Saxon Medicine*). The *Leechbook* (MS Royal 12. D. XVII, ca. 950) and the *Lacnunga* (MS Harley 585, ca. 1050) reveal native Anglo-Saxon medicine as practiced although still mixed with classical and continental elements.[18]

These texts are more practical and instructional in their organization and suggest some lay origins. The first two of the *Leechbook's* three books are arranged, respectively, from head to foot and into internal and external diseases, while the third book is different in character, containing more of the Christian-folk amalgamations of interest here. Each of the books has a table of contents for easy reference. The first two books are properly called *Bald's Leechbook*, according to the end of Book II where Bald commissioned Cild to compile the manuscript, suggesting private ownership (fol. 109a). These first two books of the manuscript may be a copy of a text from fifty years earlier, circa 900. However, the compiler may have copied the differently organized third book from a different source or sources. All three books are in the same hand, which N. R. Ker identified with the Winchester scriptorium (Cameron treats the third book as a separate text from *Bald's Leechbook*).[19] The *Lacnunga* groups remedies for the same ailment in a fashion similar to *Leechbook* III, without the same overall design found in *Leechbook* I and II.

These texts were compilations from a variety of sources, which, when their origins are traced, give the impression to a modern reader of a hodgepodge of incompatible theories; however, an underlying set of assumptions holds these remedies together. Grattan and Singer, the editors of the most authoritative edition of the *Lacnunga*, comment that a reader comparing two sections, one of Christian prayers and one of charms, "will find himself contemplating two utterly different worlds."[20] They argue, primarily on internal evidence, that the *Lacnunga* has five or six layers of compilation mixed together representing these different points of view, from pagan to Christian.[21] The circularity of their argument is disconcerting. They establish types of remedies based on the amount of Latin Christian, Teutonic Pagan, or debased classical medicine in them, on a spectrum reminiscent of the progressivist magic-religion-science. Unfortunately their label "Teutonic Pagan" conflates two types of designations, one cultural and one religious, that perhaps could be separated. They then posit different compilers for these types, ranging from very Christian and intelligent to barely Christian and semiliterate. What if, though, Anglo-Saxon standards of what was Christian and intelligent were so different as to render these categories meaningless? The existence of the manuscript with these remedies intermingled presupposes the existence of a single world in which these ideas cohabited. The analysis of these remedies in this and the next chapter examines the shared features of these diverse traditions, the overlaps between these two seemingly different worlds.

The *Lacnunga* and the *Leechbook* are both made up of recipes collected from a wide variety of sources that reveal the complex mixture of religious, medical, and folkloric ideas current in late Saxon England.[22] This complexity indicates the depth of the transformation taking place as these Anglo-Saxons blended native traditions with a Christian cosmology. Both texts, as popular compilations of recipes from earlier classical and Germanic sources, are thus rich resources for understanding late Saxon views.

The *Leechbook* and the *Lacnunga* differ, though, in several ways. Most scholars see the *Leechbook* as a much more sophisticated medical handbook, while they treat the *Lacnunga* as the basest of texts, barely Christianized, semiliterate, and with little or no medical theory. Again this valuation represents a modern scale of rationality that sets classical learning as the standard and then measures the distance between the classical and the popular; this scale in some ways distorts the standing these texts may have had in practice. The *Leechbook* is a more highly organized and elaborate text and has more classical and continental-Christian elements than the *Lacnunga*. However, the comparatively unscholarly nature of the *Lacnunga* should not lead us to disparage it as a source for understanding Anglo-Saxon medicine.[23] The *Lacnunga*, in all its perceived barbarousness, reflects more of actual practice *because* of its diverse mixture and simple approach to medicine. It is much more representative of Anglo-Saxon medicine, if what you want is the whole society and not just the narrow tradition of copied texts.

Moreover, the *Lacnunga* and the *Leechbook*, while practical and not intellectual texts, nonetheless share a certain similarity of view about disease causation and cure with their more scholarly counterparts discussed above. While the scholarly classical texts contain an intellectual theory to explain this view, as in the *Byrhtferth* text, the cures of the common texts assume the same basic premises in their practices—they simply do not articulate them in an analytical fashion.

Medical Worldview

The medical view revealed by all of these texts was nonempirical and holistic and hence appears unscientific to the modern eye. The remedies offer very few observations on symptoms or causes but place greater emphasis on alleviating the patient's distress. The majority of the remedies were natural preparations, relying on traditional knowledge of herbs and animals as found in texts such as the *Anglo-Saxon Herbal* and the *Medicina de Quadrupedibus*. The classical model of the four humors dictated the use of these ingredients, along with practices such as purgation, sympathetic magic, the use of powerful words, and symbolic transference.[24] These methods assumed an interconnection between body and soul similar to the worldview expressed in Ælfric's homilies using the dualities of seen and unseen, without and within.

The concept of the four humors (hot, cold, wet, and dry), borrowed from Greek medicine, is evident in both of the popular medical manuscripts. *Leechbook* II:xxvii, for example, discusses stomach ailments: the stomach of a hot nature digests meats well; the cold and moist stomach is susceptible to disease of the brain; the hot and dry stomach should not have honey but old wine and lukewarm meats; sex is bad for people with dry — especially cold and dry — constitutions, and most evil for those with a cold and moist nature, who should seek exercise. *Lacnunga* CLXXX (112) links the various causes of coughs with the four humors, in a rare instance where this book describes symptoms.[25] Despite its obvious deficiencies from a modern medical view, this physiological system was internally consistent, providing a logical framework for working out treatment based on balancing the four elements.

Balancing the humors sometimes led to the use of purgation to get rid of excesses. The most common form of purgation was of course bloodletting, for which there were elaborate instructions mostly concerned with the safest times for it. But purgation can also be found in practices such as pricking with a sharp object, vomiting, taking laxatives, and spitting. These kinds of practices also slid over into exorcisms or purging the body of evil, as will be shown below. These approaches lacked a clear distinction between physical and spiritual ills, particularly in cases where the malady was internal rather than visible externally.

The concept of balance and the interconnection between all things visible and invisible is evident also in sympathetic medicine. The theory of sympathy relied on the similarity between a plant or other item, or its name, and the disease's manifestation, location, or cause: for example, the use of an ear of barley thrust into the ear of a patient (unawares, no less!) to stanch bleeding, or the herb *ælfthone* for elfshot.[26] The underlying premise was as old as Pliny: "Nothing has been created by Nature without some purpose to fulfill."[27] This was easily Christianized as the Augustinian concept, expressed by Ælfric, that God gave to all things specific virtues that humans can tap. Consequently, certain herbs became associated with certain types of diseases. Herbs, animals, and other natural objects also fit into the humors scheme as having one or more of the four elements, and hence healers used them to counterbalance an excess of one of them. The *Anglo-Saxon Herbal* and the *Medicina de Quadrupedibus* list these functions for each item. For example, certain foods (animal or vegetable) have a greater strength in one or more of the four humors, and thus people used them medicinally as well as for food. In fact the boundary between medicine and food was rather vague, just as it is today, since good health was intimately connected to proper diet. Diet and medicine in the Middle Ages, however, were linked to the four humors and to the strength of a particular food. For instance, garlic, whose potency is self-evident, had the highest use as a medicinal food.[28]

Words had a virtue similar to that of herbs or animal parts; remedies frequently used written words in amulets or washed off into a drink in order to effect a cure. In this sense words were objects. Of course words also had the power to invoke the latent virtue of an herb, especially chanted words, even in an unintelligible language.[29] The wrong words, or words spoken at an inappropriate time, could cause damage, as evidenced in the instructions in several remedies to do certain actions in silence.[30] Words, then, were under the control of human agency. Knowledge of the right words and how to use them was a power a healer—or even a patient—might possess. This verbal power is evident in the use of command formulas in the first person ("I adjure you . . ."), in which it was by the power of the speaker's words and actions that the changes took place. For example, a pregnant woman unable to carry a child to term says this as she goes to bed, stepping over her husband: "Up I go, over you I step, with a live child not with a dying one, with a full-term child, not with a doomed one."[31] This remedy also employs sympathetic medicine in the instruction to step over a live man in order to produce a live child, just as, earlier in this remedy, the woman who has miscarried is told to step over a dead man's grave in a symbolic transference of death to the dead.

As in this case, symbolic transference was a type of sympathetic medicine in which disease could be transferred out of the patient into a plant or animal by some kind of contact. For example, the cure for spider bite was to make three incisions near the wound, let the blood run on a green hazel stick, and then throw the stick across the road.[32] Symbolic transference could also manifest in the other direction by invocation of power through narrative; telling the story of a fellow sufferer or a victorious person (such as Woden or Christ) transferred and then conquered the disease. For example, one dental remedy invoked the apocryphal story of Jesus healing Peter's toothache; childbearing complaints appealed to Mary and her cousin Elizabeth; and several maladies, including getting a stuck bone out of the throat, invoked the story of the raising of Lazarus.[33]

Inherent in these practices was the underlying concept of the interconnection of all things, macrocosm and microcosm. This concept can be attributed, in part, to the influence of Neoplatonic philosophy; however, this same notion of interconnectedness was implicit in Germanic belief as well. Signs had an actual, physical relationship to meaning; words naming certain real forces and actions imitating an intended goal had a direct impact on the objects themselves. This correspondence of microcosm and macrocosm, explained in Greek and Latin literature as well as by Anglo-Saxon scholars such as Byrhtferth, also formed the unstated foundation of practical medicine in classical, Christian, and Germanic societies.[34]

The elaborate diagram of the relationship of macrocosm and microcosm seen in the *Handbook of Byrhtferth* (fig. 4.1) may have been beyond the understanding of the typical Anglo-Saxon healer, but the same idea appears more simply in pictorial representations of the Creation, as in the Cædmon manuscript (fig. 4.2).[35] The Byrhtferth figure is undeniably more complex and literate, laying out specific connections between the seasons, the constellations, and the humors; the Cædmon illustration is graphic and more visually oriented, intended merely to represent the divine ordering of the days of creation. Yet the same concept comes through in both, that the natural, human, spiritual, and cosmic worlds are all interconnected and interdependent. Human beings share a little of each of the created orders, a Neoplatonic concept commonplace in early medieval writers, including Gregory the Great and Ælfric.[36]

A typical example of the application of this holistic view is the elaborate instructions concerning the proper times for bloodletting. The *Prognostics* laid out the theory behind this practice.

The old leeches set it down in Latin books that in every month there are always two days that are very dangerous for drinking any potion [drenc], or for letting blood; because there is one period in each of those days, [in which] if a man open any vein in that time then it results in

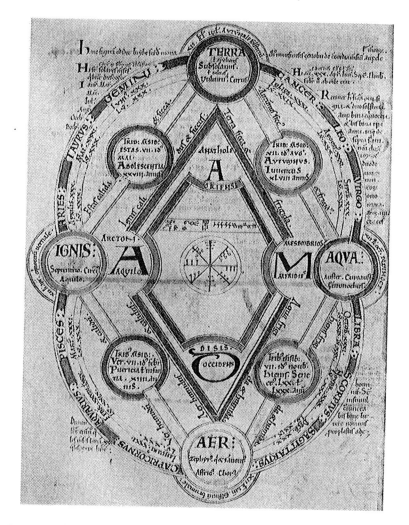

Figure 4.1. The Macrocosm, from Handbook of Byrhtferth, *ca. 1011. (Oxford, St. John's College MS 17, fol. 7v; reproduced courtesy of St. John's College)*

life lost or long pain. A leech tested this and let his horse's blood during this time and it soon lay dead. Now these are the days as it here says. . . .

Now then about the moon: it is important to beware that no one let men's blood on the fourth night of the old moon or on the fifth night, as books tell us, before the moon and the sea be of one mind. Also we heard a man say that no man lived who had blood let from him on All Saints massday; or if he were wounded. This is no sorcery [wiglung], but wise men found it out through the holy wisdom, as God Almighty directed them.[37]

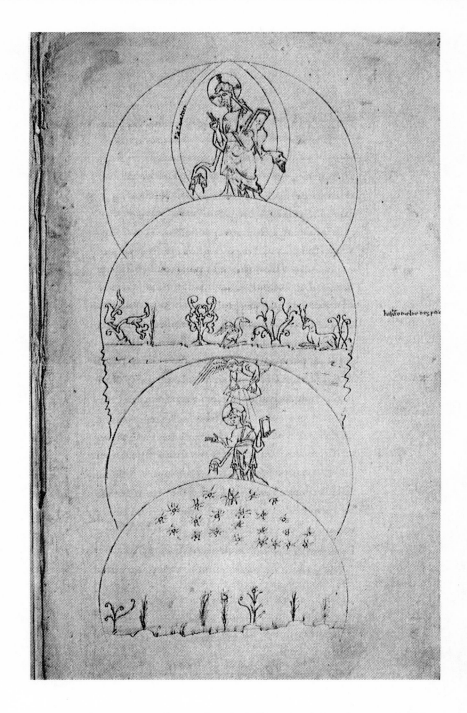

Figure 4.2. Cædmon manuscript diagram of the third, fifth, and sixth days of creation. (Bodleian Library, Oxford MS Junius 11, p. 7; reproduced courtesy of the Bodleian Library)

The *Lacnunga* contains similar information simplified into three dangerous days in the year for bloodletting or drinking prescriptions.[38] Whether complex or simple, the logic was the same, consistent with the medical view of the interconnection of microcosm and macrocosm. The larger rhythms and patterns of the cosmos affect the human body, and the healer must take into account these cosmic influences in treating the patient.

The author's assurance that the knowledge of these medicinal times was not sorcery because it came from church fathers or other Christian authorities echoes Ælfric's explanations about the rationality of the moon's patterns as part of God's design of nature (for example, trees are harder at the full moon because of the moon's pull). "Wise men found it out through the holy wisdom, as God Almighty directed them," as the *Prognostics* asserts, indicates how reason and authority worked together. True knowledge, in the Augustinian worldview, was both discoverable and revealed, as God directed wise men to find out the true nature of things. Indeed, the number of manuscripts concerned with computational knowledge demonstrates its importance in early medieval thought. Knowledge of astronomy, calendars, and computations constituted the skills of the literate few, who endeavored to create an accurate calendar, primarily for such religious purposes as the dating of Easter, but also for the healer.[39]

All of the medical manuscripts, classical and Germanic, also presumed concrete connections between certain herbs and substances and certain diseases. The *Anglo-Saxon Herbal* and *Medicina de Quadrupedibus* list these uses by herb or animal, while the *Lacnunga* and the *Leechbook* remedies demonstrate the connection in the way they consistently identify specific elements with certain types of disease. The so-called superstitious aspects of some remedies— the use of special actions and words—made the natural ingredient efficacious by bringing out its God-given powers. Practitioners had to gather and prepare certain herbs in special ways if they were to use them against some of the more mysterious ailments, particularly those with invisible causes. These special actions and words can be traced to both Christian liturgy and native folklore; moreover their correspondence with one another is especially intriguing, particularly in the elf charms explored in Chapter 5.

Liturgy

The liturgy of the Catholic Church is today a well-defined body of material found in established texts; however, in the early ages of the church, these materials were still evolving and were thus ill defined. The idea of a single book, a missal, had not yet developed; several liturgies of Roman,

Celtic, and Gallican origins and mixtures circulated in Europe by the mid-tenth century.[40] Particularly under Carolingian patronage in the eighth and ninth centuries, churchmen fought what they perceived to be the forces of illiteracy and ignorance among the clergy by establishing a textual base for a single, official liturgy. The abbeys of Fulda and Reichenau in ninth-century Germany became major centers for liturgical study and development. Thus by the late tenth century the Roman form of practice had superseded the Gallican and Celtic rites in most of Europe.[41]

Nonetheless a number of different types of liturgical books, and mixtures of types of documents within one manuscript, were in use in the tenth and eleventh centuries, including sacramentaries, so-called missals, and prayer leaflets; as well, liturgical rubrics and formulas occur throughout manuscripts with charms and exorcisms, sometimes in the margins.[42] From what remains of these texts we can see the core of Catholic liturgical tradition as it developed as well as a few anomalies peculiar to time and place, such as elaborate exorcisms, vernacular instructions in the margins, and the use of blank spaces for official records such as manumissions.[43] For example, Corpus Christi College, Cambridge 422 is a typical eleventh-century liturgical handbook with a calendar and instructions in Old English; Corpus Christi College, Cambridge 41 contains a broader mixture, including an Old English version of Bede's *Ecclesiastical History*, a sacramentary, homilies, and charms.[44] One of the best Anglo-Saxon examples of liturgical usage as well as the hybrid nature of such texts is the *Leofric Missal*. Manumissions of slaves were recorded on both ends of the manuscript. Extensive exorcisms, for things such as salt and oil, resonate with formulas found in medical manuscripts for driving out evil causes of illness.[45] So liturgical books are not straightforward texts by any means.

Furthermore, if we mean by liturgy the prescribed and repeatable formulas used in the main rituals of the church, then we find them not only in the official texts laying out the liturgy (missals) but also referenced in other textual situations, most notably the medical manuscripts, where prayers from the liturgy, ritual actions, and even whole masses are specified as part of the cure. These early medieval uses of the liturgy for "effective" purposes were classified as magic by many modern scholars, especially liturgists who shuddered at the degradation of a "pure" liturgy that in reality came into existence only later.[46] In many ways in this early medieval period, the gap between liturgical books and medical books was so small that they belong together as a single, larger group of manuals for health and well-being, along with penitentials.[47]

Liturgical Medicine

The idea of curing ailments by the use of liturgical formulas and actions or with Christian symbols and names was a logical consequence of the Christianization of Anglo-Saxon culture.[48] The high incidence of such Christian elements in the tenth- and eleventh-century medical books reflects a process of amalgamation that had been going on for some time in Anglo-Saxon England on the popular level such that it found expression in the vernacular texts. As Christianity spread through the various levels of society in the 350–400 years after Augustine's mission landed in England, especially in the tenth century with the increase in local clergy, so the availability and potential of Christian ideas increased. But these ideas did not remain static. They interacted with and were changed by native views. By the tenth century Anglo-Saxons may have unconsciously amalgamated Christian ideas with folklore notions predating Christianity, but they were conscious of being Christian—that is, they acknowledged Christianity as their religion, and it was becoming an integral part of their daily lives through the activities of the local priest. The application of Christian ritual to daily problems such as illness points to the local priest as a logical agent of change in traditional medicine because he had authority and power. One of the greatest popular needs was for remedies to fight malign forces that cause illness, especially those evils of ancient Germanic tradition. Against these the Christian liturgy was a logical and powerful tool.

Scholars such as Grattan and Singer treated the Christian elements in the medical remedies (and especially the charms) as superficial, late additions and focused instead on the strong, ancient magic of the "pagan" charms.[49] These scholars of the late nineteenth and early twentieth centuries, influenced by the development of modern science, were shocked by the primitive and magical medicine of their Anglo-Saxon forebears and focused their attention on the superstitious quality of the remedies, seen as irrational from their own modern "rationalist" and Christian view of the universe and how it functions. Current research is less grounded in a single truth emerging from the scientific worldview and is more open to alternative views as other "modes of rationality." Consequently our understanding of the relationship of Christianity and Anglo-Saxon folklore has changed in two ways: from a static to a more fluid and dynamic assessment, and from less stress on the opposition between them to more emphasis on the symbiotic nature of their relationship. For example, in the *Lacnunga* and the *Leechbook* the predominance of Christian elements over pagan references and the degree of intertwining between Christian ideas and Germanic folklore indicate not a hasty veneer by some guilty pseudo-Christian compiler but a gradual synthesis occurring over a period of time.

I see in the popular medical texts the meeting ground of a dual transference as popular remedies found their way into Christian texts and Christian rituals influenced popular practice. The presence of native Anglo-Saxon folklore in monastic texts in the vernacular, as discussed below, is evidence of the upward direction, the textualizing, of common practice. The various combinations of Christian and native folklore found in these manuscripts, though, are testimony to the synthesis of these traditions during a phase of oral transmission. That is, the wide variety of ways that these elements intertwined is evidence that they were not combined in one sitting by one person, but that this process was happening in many places over a period of time. The manuscripts reflect the diversity of what the compilers found.

The Power of Words and Rituals

Just as classically derived medicinal theory and Germanic ideas of disease were similar, so too Christian and Germanic ritual shared certain features. Both Christian theology and pre-Christian Germanic belief perceived power as resident in material objects. Words and objects were means of tapping power because of their inherent God-given virtues; human agents used words and objects to interact with spiritual forces. Knowledge of the words and rituals was a form of power held by certain people. By virtue of their ordination priests had the power of the words of the mass and other liturgical prayers, a kind of mana, just as practitioners of folk remedies such as charms had mana when they asserted, "I blow this poison away" or "I command you . . . ." Likewise the exorcisms of oil and salt preceding their blessings commonly found in early medieval liturgical books may offend modern liturgists, but they exercised a kind of power assumed by the priest. They all began, *Exorcizo te, creatura salis* (or *oleis*), that is, "I exorcise you, creature salt (or oil)." [50]

The confluence of these two kinds of power or mana, Christian and Germanic, is therefore not surprising. The Polynesian term *mana* has come into English usage as a label for either the power that can be tapped in objects or words or the power of a person. Christianity is capable of producing and maintaining a notion of mana, and this borrowed term is a useful way of understanding how the liturgy functioned in medical remedies and allows us to avoid the pejorative overtones of the word *magic*. [51]

The presence throughout Anglo-Saxon remedies of verbal or written formulas taken either directly from the Christian liturgy or imitating it after a fashion demonstrate the kind of mana held by priests. The masses, prayers from the litany, Psalms, Creed, Pater noster, and benedictions operated the same way as the verbal pre-Christian charms did. Their function was to use words to draw down power into an herb, object, or patient through their symbolism or homology. For example, *Lacnunga* CLXXXIII (114) specifies ritual actions of purity (a virgin collecting running water) in multiples of three, accompanied by the singing of the Creed and Pater noster.

> If cysts pain a man at the heart, let a virgin go to a spring which runs straight east, and draw forth one cup full, with [in the direction of?] the current, and sing thereon the Creed and Pater noster, and then pour it into another vessel; and let him/her draw again a second and sing again the Creed and the Pater noster; and do so that you have three [cupfuls]; do this nine days; soon he will be well.[52]

Sometimes Christian wording (often unintelligible Latin or Greek) displaced pagan, or at least non-Christian, wording, but more often it stood side by side with the native folklore (the number nine, the direction of the stream), demonstrating that there was little perception of a conflict. For example, the following "reduction" charm from the *Lacnunga*, CLXII (95), relied on a pre-Christian practice of the sympathetic power of words to reduce "kernels" or nodes (possibly swollen glands, cysts, or other lumps), but it also has a Christian blessing attached at the end.

> Nine were [blank]
> node's sisters, then [turned] the nine to VIII, and the VIII to VII, and the VII to VI, and the VI to V, and the V to IIII, and the IIII to III, and the III to II, and the II to I, and the one to none. Let this be medicine [*lib*] for you for kernel and for scrofula and for worm, and for every evil. Sing benedicite nine times.[53]

The Germanic elements (the number nine, the worm) fall into the category of folklore discussed below. The addition of the Benedicite to this folk remedy is consistent with both Germanic and Christian notions of the power of words to affect natural objects, and it also fulfills the dictum that medicinal remedies should use Christian words.

Words had power whether or not they were intelligible. The word and concept of gibberish arises only later.[54] The early Middle Ages probably did not have a concept of "meaningless words" (just words a given individual did not understand). Late antique and medieval attitudes toward words and meaning were thus significantly different from our own, in that understanding the language was not considered absolutely necessary to the efficacy of the word. For example, John Chrysostom defended the singing of

Latin hymns by the laity ignorant of Latin on the grounds that the sounds of praise were just as significant.[55] Charms containing garbled, untranslatable foreign language words relied on the sound of the words—their mystery and assonance—to achieve some connection with spiritual powers. Also, they were ennobled by their vague association with the venerable classical languages, Latin and Greek. Consequently the Latin prayers used with these garbled foreign charms would sound equally mysterious and powerful to an illiterate Anglo-Saxon ear.

A classic example of untranslatable language mixtures in a charm, combined with elements from the Christian liturgy, is the following popular remedy for black ulcers, found in several manuscripts. This version is from *Lacnunga* XXV (9). The first prayer is Old Irish so garbled that it is untranslatable. The second prayer in Latin is a recognizable scriptural formula.

> Sing this prayer on the black ulcers nine times, first Pater noster;

> Tigath tigath tigath calicet aclu cluel sedes adclocles acre earcre arnem nonabiuth ær ærnem nithren arcum cunath arcum arctua fligara uflen binchi cutern nicuparam raf afth egal uflen arta arta arta trauncula trauncula.

> Querite et inuenietis. Adiuro te per patrem et filium et spiritum sanctum non amplius crescas sed arescas; super aspidem et basilliscum ambulabis et conculcabis leonem et draconem. Crux Matheus, crux Marcus, crux Lucas, crux Johannes.

> [Seek and you will find. I adjure you through the father and the son and the holy spirit. Do not grow greater but dry up. Upon the asp and the basilisk you shall tread and on the lion and the dragon.] [56]

Godfrid Storms's comments on this charm in his edition are enlightening—he refuses to allow this magical use of Christian words to stand as Christian: "The first four lines of the incantation are unintelligible to me. Then we find a reference to Matthew VII, 7, followed by a Christian-worded though in reality magic adjuration of the disease-spirit not to increase but to dry up and vanish." [57] What appeared unintelligible to Storms, the garbled Old Irish, actually worked with Latin in the Pater noster and specific scriptural references to produce a powerful set of words. The Matthew reference, "Seek and you will find," combines with an exorcistic adjuration to the Trinity and a reference to Psalm 90 (91) invoking God's miraculous protection against various evils. The shrinking of the sores is compared to the confident triumph of the believer walking unscathed in the midst of terrible danger. The victory of both body and soul is here inseparable.

In Storms's reality, or from many post-twelfth-century views where natural and supernatural are separate, this kind of thing is a misuse of prayer and Scripture. But the practice was perfectly consistent with early medieval views of the power of words in relation to objects, and medieval Christianity's emphasis on the power of the liturgy to change objects and cross the boundary between this world and the next.

In addition to Christian verbal formulas, these remedies also made use of other Christian symbols and objects: the sign of the cross, the triangular symbol of the Trinity, the paten, the consecrated bread, the consecrated wine, the altar, and holy water, oil, and salt.[58] For example, in the remedy for elfshot quoted at the beginning of my Introduction, *Leechbook* I:lxxxviii.2–3 or *Lacnunga* CXVIII (60), a masspriest is instructed to sing twelve masses over dock seed and Scottish wax before placing the herbs with holy water on the horse. Words become objects as well, as in the following remedy, *Leechbook* I:lxii.3, part of a section using Christian elements to counteract mind-altering afflictions (discussed further in Chapter 5). It combines word and object by specifying that the patient consume writing in a drink.

[For fever:] A man shall write this on the housel dish [paten] and wash [it] into the drink with holy water, and sing on it:

[To the left of the following Latin quotation appears a design of eighteen crosses resembling plus signs, which surround the Greek letters alpha and omega.][59]

In principio erat uerbum et uerbum erat aput deum et deus erat uerbum. Hoc erat In principio aput deum omnia per ipSum facta Sunt.

[In the beginning was the word and the word was with God and the word was God. He was in the beginning with God and all things through him were made.][60]

Wash then the writing with holy water off the dish into the drink. Sing then the Credo, and the Pater noster.

There follows in the remedy a list of Christian songs and an exorcism in Latin beginning "I adjure you" addressed to the fevers.

The actions of this remedy are unclear to us. Although some scholars assume that the entire Gospel passage was written in some fashion on the dish, the instruction "write this" could refer exclusively to the diagram and the "sing over it" to the Latin passage from John. The table of contents entry for this remedy describes the instructions as writing "the holy and great god's name" on the housel dish. However, a similar set of instructions in the *Lacnunga*, XXIX (11), specifies the entire passage of John 1:1–5 as well as a number of other such passages taken from the liturgy, but contains no diagrams. In any case it is hard to imagine how the writing was produced on the paten, whether the symbols were inscribed on the dish itself and hence reusable, or written on something disposable—bread or a scrap of vellum—or even symbolically written by the priest with his finger in the same way that he makes the sign of the cross. Nonetheless the remedy clearly shows how Christian ritual, words, and objects together effected a cure that is indistinguishably medicinal and liturgical.

Holy objects thus added a potency to natural ingredients used in medicinal remedies. The Christian liturgy sanctified ordinary objects (water, wine, and bread) through its prayers, bringing together, as Ælfric explained, the earthly and the heavenly.[61] Once blessed in this way, these ordinary objects transferred their potency to other objects, hence their use in remedies to fight off illness. Indeed, the Christian liturgy itself contained formulas to combat disease. What better use was there for oil consecrated for anointing the sick than to administer it as a prescription?

The inclusion at the end of the *Lacnunga* of several generic Latin prayers for herbs and salves indicates the proximity of this medical text to liturgical texts that contain similar prayers for blessing water, oil, and salt. So, for example, the blessing of plants is similar in some ways to the elaborate Field Remedy at the beginning of Chapter 1 and resonates with Ælfric's explanation of the correspondence between the multiplied loaves and the miracle of agriculture discussed in Chapter 3. *Lacnunga* CXCI offers the following blessing of herbs:

BENEDICTIO HERBARUM:
Omnipotens sempiterne deus qui ab initio mundi omnia instituisti
et creasti tam arborum generibus quam herbarum seminibus, quibus
etiam benedictione tua benedicendo sanxisti eadem, nunc benedictione
holera aliosque fructus sanctificare ac benedicere digneris, ut sumenti-
bus ex eis sanitatem conferant mentis et corporis ac tutelam defensionis
eternamque uitam. per saluatorem animarum dominum nostrum
iesum christum, qui uiuit et regnat deus in secula seculorum. Amen.

[Omnipotent eternal God who from the beginning of the world insti-
tuted and created all things, both trees after their kind and herbs with

their seeds, with which by your benediction you have blessed and ordained the same; now deign with thy benediction to sanctify and bless these plants and other fruits, so that they may confer health of mind and body to those partaking (of them), and a safeguard of defense and eternal life. Through the savior of souls, our lord Jesus Christ, who lives and reigns God for ever and ever. Amen.][62]

While blessing herbs with a Latin prayer follows the liturgical pattern of blessings for holy water and oil, it does not occur in the "pure" liturgy envisioned by later scholars who find it easier to identify such blessings with pagan formulas than to locate the liturgical connections.[63] However, the remedy's similarity to Ælfric's Augustinian worldview, its context in a Christian medical manuscript, and the blessings that follow that are found in liturgical manuscripts all indicate that this prayer was predominantly Christian.

For example, the blessings that follow this one, "Benedictio Unguentum" and "Benedictio Potus sive Unguenti," have parallels in the Durham Ritual.[64] The fine line between blessing and charm, supplication and manipulation, is invisible here. The second blessing of unguents, *Lacnunga* CXCIV, reads as follows:

In nomine patris et filii et spiritus sancti et per uirtutem dominice passionis et resurrectionis a mortuis ut sanctificentur tuo uerbo sancto et benedicantur omnes fideles cum gustu huius unguenti aduersus omnes nequitias in mundorum spiritum et contra ualitudines et infirmitates que corpus affligunt.

[In the name of the Father and the Son and the Holy Spirit, and through the power of the Lord's passion and resurrection from the dead, (I pray) that all the faithful may be sanctified by your word and blessed with a touch of this unguent, against all wickednesses aimed at the spirit of pure ones and against illnesses and infirmities that afflict the body.]

Both the blessings of herbs and of unguents found in these closing folios of the *Lacnunga* combine physical and spiritual issues, blurring the boundary between medicine and liturgy. The herbal prayer addresses ills of both mind and body as well as the spiritual life of the soul in eternity. The prayer for the unguent indicates that both the word as spiritual force and the blessed natural ingredient work together. For this blessing it did not matter whether the attack was spiritual or physical or whether that distinction even needed to be made. The identification of spiritual evil with physical illness was very close here; hence the use of both a natural element (the unguent) and the spiritual invocation.

Categorizing this kind of practice as "Christian magic" ignores the context in which it was produced. When charms call on sympathetic identification to cure a disease, previous scholars such as Grattan and Singer called it magic. From a modern view these blessings invoking God's creation of all things and Christ's death and resurrection seem to manipulate the power of prayer for effective, and hence magical, purposes; yet sympathetic identification was, and is, a Christian concept as well—the believer is supposed to identify with and participate in Christ's death and resurrection.[65] That this was applied literally, rather than figuratively as in later Christian theology, should not suggest a lesser understanding of Christian truth or a degradation of Christianity by the influence of paganism. In the early medieval Christian worldview where microcosm and macrocosm were so closely linked, physical and spiritual medicine functioned in harmony.

The most potent liturgical combination of act and words, therefore, was the recitation of the whole mass, in which the verbal power of the priest ordained by the holy church opened a doorway through the natural elements to heavenly power. Masses said over the herbs in a remedy called down God's blessing on his natural creations (the bread and wine for spiritual cure or the herb for physical cure) and served to drive out evil forces (worm, elf, or demon), just as a mass of exorcism did.

The power resident in the church, once its presence was felt, had a tremendous impact on everyday belief and practice. The example cited above from *Lacnunga* CXVIII (60), using twelve masses to bless herbs for elfshot, concludes, "Have the herbs always with you." It would seem that priests or parishioners regularly placed herbs under the altar and then kept them for medical emergencies. The frequent inclusion of the mass in the folk remedies examined below leads one to believe that church altars had an assortment of items under them, despite the canonical prohibitions against bringing unseemly things into church. This practice is not uncommon in churches today. Parishioners, particularly in cultures Christianized since 1500, are in the habit of bringing all kinds of significant household items to the church for the priest's blessing. The modern church has not overtly discouraged this practice because it reinforces the power resident in the church and diverts attention from other potential sources of spiritual power to which someone might turn. Indeed, this practical side has been a part of the Christian tradition throughout the ages. For example, Peter Brown has argued for late Antiquity that Christianity transferred evil ailments from human agency (sorcerers) to spiritual forces (demons) in a cosmological shift that changed the way people responded to the bad things that happened to them.[66] This cosmology of demonic forces was operative in late Saxon England as well, evident in the medical manuscripts.

Since most remedies in the medical manuscripts did not contain liturgical formulas, this raises the question of why some did and some did not. Most of the remedies in the medical texts are, to use a modern category, "natural"; that is, they consist entirely of visible ingredients and their preparation without calling on invisible forces. On the other hand, the remedies with heavy use of the liturgy, and also remedies with charms, form a separate category—not because they are in some modern sense "supernatural" or "magic" (as opposed to natural and therefore scientific) but because they are associated with spiritual forces and thus require a remedy employing words of power.

The clustering of such remedies in the medical texts, especially the *Leechbook*, is a result of the organization of the manuscript by disease or body part. For example, most of the remedies in *Leechbook* I:xlv–lxvi include Christian elements for diseases such as flying venom, dry disease, fever, demon possession, elvish tricks, and folly. Remedies elsewhere for these same ailments frequently include Christian elements also.[67] The *Lacnunga* has numerous salves that require Christian liturgy or holy elements in order to be efficacious, including remedies against elves, dwarves, black ulcers, cysts, and cattle theft.[68] Most of these problems required powerful words and rituals because they had an invisible or internal cause that might be attributed to some spiritual agency, demonic in the Christian view. This correlation suggests a conflation of Germanic and Christian views, as demonstrated in the next section on Germanic folklore.

Folklore

The correlation between liturgical elements and native remedies is perhaps the most significant factor indicating an amalgamation occurring in late Anglo-Saxon England between Germanic folklore and Christianity. The combination of these two elements represents both a Christianization of folklore and a "folklorization" of Christianity. This dual process can be seen in action: in the high incidence of Christian elements in remedies for traditional Anglo-Saxon ills, in the association of these native ills with remedies for spiritual attacks (such as demon possession), in the inclusion of folk elements in recipes for such spiritual ills (temptation, for example), and most of all, in the variety of ways different remedies found together in the same manuscript combined these elements, without any sense of progressive Christianization through time. A completely Latin remedy can be found next to a completely folkloric remedy lacking any Christian elements. Were the compilers just ignorant? confused? not fully Christian? Instead of assuming that the producers and users of these remedies were entirely illogical, we need to seek a logical answer by examining their point of view in an appropriate cultural context.[69] A contextual analysis of these folklore elements reveals a clear pattern of accommodation that preserved Germanic folk knowledge of the natural world while maintaining the integrity of the Christian cosmology.

Four unique elements characterized Germanic ("native") medicine transmitted through folklore: flying venoms, the worm, the number nine, and the elf. Any occurrence of one of these four in a remedy is a fairly clear indication that it is in part or whole a native remedy, as opposed to a copy or translation of a classical remedy. "Germanic" is a more appropriate, if generic, label, rather than "Anglo-Saxon," because remedies with such elements may not be specifically Anglo-Saxon but shared by other Germanic peoples. Such remedies, or portions of remedies, could have come into usage in England either through the Anglo-Saxon migrations or later through adaptation from continental sources. In addition the Anglo-Saxon medical manuscripts borrowed heavily from Irish traditions and incorporated some Scandinavian elements as well. As pointed out in Chapter 2, the Anglo-Saxons did not exist, strictly speaking, as a cohesive and separate culture occasionally interrupted by outsiders; rather, they are one complex ethnic amalgamation existing in a network of evolving groups. These four Germanic folk-medical elements, then, emerge in a larger context of contact and mingling between a variety of pre-Christian traditions, in addition to the contact and mingling with the classical and Christian traditions.[70]

What is intriguing about remedies with identifiable Germanic traits is not so much the survival of pre-Christian ideas about the causation of disease, but the way in which the Christian elements were used along with them. The majority of these Germanic remedies in the *Leechbook* and the *Lacnunga* contain at least some Christian wording or action. This correlation indicates a long-standing effort to meet the dangers of traditional evils with the power of the Christian religion that had taken hold by the mid-tenth century. Given the variety of combinations of folk and Christian traditions in the medical manuscripts discussed below, this amalgamation was not just a unilateral imposition from above but was a synthesis occurring throughout Anglo-Saxon society as Christianity spread in the growing numbers of local churches. This synthesis percolated upward into the increasingly vernacular texts produced in the scriptoria of the late Anglo-Saxon period.

Lays of the Nine

Illnesses associated with worms and venoms (or poisons) are frequently found together in medical remedies, while the number nine is all-pervasive. (The elf will be dealt with separately, in Chapter 5). The "Lay of the Nine Herbs" and the "Lay of the Nine Twigs of Woden," *Lacnunga* LXXIX–LXXX (45), together with the instructions that follow (LXXXI–LXXXII), are the best examples involving these first three native elements in a fairly un-Christianized form.[71] The first lay is a kind of herb list, like the *Anglo-Saxon Herbal*, and the second specifies natural substances effective against various poisons. These lays were more than a written record of the oral formulas a healer would memorize in order to remember herbs and their function; they were also chants to sing over them during preparation procedures, to activate their inherent virtues.

[LAY OF THE NINE HERBS][72]

Be mindful, Mugwort,   what you revealed,
What you established   at the great proclamation
Una you are called,   oldest of herbs,
you are strong against three   and against thirty,
you are strong against poison   and against onfliers [flying venoms]
you are strong against the foe   who goes through the land.

And you, Waybroad [Plantain],   mother of herbs,
open from the east,   mighty within.
Over you chariots creaked,   over you queens rode,
over you brides cried out,   over you bulls snorted.
All this you withstood,   and confounded.
So you withstand   poison and flying venom,
and the foe   who goes through the land.

Stune this herb is called,   she grew on a stone,
she stands against poison,   she attacks pain.
Stithe [hard] she is called,   she confounds poison,
she drives out evils,   she casts out poison.
This is the herb   that fought against the worm,
this is strong against poison,   she is strong against flying venoms,
she is strong against the foe   who goes through the land.

Rout you now, Attorlathe [Venomloather],   the less the more,
the more the less   until there be a remedy for him against both.

Remember you, Maythe [Camomile],   what you revealed,
what you accomplished   at Alorford,
that never for flying venom   did he yield life
since for him a man prepared   Maythe for food.

This is the herb   that is called Wergule.
This a seal sent   over the sea ridges,
as a remedy   against the harm of another poison.

[Two herbs, chervil and fennel, are missing]

[LAY OF THE NINE TWIGS OF WODEN]

These nine go   against nine poisons.
A worm came crawling,   he wounded nothing.
Then Woden took   nine glory-twigs [wuldor tanas]
smote then the adder   that it flew apart into nine [parts].
There apple and poison   brought it about
that she never would   dwell in the house.

Chervil and Fennel,[73]   very mighty two,
these herbs he created,   the wise Lord
holy in heaven   when He hung;
He established and sent them   into the seven worlds,
to the poor and the rich,   for all a remedy.

She stands against pain,   she assaults poison,
who has power against three   and against thirty,
against enemy's hand   and against great terror[74]
against the bewitching   of little/vile wights.
Now these nine herbs have power   against nine evil spirits
   [wuldorgeflogenum, "fugitives from glory"],
against nine poisons   and against nine flying venoms:
Against the red poison,   against the foul poison,
against the white poison,   against the purple poison,
against the yellow poison,   against the green poison,
against the dark poison,   against the blue poison,
against the brown poison,   against the crimson poison.

Against worm-blister,   against water-blister,[75]
against thorn-blister,   against thistle-blister,
against ice-blister,   against poison-blister.
If any poison   flying from the east,
or any from the north   . . . come
or any from the west   over humanity.
Christ stood over the old ones,   the malignant ones [?].[76]
I alone know   running streams
and the nine adders   now they behold [?].
All weeds must now   give way to herbs
the seas slip apart,   all salt water,
when I this poison   blow from you.

[THE PREPARATION]

Mugwort, waybroad open from the east, lamb's cress, attorlathe, maythe, nettle, crab-apple, chervil and fennel, old soap; work the herbs into dust, mix them with the soap and the apple juice. Work then a paste of water and of ashes; take fennel, boil it in the paste and beat with the [herbal] mixture when he applies the salve both before and after.

Sing the charm [galdor] on each of the herbs three times before he prepares them, and on the apple likewise. And let someone sing into the mouth of the man and into both his ears, and on the wound, that same charm [gealdor] before he applies the salve.

According to this lay and other remedies, these nine herbs were effective against various kinds of invisible, malicious ills, such as poison, worms, and "flying venoms," possibly airborne infections. However, the activation of the herbs' inherent virtues in combating such spiritual ills required the mana of a trained person relying on ancient knowledge. On the one hand, addressing the herbs directly indicates that potency resided in the plant itself—in a Christian view, God placed this virtue there, although the lay does not make this assumption explicit. The tone is much more reminiscent of animistic or polytheistic belief in the way the lay personifies the herbs as warriors, consonant with references to the battle-laden Æsir. On the other hand, the speaker or healer speaks with his or her own authority or power: "I alone know" and "I blow this poison from you." Clearly power runs through this human channel, the one who knows the right associations between the microcosm of the herb and the spiritual macrocosm.

The single mention of Woden as a pagan reference is not that radical when we consider that Anglo-Saxon kings still claimed descent from this mythical figure. The inclusion of Christ in a parallel function to Woden, as sympathetic magic and an appeal to a past event of power, demonstrates an awareness of a shift in the scheme of power toward a Christian orientation. Likewise the Germanic pantheon hovers in the background in the Germanic battle imagery of spears, the herbal weapons counteracting those of the elves, the Æsir, or other Germanic spiritual agents. This reorientation in the macrocosm was not great enough, however, to necessitate a revolution in the microcosm of plants and animals.

These lays, really a set of charms, one for each plant, have the most pagan references found in Anglo-Saxon medicine, and only a brief mention of Christ. In other words, this set represents the extreme end of a spectrum of remedies ranging from "pagan" to fully Christian. However, I do not think it is pagan in a religious sense so much as it is a type of highly conservative folklore. This kind of memorized and performed remedy lived a long life, gradually absorbing, as this one had begun to, the new religious overtones.

Venom and Worms

Other remedies for worms and venoms contain more Christian elements than the lays, indicating a long-standing, ongoing process of Christianizing what was clearly a widely known set of afflictions demanding attention from healers. Remedies for flying venom—perhaps a kind of epidemic—occur throughout all of the medical texts, and almost all those in both the Leechbook and the Lacnunga have some Christian elements to combat this invisible, hence spiritual, ailment. Lacnunga XVIII (6), for example, prescribes a salve made of herbs over which one mass has been sung.[77] Lacnunga CXXXIII (74) offers the following heavily Christian remedy:

> Against flying venom, slash four strokes in the four quarters with an oaken brand; make the brand bloody, throw it away; sing this on it three times: [making the sign of the cross as drawn in the manuscript]

> matheus me ducath, marcus me conseruæth, lucas me liberat, iohannes me adiuuat semper. amen. Contriue deus omnem malum et nequitiam per uirtutem patris et filii et spiritus sancti sanctifica me emanuhel iesus christus libera me ab omnibus insidiis inimici; benedictio domini super caput meum; potens deus in omni tempore. amen.

> [Matthew guide me, Mark protect me, Luke free me, John aid me, always, amen. Destroy, O God, all evil and wickedness; through the

power of the Father and the Son and the Holy Spirit sanctify me; Emmanuel, Jesus Christ, free me from all attacks of the enemy; the benediction of the Lord (be) over my head; mighty God in every season. Amen.]

Grattan and Singer note that "the words of the spell are Christian but the form is Northern Pagan."[78] This is a trenchant observation concerning origins, but it is not of much help in identifying what this mixture of form and content meant in an Anglo-Saxon Christian context. Which is dominiant? Which gives meaning? The implication that somehow the Christian words used in this pagan form represent a degeneracy of Christian meaning is, I think, erroneous, because it makes a distinction between Christian and pagan, word and form, that may not have been operative in this context. From an Anglo-Saxon view, nothing here indicates magic as an appeal to demonic forces; rather, the remedy seeks to drive out evil spirits using Christian prayers. This prayer "pertains to God," in the qualifying words of the *Penitential of Egbert*, more than it pertains to anything else.[79]

The ability of the disease to spread through the air (the reference to cardinal directions suggests winds blowing the poison in) gave this ill a spiritual quality requiring appeal to unseen forces, available through Christian symbols and the protection of the four gospelers, to add potency to the herbs or to ward off the evil. In some ways this Latin, highly Christian remedy sought to accomplish the same aims as the "Lay of the Nine Herbs" and operates on the same principles. Why is one pagan and the other Christian, while both are in the same manuscript? The question of labeling these remedies as pagan or Christian is irrelevant to the context in many ways. What was significant in the context of the *Lacnunga* manuscript was the way in which the compiler dealt with a popularly recognized affliction through a variety of means, revealing a shift in cosmology that led to changes in practice but not necessarily conflicts or a crisis of conscience for these practitioners.

The same kinds of accommodation processes were at work with another Germanic affliction, worms. Much speculation surrounds the idea of worms as a cause of disease, given the large number of references to them in all the medical texts and herbals. The usual Anglo-Saxon terms were *wyrm* or *adder*, but also the reptilian *dracon* and its associations with the gem *draconitis*.[80] This creature or affliction of Germanic folklore has an immediate and obvious identification with the serpent of Genesis and the Devil; it clearly is associated with internal, hence invisible, illnesses that therefore have an unseen, probably spiritual, cause. That illnesses caused by tapeworms or other known worms were common—witness the number of remedies—is not surprising from the experience of modern medicine in areas of poor sanitation. As with flying venoms, worms account for a variety of mysterious illnesses necessitating a wide range of remedies that became Christianized in different ways. For example, Leechbook I:xlviii–li offers a series of remedies for worms, varying in their description and technique. The cures generally involve driving out or reducing the worm through a combination of herbs, salves, charms, and prayers.[81]

As a less visible, internal illness worms necessitated strong words of power. Lacnunga XXVI (10), which follows the "Tigath, Tigath, Tigath" charm quoted above and precedes one against elf attack, prescribes a song for a human or an animal that has swallowed a worm in a drink, for a penetrating worm, or for poison that has been drunk. The lay is sung nine times, along with a Pater noster. Its words appear unintelligible to us but exhibit Celtic traits: "Gonomil ongomil manbumil manbrai namum tofethtengo docuillo binam cuithæn cæfmul scuiht cuillo scuiht cuib duill manbrinamum." This worm charm seems to have been popular, because it is referred to in a later remedy, Lacnunga LXIII (29), a "Holy Salve" made up of numerous herbs that also uses holy water, the four gospelers, and many psalms and litanies as well as another untranslatable word series: "acre, arcre, arnem nona ærnem beothor ærnem." The use of Celtic elements shows the local origins of this remedy and the pervasiveness of this concept of disease in early medieval Europe.

These examples of poison and worm remedies show not only the prevalence of these diseases but the variety of approaches taken to cure them. Because they were part of popular folklife and because they involved unseen powers, they required appeals to spiritual power through rituals. These Germanic afflictions by their very nature, then, are the most subject to Christianization, as these manuscripts demonstrate. Christian words and rituals began to have weight equal to or greater than pre-Christian remedies and were becoming part of Anglo-Saxon folklore.

Conclusions: Intertwining Contexts

Medicine, liturgy, and folklore intertwined in the literate communities of late Saxon England. This textual intertwining represents popular culture and religious practices in two ways. First, the diverse fusions of Germanic, classical, and Christian traditions in these texts predate their written form and reflect an oral tradition of synthesis in everyday practice. Second, the production of these manuscripts shows an effort to meet popular needs by recording and spreading these remedies. Just as penitentials, liturgical manuscripts, and homilies functioned as aids to the clergy, so too the medical books served as manuals of instruction and transmission of Anglo-Saxon religious folklore concerned with alleviating people's physical and spiritual ills. The overlap between physical and spiritual well-being is obvious in these texts; the development of Christian remedies was therefore very much part of the effort to create an Anglo-Saxon Christian tradition that met the needs of the populace.

The worldview evident in these remedies, while unscientific to a modern reader, was not that different from the Augustinian worldview propounded by Ælfric and certainly should not be labeled pagan or magic out of hand. The inclusion in these manuscripts of Germanic ideas of disease and cure predating Christianity does not in itself indicate the survival of paganism as a religious system or of magical beliefs opposing religious rationality. Rather, the similarity of belief about nature and spiritual agency found in both the Augustinian worldview and Germanic medical folklore set the stage for a relatively easy assimilation between the two.

5

ELVES, DEMONS, AND OTHER MIND-ALTERING AFFLICTIONS
EVIDENCES OF POPULAR PRACTICES

The creation of a popular Anglo-Saxon Christianity involved not only the displacement of older traditions (paganism) but also the synthesis of native and Christian beliefs, consciously or unconsciously. The process of cultural accommodation went on piecemeal, growing in the same organic fashion as the local churches and influenced by that developing local environment. The adaptation of folk practices to Christian ideas in the medical manuscripts followed no prescribed plan, unlike the clear reform agenda of Ælfric or Wulfstan. Rather, as the *Leechbook* and the *Lacnunga* show, various ways of combining these divergent traditions occurred side by side in the same manuscript, offering several alternative ways of understanding a given problem. Nowhere is this clearer than in the transformation of the Germanic conception of elves by Christian ideas, and vice versa, the inclusion of elves in the Christian cosmology.

Remedies against the attack of elves on humans or cattle form a distinct group, although they overlap with the other three Germanic elements discussed in the previous chapter. Elf remedies sometimes appear in medical manuscripts collected together, often accompanied by remedies for demonic and other mind-altering afflictions, indicating a consciousness of a similarity between these ailments. These remedies not only contained Germanic elements, particularly charms, but also included a large amount of Christian material, particularly the saying of masses. The various ways in which these traditions, elfin and demonic, charm and mass, intermingled reveal to us the gradual amalgamation process at work in late Anglo-Saxon England.

This chapter first examines the problematic nature of elves as a Germanic concept revealed to us only in Christian sources. The majority of the chapter then explores the diversity of elf charms within the context and ideology of the medical manuscripts. The few elf charms scattered in the *Lacnunga* reveal a wide variety of accommodations made between Germanic folk remedies and Christian cosmology and liturgy that demonstrates not the retention of paganism in popular thinking but the active Christianization of local culture occurring on an ad hoc basis in Anglo-Saxon England. The more systematic collection of elf remedies in the *Leechbook* reveals not only a diversity of accommodations but also the congruence between folk and Christian cosmologies in the association of elves, demons, fevers, and madness. The *Leechbook* remedies, so diverse and yet so organized, best represent the new cosmological synthesis of late Saxon popular Christianity.

The aim of this chapter is to reread the elf charms using an approach drawn from cultural history that is more sympathetic than previous treatments. This in part involves critiquing some of the older interpretations. Because the focus is on reading the texts in their appropriate contexts, this chapter quotes extensively from the table of contents of the *Leechbook* and includes entire remedies from the *Lacnunga* and the *Leechbook*. Rather than thinking about these remedies according to modern categories, the reader should place them in an early medieval context. Rather than attempting to label these practices as pagan or Christian, magic or religion, I explore the dynamics of these middle practices as expressions of an Anglo-Saxon Christian worldview.

Elves

Elves were ambivalent, amoral creatures in Anglo-Saxon folklore. *Beowulf* lists them along with other monsters, but the prefix *ælf-* occurs in many positive, feminine compounds expressing beauty or light.[1] In addition to disease suffixes attached to the root word, numerous prefixes indicate elves' association with the natural world in such compounds as mountain-, sea-, wood-, down-, and field-elves.[2] Old Icelandic lore contains several references to elves as part of the Scandinavian cosmology. Elves, along with land spirits, are associated with the god Freyr who rules over "Alfheim" (Elfland); they are linked also to the Norns and the Æsir.[3] For example, Snorri Sturluson quotes *Reginsmal*:

> Of different origins
> are the Norns, I think,
> not all of one kindred;
> some come from Æsir-kin,
> some from the elves
> and some are the daughters of Dvalin.[4]

Snorri Sturluson also draws a distinction between light and dark elves, but this may reflect Christian influence.[5]

Elves were thought to be invisible or hard-to-see creatures who shot their victims with some kind of arrow or spear, thus inflicting a wound or inducing a disease with no other apparent cause (elfshot). They appear to be lesser spirits than the Æesir deities, but with similar armaments in spears and arrows. Remedies treat such attacks with medicinal salves and drinks made with specific herbs or with purgative methods, such as smoking the elf out or pricking. All of these types of remedies included the use of charms or liturgy.[6] This attack by elves was eventually linked with Christian ideas of demons penetrating or possessing animals and people, who then needed exorcism.

We have deduced this much from the available linguistic evidence, but because the medical remedies generally lack symptoms and observations of disease, we do not know exactly how the affliction manifested itself externally or internally (or both). However, one of the rare instances of a diagnostic description of symptoms occurs in the set of elf remedies at the end of *Leechbook* III, a series analyzed at the end of this chapter. Some of these variations on elf attack give symptomatic descriptions. *Ælfsogotha* (elf-juices, heartburn?) manifested itself in yellowish membranes in the eyes and differentiated between men and women with separate symptoms. The remedy further distinguished curable from incurable manifestations of the disease; it also determined treatment according to the length of time the patient had suffered. "Water elf" disease was manifested in livid fingernails, tearful eyes, and looking downward, and yet the remedy prescribed a poultice for the wound, indicating some visible manifestation and location associated with the cause (an elf arrow?). Storms speculates that the illness was chicken pox (see below).[7] As with many early medieval remedies, then, the authors or compilers usually assumed that the person using the text was able to diagnose the type of ailment. The practitioner used the text to locate and then experiment with that cluster of remedies (herbs and charms) associated with the type.[8]

Elf-disease remedies appear in close proximity to or combined with remedies for demon possession, nightmares, madness, fevers, and other mind-altering afflictions of seemingly malevolent origin that aggressively attacked humans or cattle. The remedies used herbs or purgative techniques to guard against or drive out elvish attacks. The efficacy of medicinal herbs in a salve or drink was enhanced with rituals of power, frequently Christian, known to bring out the herbs' virtues against these creatures.

Some of the most commonly used herbs occurring in these elf- and demon-related remedies include lupin, bishopwort (betony), fennel, and cropleek. Also appearing frequently are feverfew, waybread, attorlathe ("venomloather"), garlic, *heahhiolothe* or *helenium* (possibly elecampane), pennyroyal (*pulegium*, *pollegian*, or *dwarf dwosle*), hassock (*cassock*, grass), rue, wormwood, libcorn and *ælfthone*.[9] Many of these herbs Ælfric glosses in his Latin-Anglo-Saxon glossary, and most appear in the *Anglo-Saxon Herbal*.[10] The presence of these herbs in these texts indicates a classical medical connection through a translation process. Some of these herbs have strong Germanic associations: waybread, attorlathe, and fennel occur in the "Lay of the Nine Herbs" (see Chapter 4), and *ælfthone* is specifically Germanic, lacking a clear identification in classical medicine.

In addition to lupin (*eluhtre*, Lat. *electrum*), bishopwort or betony was the most commonly used herb in the elf remedies (appearing almost twenty times). Either the Anglo-Saxon *bisceopwyrt* or the Latin *betonica*, or sometimes both, recur in most of the herbal preparations studied in this chapter.[11] This herb is also the first entry in the *Anglo-Saxon Herbal*, and the remarks there accord remarkably well with the spiritual/physical duality found in elf- and demon-related illnesses.

This herb, which men call betony, grows in meadows, and in clean downlands and in protected places. It [is good] either for a man's soul or his body; it shields him against dreadful nightgoers [*unhyrum niht-gengum*] and against fearful visions and dreams [*egeslicum gesihthum ond swefnum*]. This herb is very holy [*haligu*], and thus you should gather it.[12]

The entry then specifies exact procedures (cut it in August without the use of iron) and lists almost thirty different uses for the herb, virtually covering head to toe. It is used against poisons and snakebite, although that is true of a large number of the herbs in this treatise.

Other elf-remedy herbs similarly known from other texts share these associations. Waybread (Lat. *plantago*, plantain), the second herb in the *Anglo-Saxon Herbal* and also included in the "Lay of the Nine Herbs," is likewise effective against poisons, worms, and·fevers; hence its use against elf, demon, and feverish ailments in the medical texts. Wormwood (absinthium), which also appears frequently in elf charms, the *Herbal* recommended for poultices on sores and with lupin for worms; like *ælfthone* (not in the *Herbal*), its name indicates its use.

The intended effect of many of these herbs—taken in a drink, mixed in a salve, or smoked—was to purge or exorcise the internal evil. Libcorn, for example, was probably "purgative seeds" of the castor-oil plant; dill, occasionally recommended in these remedies, had perhaps a gas-reducing effect.[13] Other purgative methods involved certain actions and preparations that would drive the elf out—by pricking the afflicted animal with a knife or by exorcising it with words of power similar to liturgical exorcisms against demons. The remedies presumed that the practitioner knew how to carry out many of the actions accompanying the charms. While some specified exact procedures, others, such as the "With Færstice" charm below, simply recorded the words and then referenced the actions ("dip the knife in the liquid"), assuming the leech knew what to do then.[14]

This kind of diversity in manifestation and treatment of elf afflictions was further complicated by their synthesis into the Christian-oriented view of the microcosm and macrocosm. Amoral creatures such as elves were gradually "demonized" to fit into the Good-Evil paradigm of the Christian moral universe. This process enhanced their similarity to demons. Their invisibility, their malicious attacks, and the need to "charm" them away all took on new meaning in Christian eyes so that elves began to resemble the fallen angels who seek to inflict internal and permanent harm on humans and their works, demons for Christian ritual to exorcise.

This influence of demons on elves worked the other way as well. Early medieval conceptions of demons reflected not only Christian ideas of evil but also Germanic views of spiritual agency, in art and story.[15] One intriguing and problematic example of representing evil agency in a monotheistic worldview to a Germanic, formerly polytheistic people can be seen in the *Canterbury* or *Eadwine Psalter* (Trinity College, MS R.17.1, fol. 66a, ca. 1150), based on the *Utrecht Psalter*. Figure 5.1, picturing Psalm 37 (38), "Oh Lord, thy

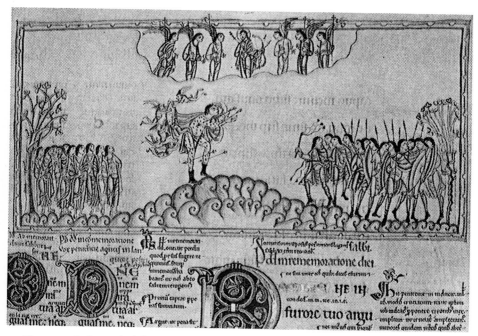

Figure 5.1. Psalm 37 (38) from the Eadwine or Canterbury Psalter, ca. 1147. (Cambridge, Trinity College MS R.17.1, fol. 66a; reproduced courtesy of Trinity College)

arrows have pierced me. . . . There is no health in my flesh. . . . My wounds putrefy. . . . I am greatly bowed down," shows a man pierced presumably by the arrows of Christ, who is standing above with a bow, but with demons tearing away the man's cloak.[16] Numerous illustrations in this and related psalters show demons, often with arrows attacking people or with pitchforks prodding folks into hell, represented in a uniquely Anglo-Saxon way by a monstrous dragon mouth.[17] Most of the demons or devils in this manuscript have a fairly human or angelic appearance (a few illustrations have the all-black, monstrous appearance associated with the Devil).[18] The angels tend to be taller and better dressed, their drapery giving a more elongated appearance than the squatter, nearly naked demons. Nonetheless the angels and demons seem to function similarly as spiritual agencies acting out the parts assigned to them by the divinity presiding at the top.

The demons in this illustration for Psalm 38 have a more elflike appearance in view of later iconography; the rotund little shapes with spritely grins and little hats (hair?) appear to us to resemble elves or sprites rather than demons.[19] In fact, Grattan and Singer chose this illustration for their frontispiece and referred to these spritely demons as elves, noting that this was a "confusion" between elfshot and Christ's arrows; Cameron also thinks the figures portray elfshot.[20] However, I am not sure we are reading the iconography correctly or understand the worldview implicit in this picture. It is easy to call it confusion on the part of the Anglo-Saxons when we are confused by it. Afflictions such as that suffered by the psalmist had macrocosmic as well as microcosmic dimensions. In the larger spiritual realm all things are God-directed, including afflictions that have some divine spiritual purpose. However, on the localized, human level, the experience of affliction had its sources in a variety of spiritual agencies, elves or demons. The apparent similarity between the appearance and behavior of elves and pictures of demons helps illustrate the convergence of elves and demons found in the medical remedies examined below.

Diversity of Approach

The variety of levels of Christianization in these elf remedies, all occurring together in the manuscripts along with other Christianized remedies, indicates the long-term and unconscious process of amalgamation between folk and Christian traditions. The *Lacnunga* and the *Leechbook* contain sixteen remedies for elf affliction, although other remedies for similar ailments and using similar ingredients could also belong to this category. A few of the elf remedies are untouched by Christian elements. Most, however, exhibit some degree of Christianization — not in any self-consciously organized way, but more haphazardly; not as if one conscientious compiler or copier systematically added Christian elements, but as if he or they copied these remedies from different sources that others, at some point in the past, had altered or developed in different ways to accommodate Christianity. In order to demonstrate this diversity of accommodation, the following sections examine elf charms within their manuscript context, first those scattered in the *Lacnunga* and other miscellaneous texts, then the sets in the *Leechbook*, culminating with an analysis of a significant and revealing long section of elf charms at the end of Book III.

The Lacnunga

The *Lacnunga* has four elf remedies that range from one completely free of Christian elements to another almost completely liturgical. Since several compilers worked on this manuscript, this text offers various remedies from different sources, giving a wider perspective on this illness and the cures developed for it.

For example, *Lacnunga* CXXXIV–CXXXV (75–76), which follows directly after the flying venom remedy using the four gospelers, quoted in Chapter 4, offers a simple herbal preparation, apparently for the shot of an elf, followed by a lay charm narrating how the Æsir and elves attack.[21]

WITH FÆRSTICE [FOR A SUDDEN STITCH][22]
Feverfew and the red nettle that grows into a house [or "in the grain"] and waybroad; boil in butter.
Loud were they, lo loud,   when they rode over the mound, they were fierce   when they rode over the land.
Shield yourself now   that you may escape this evil.
Out, little spear,   if herein you be!
Stood[23] under linden,   under a light shield, where the mighty women   readied their power, and they screaming   spears sent.[24]
I back to them   again will send another, a flying dart   against them in return.
Out, little spear,   if herein it be!
Sat a smith,   forged he a knife, little iron   strong wound.
Out, little spear,   if herein it be!
Six smiths sat,   war-spears they made.
Out, spear,   not in, spear!
If herein be   a bit of iron, hag's [hægtesse] work,   it shall melt.
If you were in the skin shot,   or were in flesh shot, or were in the blood shot,   or were in bone shot, or were in limb shot,   may your life never be torn apart.
If it were Æsir shot,   or it were elves' shot, or it were hag's shot,   now I will help you.
This your remedy for Æsir shot,   this your remedy for Elves' shot;
This your remedy for hag's shot;   I will help you.
It fled there into the mountains. . . . no rest had it.[25]
Whole be you now!   Lord help you!
Then take the knife; dip into liquid.

There are no overtly Christian elements here, other than the closing benediction; indeed, this remedy seems overwhelmingly not Christian, at least from any modern notion of that religion's ideals. It contains manipulative invocations indicative of magic from a traditional anthropological definition, and references to Germanic spiritual agencies and mythology (the spear-laden Æsir, elves, hags, and the smiths) reminiscent of paganism.[26]

The remedy contains an abundance of "untouched" folklore to delight those seeking a pure Germanic practice, despite its Christian context in this manuscript.

We need to be careful about two erroneous assumptions, however: first, that the lack of Christian elements (and the presence of "magic" as we see it) means it was not Christian and, second, that if the origins of the material predate Christianity or represent an older tradition, the remedy was therefore pagan. These so-called magic or pagan elements represent areligious folklore, transferable from one religious tradition to another. This charm was evidently practiced by people in late Anglo-Saxon England who considered themselves Christian (it is in a manuscript of clerical origin) and who apparently felt no compulsion to Christianize this charm in any way beyond a brief, vague benediction.

The strong storytelling element in this remedy is compelling and may account for its retention in a relatively un-Christianized state. The song invokes ancient stories of powerful heroes and spiritual battles, particularly the image of the militant Æsir, but portrays the pagan pantheon as malicious aggressors defeated by superior power. Like miraculous victories of monks over evil temptation, or good Christian kings over pagan monarchs, this lay countered evil spiritual agencies with stronger spiritual power, knife against knife. Whether the shot was external or internal, in the skin or in the blood, this remedy undid the poison working in the body in the same way as the venom and worm remedies, by a verbal purgation using words of power spoken with authority. The knife thus empowered was presumably used then to perform some kind of surgery, perhaps to remove a fragment, lance an infected place, or let blood.

Another remedy for the same affliction in this same manuscript does include more direct Christian references and is thus attributed to the Christian stratum by Grattan and Singer. *Lacnunga* XXIX (11) (after a series of worm and poison charms) offers the following remedy, which uses writing on a Eucharist dish washed off into a drink, similar to the *Leechbook* remedy for fever (I:lxii.3) discussed in Chapter 4.

> This is the holy drink against elf-influence [*ælfsidene*] and against all the fiend's temptings. Write on a housel dish:
> "In principio erat uerbum" usque "non comprehenderunt" et plura: "et circumibat Jesus totam Galileam docens" usque "et secuti sunt eum turbae multae." "Deus in nomine tuo" usque in finem. "Deus misereatur nobis" usque in finem. "Domine deus in adiutorium" usque in finem.

["In the beginning was the word" up to "they did not comprehend" and again: "Jesus went round all Galilee teaching" up to "and a great crowd followed after him." "God in your name" up to the end. "God have mercy on us" up to the end. "Lord God to our aid" up to the end.][27]

Take cristalan and tansy and zedoary and hassock and fennel, and take a sester [pitcher?] full of hallowed wine.

And order an immaculate [unmælne, "spotless"] person to fetch silently against the stream half a sester of running water.[28]

Take then and lay all the herbs in the water, and therein wash the writing from the housel dish very cleanly. Pour then the hallowed wine over the other.

Bear it then to church; have Masses sung over [it], one Omnibus, another Contra tribulation, a third Sanctam Marian.[29]

Sing these supplicatory psalms: Miserere mei Deus, Deus in nomine tuo, Deus misereatur nobis, Domine deus, Inclina domine.[30] And the Creed, and Gloria in excelsis deo, and the litanies, Pater noster.

And bless earnestly in the Almighty Lord's name, and say In nomine patris et filii et spiritus sancti sit benedictum. [In the name of the Father and the Son and the Holy Spirit, be it blessed.]

Use it then.

I would like to compare my interpretation of this charm to that of an earlier interpreter of Anglo-Saxon charms who reflects the values of his own time. While Godfrid Storms's work on the charms has provided a sound basis for examining the roots of Anglo-Saxon charm medicine, nonetheless his work is the product of the nineteenth-century desire for origins and the bias of a modern rationality. My intention is not to reject the work he has done but to examine the impact of modern perceptions on primary sources such as the charms, which display such a clear difference in worldview from our own.

Storms is very explicit in his commentary on this remedy as to what is Christian and what is pagan. The housel dish, hallowed wine, masses, and prayers are obviously Christian; "pagan is the washing off of writings into the drink and the manner in which water has to be drawn from a stream."[31] However, here he confuses folklore with pagan religion, form with content. The remedy's instructions concerning the use of words and the fetching of running water were not overtly pagan even if they predated Christianity, and they were rational within an early medieval worldview. Words, in Christianity as well as in Germanic belief, had power in and of themselves; the basis in Christianity for this focus on the power of words is found in the theology of Christ as the incarnate Word and the consequent power associated with the Scriptures as revelation. Monastic Christianity in particular respected the power inherent in an immaculate person (or virgin) and the spiritual benefits of silence, and the use of running water, purer than standing water, is common sense in any age.

Storms then suggests in this pagan vein that the medicinal use of the mass, however innocent at the time, may have contributed to excesses such as the Black Mass; he erroneously attributes this satanic perversion of the Catholic mass to the later Middle Ages.[32] These comments indicate his train of thought: working backward, he traces later "magic" to earlier paganism, ignoring the immediate, Christian context of the text in front of him.

His translation of *gebed sealmas* in line 18 as precatory "charms" — usually the translation of *galdor* throughout the text — instead of the literal "psalms" is an indication of his bias. Because he sees the context as manipulative and therefore magical, he is loath to use the specifically Christian wording. However, this remedy is distinctively clerical. Although it was not written by or for a priest, since it directs the reader to have the masses sung, it was probably monastic in context, since it instructs the reader to sing the various litanies and prayers.

Eliminating the words *pagan* and *magic* from a discussion of this remedy, and using instead *folklore* to describe the remedy's action, enables us to achieve a more realistic picture of such liturgical medicine.[33] It shows us the strength of the Christian liturgy as it was combined with herbs known to be effective against this traditional evil, and the proper procedures for preparing them. This remedy could then be classified as folk Christianity or Christian folklore.

As such, this remedy is clearly on the clerical end of the spectrum because of the high use of ritual and equipment available only in a minster setting. Moreover, it represents a highly demonized form of the elf, here associated with demonic illusion and temptation. The remedy's strongly liturgical flavor dominates the folklore elements and leaves one wondering what kinds of combinations might have been made in a rural, isolated setting by a local priest.

A good comparison to demonstrate the potential for this kind of variety in the amalgamations of folklore and Christianity appears in the two other elf remedies in the *Lacnunga*, both for animals afflicted by elves. *Lacnunga* CXVIII (60) and its near duplicate in the *Leechbook* (quoted in my Introduction) prescribe the following liturgical-folk medicine: "If a horse be shot, or other animal, take *ompran* [dock] seed and Scottish wax. Have a masspriest sing twelve masses over them, and put holy water on them, and put that on the horse or on whatever animal it be. Have the herbs always with you." This remedy functioned on a simple premise, that invoking God's blessing makes natural ingredients efficacious for healing (as opposed to eating for sustenance). The *Leechbook's* addition to this remedy may have been even more efficacious: "For the same: take an eye of a broken needle, give the horse a prick with it in the ribs, no harm shall come."[34] Some modern scholars speculating on these remedies have tenuously identified this ailment as colic (a buildup of intestinal gases), in which case the pricking with a knife in the intestinal region suggested here just might be medically effective, although risky.[35] This purgative treatment probably reflects actual folk veterinary practice, as does its counterpart ahead of it, the herbs with twelve masses. The temptation to speculate about what formulas Anglo-Saxons said over these herbs before Christianity came along obscures the point that Christian liturgy now played a dominant role in medicinal practice. Getting twelve masses said over a few herbs was beyond the reach of many; producing a large batch of herbs thus blessed and "keeping them with you" seems to indicate some clerical traffic in veterinary medicine—perhaps many minsters supplied more than chrism to their daughter churches and priests in their dioceses.

The clerical quality of these elf remedies reaches its extreme in the fourth *Lacnunga* elf remedy, CLXIV (97); it follows fairly closely after the reduction "kernels" remedy discussed in Chapter 4. Like *Lacnunga* XXIX (11), its use of liturgical formula, wholly in Latin, suggests a minster or monastery environment; Grattan and Singer assign it to their Latin Christian stratum dominant at the end of the manuscript.[36]

IF A HORSE BE SHOT:[37]

Sanentur animalia in orbe terre et ualitudine uexantur; in nomine dei patris et filii et spiritus sancti extinguatur [extingunt] diabolus per impositionem manum nostrarum; quis [quas] nos separabit [separavimus] a caritate Christi; per inuocationem omnium sanctorum tuorum; per eum qui uiuit et regnat in secula seculorum. Amen.

"Domine quid multiplicati sunt" III.

[May the beasts on earth be healed, they are vexed in health; in the name of God the Father and the Son and the Holy Spirit let the Devil be expelled through the imposition of our hands; who shall separate us from the love of Christ; through the invocation of all your saints;

through Him who lives and reigns forever. Amen. "Lord, wherefore they are increased" thrice.]

The words of this remedy seem to be quotations entirely from other sources, put together here to invoke considerable spiritual power. The first line of this remedy is a statement of mana, commanding and describing simultaneously. This is followed by an invocation to the Trinity that the Devil be cast out by the laying on of hands, an exorcism.[38] The remedy concludes with some scriptural references and a Christian benediction.[39] The remedy is a purgative exorcism that assumed the shot, presumably from an elf, came from a demonic force that needed driving out.

While this remedy, from a modern standpoint, seems to be a confused mix of religion and magic, it represented to an Anglo-Saxon mind an essential Christian view applied to folk tradition, the use of Christian power to cure an ancient evil affliction. The commanding voice in the first line evokes images of an ancient sorcerer manipulating the elements; the second line of Christian exorcism seems, in this context, to be equally magical. Yet, looked at from another direction, the Latinity, the use of Christian formulas and Scripture, puts this remedy very much within the literate formal church. In order to see the synthesis here, rather than the unhappy marriage of "Christian magic," we need to see the common ground shared by both formulas, that words have power. These words are Latin, addressed to God, and carry the authority of Christian tradition. It is as Christian as it can get.

The existence in this one manuscript of all these remedies using different methods to heal the same ill indicates that the conversion of various Germanic folklore medicines occurred in appropriate ways as herbal remedies added Christian blessings and invocative remedies gravitated toward Christian exorcism. The parallel remedies in the Leechbook show not only the frequency of this diagnosis but also the variety of ways elf affliction was handled, indicating some uncertainty about the ailment or its cause: Was it a wound from an invisible arrow, requiring treatment with a salve? Was it some buildup of evil fluid that needed releasing? Was it possession by an evil being (demon or elf) that needed exorcising? Or all three?

This demonic connection to elf ailments through exorcism is strong in the surviving manuscript evidence, and not only in the medical treatises. Another sample in a manuscript marginalia against demoniacal possession adds the Anglo-Saxon word elf to the Latin exorcism.

Eulogumen. patera. cae yo. cae agion. pneuma. cae nym. cae ia. cae iseonas nenonamini.

[Apparently a Greek transcription of the benediction usually done in Latin, "Gloria Patri et Filio et Spiritui Sancto, sicut erat in principio et nunc et semper et in saecula saeculorum," most commonly heard in English as "Glory be to the Father and to the Son and to the Holy Ghost, as it was in the beginning is now and ever shall be, world without end."]

Adiuro te satanae diabulus aelfae. per deum unum ac uerum. et per trementem diem iudicii ut refugiatur ab homine illo qui [h]abeat hunc a Cristo [Chrysostom? aepistolam?][40] scriptum secum.
In nomine dei Patris et Filii et Spiritus sancti.

[The sense of this rough Latin is approximately, "I adjure you Devil of Satan, Elf, through the one true God and through the fearful Day of Judgment, flee from the man who has this letter from Christ with him. In the name of God the Father and the Son and the Holy Spirit."][41]

This written amulet containing an exorcism ("I adjure you") has only the one Germanic element, aelfae, added as an appositive to Satan.[42] Storms considered this remedy magical because the words of power in Latin and Greek were unintelligible; thus he ignored the fact that the early medieval religious view about the power and use of words was not necessarily concerned with intelligibility. This remedy is evidence of how the Christian cosmology accepted a new being, the elf, just as the Lacnunga remedies above added Christian ideas to folk medical remedies.

The Lacnunga as a "popular" medical text displays a variety of treatments for afflictions caused by elves, indicating a certain ambivalence about the elf and its associated diseases in the Anglo-Saxon views of the microcosm and a diversity of approaches for curing such ailments—all involving, however, verbal appeals to spiritual powers. The folk-Christian synthesis occurring in these remedies indicates the dual processes of transmission at work in late Anglo-Saxon England. These processes created a middle ground between folk and clergy, Germanic and Christian, and spiritual and material concerns that formed the basis of popular religion.

Bald's Leechbook

The Leechbook illuminates even more than the Lacnunga this amalgamation of folk, medical, and Christian traditions in remedies for afflictions brought on by such mysterious beings as elves and demons. Because the compiler organized it by type of disease, the book has definite sections treating elf ailments or elf-related diseases such as devil sickness, dementedness, fever, and other illnesses that required Christian liturgy. What all of these ills had in common was a concern for the mental and spiritual condition of the patient, based on a holistic belief in the interconnectedness of physical and spiritual health.

Although the symptoms are not entirely clear to us, and thus these associations seem confused in our thinking, early medieval minds found a logical coherence in the treatment required. Spiritual forces must be invoked to counteract ailments involving the mind or soul. In this medieval view, human beings are multifaceted creatures with a complex interaction of body and soul, a mixture of matter and spirit in the Neoplatonic scale of being. Because of this duality humans are connected with the entire cosmos, so that they are affected by it and capable of interacting with it and the spiritual forces inhabiting it.

Seen in this light the elf- and demon-related remedies found at or near the ends of the three books of the Leechbook do form a coherent category as demonstrated in the organization of the remedies and in the table of contents. Consequently it is very important to see these remedies in the context established by the compiler, in order to understand the logic he saw in the remedies. For example, Book I:lxiv offers a set of remedies against several evils, including elves and nightmares. It is found in the context of other illnesses requiring the liturgy. The Leechbook's Book I table of contents lists the section in this fashion:

lxii   Leechdoms for fever-disease [feferadle], to heal it; drinks for that; against a third day's fever, and a fourth day's fever, and against any day's fever; and against Lent disease, that is fever,[43] and how a man must against this disease write on a housel dish the holy and great God's name, and wash it into the drink with holy water, and sing over it a holy prayer and the Creed and Pater noster. Ten leechdoms.

lxiii   Leechdoms for a fiend-sick man, drinks for that, and how a man must sing masses and prayers and psalms over the drink, and drink from church bells; and for a man with falling-sickness [brœcseocum men, "epileptic"], and for the wood heart; and for all these, six crafts.

lxiv   Leechdoms against every evil wise woman [leodrunan] and elf-trick [œlfsidenne], that is, galdor for a type of fever; and powder and drinks and salve; and if the disease be on animals; and if the disease injure a man, or if a mare ride and injure him. In all seven crafts.

lxv   Leechdoms again for Lent disease; and the four gospelers' [evan-
       gelists] names; and writings and prayers; and silently must a man
       write some writing. Five crafts.

lxvi   Leechdoms for the out-of-mind [*ungemynde*] and the foolish [*dysigum*].

These sections are much more descriptive than other parts of the table of
contents. They seem to "give away" more of the remedy than the other
sections that list only the type of disease and the type of remedy (salve
or drink). This section near the end of Book I specifically mentions the
liturgical elements used, indicating that these Christian ingredients played
a larger role in defining the remedies as a type. Someone assembled these
remedies together because they all used liturgy, and they all used liturgy
because these kinds of ailments required such intervention. Note, for instance, the connection in lxii between fever and the use of church materials; the association in lxiii of demonic possession (fiendsickness), epilepsy,
and exorcistic rituals; in lxiv, the linking of elfsickness with sorcery, fever,
and nightmares; and in lxv and lxvi, the continued association of fever
with mind-altering afflictions such as madness that require some powerful
agencies to cure.
   The elf remedies in *Leechbook* I:lxiv thus occur in the midst of a series of
remedies (from lxii to lxvi) concerned with demonic afflictions. *Leechbook*
I:lxii, discussed in Chapter 4, used writing on a housel dish washed into
a drink for a fiendsick man. Likewise, the remedies in I:lxiii for fiendsickness and madness use ingredients similar to those found in remedies for
elfsickness.

       lxiii   For a fiend sick man, when the Devil feeds the man or controls
       him from within with disease. A spew drink: lupin, bishopwort, hen-
       bane, cropleek; pound together, add ale as liquid; let stand for a night;
       add fifty libcorns in, and holy water.

Notice in this remedy the concept of possession as effected through an internal illness accomplished through the Devil "feeding" him, for which,
naturally, a purgative remedy is recommended. An alternate drink follows
it for the same ailment.

       A drink for a fiend sick man, to drink from a church bell: githrife,
       glæs [cynoglossum?], yarrow, lupin, betony, attorlathe, hassock, fane,
       fennel, church lichen, lichen from Christ's mark [a cross], lovage. Make

the drink from clear ale, sing seven masses over the herbs, add garlic
and holy water to it, and drip the drink into every drink which he will
after drink. And let him sing the psalm, "Beati immaculati," and "Ex-
urgat," and "Saluum me fac, deus."[44] And then let him drink the drink
from a church bell; and after the drink let the mass priest sing over him
this: "Domine, sancte pater omnipotens."

This was strong medicine. The church bell, hallowed lichens, and masses
and prayers draw on material and verbal sources of Christian power; the
garlic, in combination with herbs familiar in all these remedies for poisons,
fevers, and other evils, works internally to cleanse or purge the patient of
this ill.

For a man with falling-sickness [brœcseocum].[45] Costmary, goutweed,
lupin, betony, attorlathe, cropleek, holecersan, hove, fennel. Let a man
sing masses over them; make it from foreign ale and from holy water;
let him drink this drink fresh each time, for nine mornings; and no
other liquid that is thick and still. And let him give alms, and pray God
earnestly for mercies on him.

This remedy employs a skillful combination of folk remedies: the familiar
herbs, the use of ale and holy water as "pure" liquids (both able to neu-
tralize harmful invisible agents), and the number nine, then the masses, the
giving of alms, and prayers as spiritual exercises. If this is epilepsy or something similar, it is perceived as a disease of the mind and spirit requiring,
as the remedy before, both material and spiritual cures.

For the wooden heart [frenzy?]. Bishopwort, lupin, bonewort, ever-
fern, githrife, heahhiolothe. When day and night divide, then sing in
church litanies, that is the names of the saints, and the Pater noster;
with the song go, so that you may be near the herbs, and go around
[them] three times; and when you take them, go again to the church
with the same song. And sing twelve masses over them, and over all the
drinks which belong to this disease, in honor of the twelve apostles.

The identification of this "wooden heart" with "frenzy" seems to fit the context here. The disease and its herbs, along with the specific rituals, may be
imported Roman Christian — there is little specifically Germanic material.[46]
The circling ritual seems to our eyes magical in its methods, yet the context and intention are clearly Christian. The twelve masses specified at the
end were sung over all the drinks for such ailments, suggesting numerous
herbal preparations on or near the altar.

lxiv   Against every evil wisewoman [*leodrunan*],[47] and against elf trick [*ælfsidenne*], write this writing for him with these Greek letters:

    +   +   o
+ A + O + γHρBγM ╫╫╫ BερρNN | κNεTTAN |
[crosses with alpha and omega, possibly *huios*, *ichthus*; Veronica][48]

This brief remedy shows the rich mixture of traditions in Anglo-Saxon England. Here are Greek words of invocation, written on an amulet to be used against very specific Germanic ailments, evil enchantments from sorceresses and elvish illusions that suggest Christian demonic forces.

> Again, another powder and drink against a *leodrunan*. Take a bramble apple, and lupin, and pollegian; pound, then sift; put in a pouch, lay under the altar, sing nine masses over them; put the powder into milk, drip thrice on them holy water; give to drink at three times, at undern [9 A.M.], at midday, at nones [3 P.M.]. If the disease be on animals, pour the same powder with holy water into the mouth.

The mental picture of a church altar area crowded with herbal preparations to be blessed grows stronger here, a fulfillment of Ælfric's suggestion that the sick should seek health at church, not at pagan sites. The nine masses and the hours indicate a monastic or minster setting, yet one that clearly has agricultural concerns in common with the rural lay population.

> A salve. Lupin, hedgerife, bishopwort, the red magothan, armelu, cropleek, salt. Boil in butter for a salve. Smear it on the head and the breast.
> A drink. Haransprecel, alexanders, rue, lupins, hedgerife, bishopwort, magothe, cropleek, armelu, the knotty wenwort. Put into holy water.

These two remedies, salve and drink, seem to be alternate preparations that would also end up under the altar, for similar mind-altering afflictions of evil origin.

> If a mare ride a man. Take lupin, and garlic, and betony, and frankincense. Bind them on a fawn's skin. Let a man have the herbs on him, and let him go inside.

Nightmares, or the idea that "hags" ride a man during the night, causing this mental disturbance, are treated as a physiological and spiritual problem. Grendon suggests "incubus"; in the clerical setting implied by these remedies, such nightmares have overtones of temptations to lust.[49]

lxv   Again, a drink against Lent disease [*lencten adle*]. Feverfue, ram's gall, fennel, waybread. Let a man sing many masses over these herbs. Soak with ale, add holy water, boil very well. Drink then as hot as he may a great cup full, before the disease will be on him. The four gospelers names and a charm [*gealdor*], and a prayer. ✠✠ Matheus +⁺+⁺+ Marcus +⁺+⁺+ Lucus ✠✠ Iohannes ╫╫╫. Intercedite pro me [Intercede for me]. Ticeon, leleloth, patron.[50] adiuro vos [I adjure you].

This remedy treats fever as a mind-altering affliction with spiritual implications. The power of the cross, masses, and the names of the gospel writers are brought to bear in somewhat of an exorcism ("I adjure you") of this apparently recurring fever (as indicated by the instructions to drink before it comes on).

> Again, a godly [*godcund*] prayer: In nomine domini sit benedictum [In the name of the Lord be blessed]. beronice, beronicen [Veronica] et habet in vestimento et in femore suo. scriptum rex regum et dominus dominantium [she? has on her garment and on her thigh? (It is) written king of kings and lord of lords].
> Again, a godly prayer: In nomine domini summi sit benedictum [In the name of the most high Lord be blessed].

[transcribed Greek letters]

> Again, a man must silently write this, and put these words silently on the left breast, and he should not go indoors with the writing or bear it indoors. And also silently put this on: [EMMANUEL, VERONICA, in transcribed Greek letters].

These "godly" prayers emphasize their Christian roots, using Latin, Hebrew, and Greek in a none-too-clear manner and appealing in sympathy to a powerful story. St. Veronica's name invokes the cloth of the saint, which touched the face of Christ and bore his image; the invocation of the relic acts as a kind of written amulet that may have been worn on the thigh or hip.[51] Throughout, silence and prayer evoke a monastic setting.

This set of remedies is much more clerical than those found in the *Lacnunga*. The authors or compilers seem to live according to a monastic routine, with ready access to a church, church equipment, and a priest. These *Leechbook* I remedies are very much products of a literate community who nonetheless reflect their Anglo-Saxon roots by using native oral traditions.

These Anglo-Saxon clerics "textualize" as well as Christianize this folk tradition by merging it with classical Christian material accessible to them in the minster, or vice versa, they adapt the Christian texts to local conditions by modifying classical remedies to include Anglo-Saxon practices. Both processes appear to be at work. The mixture of *galdor* and prayer, even in the same line, and the combination of Greek and Latin with Anglo-Saxon indicate the literate synthesis taking place in the *Leechbook*, a synthesis that we can well imagine took place in a cruder fashion in local churches with priests without access to all of this liturgical equipment or source-texts.

This series demonstrates quite clearly, then, how the *Leechbook* treated the folk ailment of elf affliction with liturgical medicine and demon possession with folk remedies. The first remedy in I:lxiii gives a fiendsick man (demon possessed) a Germanic purgative drink of herbs, while it recommends for elf afflictions, fevers, and epilepsy liturgical medicines resembling exorcisms in some cases. This two-way transmission blurs the line between liturgy and medicine in the same way that these remedies make no absolute distinction between spiritual and physical illness. The overlap of spiritual and physical in the remedies resonates with the frequent pairing of body and soul, visible and invisible, in discussions of health and well-being, as seen for example in the sermons of Ælfric. The coherence of this worldview, evident in the association of elf disease with other illnesses requiring similar Christian elements, is quite striking throughout the *Leechbook*.

The *Leechbook*'s tendency to collect such remedies together, mixing Germanic spiritual agencies with Christian elements, is visible again at the end of *Leechbook* II:lxiv–lxv, folios 105a–108a (after a break of several missing folios). The remedies appear to be odds and ends added at this juncture. They may have been assembled here because they were local submissions, native remedies given to the compiler by a number of contributors, perhaps collected on scraps of manuscript pages and then copied at the end of Book II. However, they have a basic similarity in that they all have identifiably Germanic as well as Christian traits.

The section begins (II:lxiv) with a series of remedies sent "by the Patriarch of Jerusalem to King Alfred," thus establishing this part as an Anglo-Saxon contribution with roots in the East. The Germanic influence is confirmed by the inclusion of a prescription for flying venom. The remedies treat disorders of the mind (delusions, fever, and apparitions) with the usual mixture of herbs and Christian ritual. The following section, II:lxv, is a collection of five sets of remedies, described in this way by the table of contents:

Leechdom if a horse be [elf]shot [ofscoten], and for dysentery, and if the evacuation be obstructed, and for the lent disease; again for dysentery, and for poisons [unlybbum], and for the yellow disease, and if on a man there be sudden evils; and to keep the body's health; and for itch and elf; and for land disease and for bite of gangway weaver [spider]; and for diarrhea; and head salves.

The connections between these ills are not immediately clear, especially how bowel disorders relate to fevers and various poisons that in other sections, as here, have links to malevolent causes. The remedies all contain both folklore and Christian elements. Moreover, purgation is a common remedy, which may provide the connection to the bowel ailments.

The first remedy (II:lxv.1), for a "shot" horse, takes a purgative approach to elfshot, attempting to drive out the evil through various actions enhanced by Christian material.

If a horse is [elf]shot [ofscoten]. Take then the knife of which the haft is a fallow ox's horn, and on [which] are three brass nails. Write then on the horse's forehead Christ's mark [cross], and on each of the limbs that you can press. Take then the left ear, prick through [it] in silence. This you must do. Take one staff, strike on the back. Then the horse will be whole. And write on the knife's horn these words: "Benedicite omnia opera domini dominum." [Blessed be all the works of the lord of lords.] Whatever elf is on him, this can be a remedy for him.

Not only do these ritual actions, Germanic in origin, purge or exorcise the shot of the elf, but the Latin words of blessing invoke a Christian idea expounded by Ælfric, that God created all animals and herbs and thus they are worthy of blessing, not cursing. Calling on that blessing establishes the Creator's superiority over the power of evil spiritual agencies such as elves and banishes them.

The rest of the remedies collected here in II:lxv include numerous Christian as well as folklore elements to alleviate bowel disorders, lung disease, yellow disease, fever, and poison as well as another elf attack. This collection combines physical and spiritual ailments and remedies, using both classical medicine of the four humors and local folk remedies. The recommendations flow one into another without much distinction between type.

The dysentery and bowel obstruction remedies recommend comforting medical treatments including rest and warmth as well as herbal brews. The bramble root used for dysentery required preparation with specific Latin prayers (nine Pater nosters, for example). Likewise the lung disease remedies follow the medical system of humors, recommending herbal drinks and restricting the diet as well. After this lung remedy, another for dysentery and one for poisons both use dairy products and honey combined with specific instructions about preparation (silence, not bringing the ingredients into the ill person's presence) that suggest folk origin.

After some herbal brews for yellow disease come two general prescriptions for health, one spiritual and the other material, that demonstrate the connection between the two approaches (II:lxv.3). "If a man is made suddenly ill (evil)," a trinity of cross marks, on the tongue, the head, and the breast will soon make him well. "To keep the body whole with prayer of the Lord, this is a noble leechdom." The prescription then recommends myrrh and wine as not only preventing illness of the body but also "for the fiend's evil temptations." The following section (II:lxv.4) continues this same theme of noble preventative powders using frankincense and myrrh but adding holiday masses in sets of three. The drink prepared from this powder is efficacious against all kinds of ills, including fever, Lent disease, poison, and evil air—in short, against all those ills and evils that move invisibly in the air. In an added bonus the remedy concludes by asserting that the sources say that this medicine is able to preserve a man who uses it for twelve months against all infirmities [untrymnessa]. This preventative medicine, as with the other specific remedies, refuses to make a clear distinction between the physical and the spiritual when treating what troubles an individual.

The brief remedy for an elf (II:lxv.5) comes in the midst of a curious collection of remedies involving, for the most part, skin ointments and some Christian elements. First is a remedy for itch and general skin care (a salve of oil and wine dregs applied in the sun for a clean, shining, bright body color). The elf remedy is also to cure "a strange custom" or possibly "charm" [uncuthum sidran]; it uses, as the preventative drinks above did, myrrh and frankincense along with agate stone shavings in a morning drink for three, nine, or twelve days.[52] The ointment for "land" disease (Cockayne suggests "nostalgia" or homesickness) uses the oil of extreme unction (oleo infirmorum) applied in front of a fire by a masspriest "if a man has" one. There follow remedies for spider bite and diarrhea, and two head salves, one using holy oil, water, and salt as well as "nine English herbs" (many of them familiar and clearly perceived as local: polleie/pulegium, bramble apple, lupin, bishopwort, fennel, rough waybread, haransprecel, harewort, and lithewort). In both cases where holy oil is mentioned, Cockayne notes that the word infirmorum has been "paled away purposely"; clearly, though, holy oil was originally meant, since the remedy refers later to "other" oil.

The uncertainty about the availability of a masspriest, the specifically identified "English" herbs, and the erasures of holy oil suggest origins for these remedies partly outside the minster or monastery environment where this manuscript was compiled. The sometimes dubious connections between these remedies enhances the feeling that someone collected these remedies here somewhat haphazardly. The preceding sections (II:lx–lxiii) are missing in the manuscript; they included women's remedies, according to the table of contents.[53] The two sections that finish Book II after this odd collection in II:lxv are straightforward copies of information (rather than remedies), one on the eight virtues of agate (II:lxvi), the other on measurements (II:lxvii). The remedies in II:lxv stand out by their placement in this isolated section but also because they contain a vague sense of interconnection in their Germanic origins and their respect for the power of the Christian liturgy and rituals. What this section at the end of Book II appears to be, then, is a rather raw set of folkloric remedies imported into the text but not yet fully assimilated into either the organization or the medical scheme of the *Leechbook*.

A more integrated sequence of remedies in *Leechbook* III:xli reinforces the notions displayed in Books I and II about mind-altering afflictions crossing the boundary between the physical and the spiritual. The demonic temptation remedies in this section demonstrate the folklorization of Christianity in the importation of elves into Christian demonology. The remedies leading up to and following this set reveal similar concerns about Germanic and other afflictions of the mind. *Leechbook* III:xxxix contains salves for worms; the remedy in III:xl is a favorite for scholars to quote: "In case a man be lunatic; take the skin of a porpoise [*mere swines*], make it into a whip, and whip the man with it; he will soon be well [added in a different hand: Amen]." The two prescriptions in *Leechbook* III:xlii and III:xliii, after the demonic set, are both drinks against poison using medicinal preparations without the aid of ritual or words of power.[54]

The remedies against temptation in III:xli fit into this context of Germanic ailments not only because of the inclusion of the elf but also because of the folk knowledge used—the familiar herbs and the number nine. The association of temptation with elves and fever and the use of masses and purgative drinks all indicate a coherent synthesis of Germanic and Christian medicine for mind and body.

Work a good drink against all the fiend's temptations. Take betony, bishopwort, lupin, githrife, attorlathe, wolfscomb, yarrow.[55] Lay them under the altar, sing nine masses over them. Cut the herbs into holy water. Give him [the patient] a cup full to drink at night while fasting, and put the holy water on all the food that the man eats.

Work a good salve against the fiend's temptations. Bishopwort, lupin, hara[n]sprecel, strawberry plant, the cloved wenwort, earth rime, bramble apple, polleian, wormwood. Pound all the herbs, boil them in good butter, wring through a cloth; set under the altar, sing nine masses over. Smear the man with (this) on the temples, and above the eyes, and on top of the head, and the breast, and the sides under the arms. This salve is good against every temptation of the fiend, and elf-trick [ælfsidenne], and against Lent disease [typhus].

These two parallel remedies for the same problem, temptation from the Devil, use two different approaches using similar ingredients drawn from folk herblore, and each using nine masses. The addition of ælfsidenne and typhus fever confirm the connection between physical ailments requiring herbs and spiritual attacks requiring words of power. In the next remedy, madness as another mind-altering affliction utilizes both drink and salve in a powerful combination.

If you will heal a wit sick man [gewitseocne man], take a tub full of cold water, drop thrice into it some of the drink. Bathe the man in the water, and let the man eat hallowed bread, and cheese, and garlic, and cropleek, and drink a cup full of the drink. And when he has been bathed, smear him with the salve thoroughly. And when it is better with him, then work for him a strong purgative drink. Work thus the drink: take libcorn leaves, and celandine roots, and gladden roots, and [holly]hock's root, and [dwarf]elder's root rind;[56] boil in ale, let stand for a night; clarify then, and warm; add butter and salt to it. Give to drink.

This series offers a course of treatment to restore the person suffering from some mental dislocation. It starts with external treatments—a bath using the drink, and the salve. Only when the patient is stronger is a purgative, internal method used. Purgation, like an exorcism, continues to be an effective cure in the following remedy, a drink that apparently induces vomiting (as opposed to the presumed laxative effects of other purgative drinks).

Work a purgative spew drink. Take forty libcorns, rend them well, and rub them on the bottom part of celandine and [holly]hock root, and two cloves of the cloved wenwort, and a small part of the lower part of cucumber, and a moderate part of homewort root. Make all the herbs thoroughly clean, and pound; put in ale, wrap up, let stand for a night. Give a cup full to drink.

The purgative methods in the last two parts contain no Christian elements or, indeed, any ritual actions or words; rather, they rely on medicinal preparations designed to cause a physical reaction. Nonetheless they remedy a spiritual ailment, temptation, that requires physical as well as spiritual means of cure.

Thus a basically Christian "spiritual" or moral ailment, temptation, is treated with remedies that, from our perspective, combine natural with spiritual elements. However, the early medieval Christians this manuscript represents did not see the two as separate. Just as they tended to see spiritual power in natural objects, they saw natural objects as capable of influencing spiritual matters. Christian ritual thus easily accommodated folklore in this set of remedies. The variety of treatments available for such physical/spiritual ailments is too easily read by modern eyes as confusion over treatment of nonexistent or misdiagnosed ailments. However, within their own context, these remedies represented different options for a complex of ailments attributable to spiritual forces. The process of coming to grips with these forces involved experimenting with a number of different prescriptions, as shown in the variety of recipes in the Leechbook.

Leechbook Book III

The best evidence of this variety of remedies representing the amalgamation of Christian ideas and Germanic folklore is found at the end of Book III of the Leechbook in a series of elf- and demon-related remedies. Book III of the Leechbook (folios 109a–127b) is generally held to be a separate entity from the first two books known as Bald's Leechbook. This third book appears to be a compilation of different sources rather than a copy of a single earlier text, as the first two books are.[57] Folios 122b–127a contain fourteen remedies, of which nine are for elves or demons, while two others are for related ailments requiring Christian elements.[58] What is striking about these charms is the variety of treatment and the different ways native Anglo-Saxon remedies and Christian ideas were integrated.

The remedies occur in the order given below, summarized from Leechbook III's table of contents (with quotation marks indicating direct translation from the contents).[59] For those remedies not discussed below I have included some brief comments and have indicated by the word natural that the remedy contains only material ingredients. Those remedies that include unseen forces such as elves and use Christian liturgy, III:lxi–lxiv, are analyzed below. This listing of the contents shows the logical ordering of these remedies and the emphasis the compiler placed on those using special masses to counteract spiritual or mental ills.

liv   Salve against "night" visitors (nihtgengan), using only natural ingredients, herbs traditionally associated with elves and other such evils (such as lupin and bishopwort).

lv   For a "bound" or possible "ridged" skull, with bizarre treatment.[60]

lvi   An all natural drink for inability to digest meat.

lvii   Against a woman's speech (wif gemædlan), radish taken at night prevents harm from her talk the next day. Cockayne's translation of wif gemædlan as "woman's chatter" gives the wrong impression. Grendon's translation as "witch's spell," while not in keeping with the literal meaning, does convey a better sense in this context, that of words of power spoken to harm.[61]

lviii   Against temptation of the fiend: a preventative amulet made of red mullein carried, placed under the pillow, or put over the door.[62]

lix   For an ulcer (theor wenne) on a joint, a hot plaster using only natural ingredients.

lx   A good ear salve, all natural ingredients wrung into the ear.

lxi   "Against elf kind [ælf cynne], a salve; and against nightgoers, and for the ones that the Devil lies with."

lxii   "Against elf disease [ælf adle], leechdom; and again, how a man must sing on the herbs before a man take them, and also how a man must put the herbs under the altar and sing over them; and also signs [tacn] of this, whether it be elf hicket [ælfsogotha]; and a sign by which you might understand whether a man may heal him; and drinks and prayers against each temptation of the fiend [feondes costunge]."

lxiii   "Signs [tacnu] how you might understand whether a man is in the water-elf disease [wæeter ælf adle]; and leechdom for that, and charm [gealdor] to sing on it; and the same a man may sing on wounds."

These two, lxii and lxiii, are unusually long descriptions in the contents, reminiscent of the lengthened content entries in Book I for this kind of ailment. Section lxii is a long set of four remedies.

lxiv   "Against the Devil, a mild drink; and for madness [*ungemynde*] and against the Devil's temptation."

lxv   If a man be cut, with instructions as to whether to even attempt to heal him; it recommends an herbal drink, lard, or butter for the wound, cleaning procedures, and a "good red leech" to pull it together.

lxvi   Drink for ulcers (*theor*), using herbs (including fennel, bishopwort, and betony) blessed with three masses.

lxvii   For Devil sickness and against the Devil, several purgative drinks made with familiar herbs (bishopwort) and holy water.

lxviii   A light drink for "wood heart" (*weden heorte*) using herbs reminiscent of elf and demon remedies and much liturgy, very similar to I:lxiii.

lxix–lxx   For various stomach ailments, using natural ingredients.

lxxi–lxxvi   Ointments, salves, and drinks for a variety of ailments, including poisons, yellow disease, bowel problems, and other "inward" diseases, ending the book, according to the table of contents, with a holy salve. However, the manuscript breaks off after lxxiii. One herbal salve for a sore (lxxi) has Pater nosters sung over the boiling mixture.

The specifically elf-related remedies thus fall into the context of herbal remedies (salves, drinks, or amulets). Several are for demonic afflictions, and others (for dry disease and wood heart) require Christian elements. The section III:lxi–lxiv forms a coherent series of remedies against spiritual, malevolent forces, which, nonetheless, are manifested in physical symptoms and can be cured with natural ingredients properly brought into relation with the spiritual macrocosm.

The salve recommended in *Leechbook* III:lxi, like lvii against a woman's speech, is a preventative remedy, in this case against an assortment of evil beings grouped here.

Work a salve against elfkind and nightgoers [ælfcynne, nihtgengan], and the people with whom the Devil has intercourse.[63] Take eowohumelan, wormwood, bishopwort, lupin, ashthroat, henbane, harewort, haransprecel, heathberry plants, cropleek, garlic, hedgerife grains, githrife, fennel.[64] Put these herbs into one cup, set under the altar, sing over them nine masses; boil in butter and in sheep's grease, add much holy salt, strain through a cloth; throw the herbs in running water. If any evil temptation, or an elf or nightgoers, happen to a man, smear his forehead with this salve, and put on his eyes, and where his body is sore, and cense him [with incense], and sign [the cross] often. His condition will soon be better.

The conflation of folklore evils such as elves with the Christian cosmology of demonic beings is clear and logical in its own way. These are all things that go bump in the night—invisible, malicious beings who harm not only physically but also spiritually in the form of temptation. Christian ritual blessed the traditional herbs in a number (nine) known in Germanic lore to have special effect. The used herbs are disposed of in running water, their blessed virtue having passed into the salve through boiling. The salve works with incense and the sign of the cross to drive or smoke the elf out. The locations for smearing the salve are significant for the nature of the ills mentioned—the forehead or the mind, the eyes as gateways of perception, and the points of entry in the sores on the body. The separate folk and Christian elements are identifiable, but their intertwining here is so complete that removing either set distorts the remedy. Storms insightfully comments on this charm that those who try both natural and supernatural medicine did not make such a distinction, so that "salves, drinks and charms are all on the same plane." However, his translation of recelsa as "smoke" rather than "cense" pushes too hard for the pagan idea of smoking an elf out, rather than the clearer liturgical meaning here of "cense and sign."[65] In the same way that the remedy lacks a supernatural and natural distinction, so too it defies categorization as medicine or liturgy, magic or religion, physical or spiritual. As a preventative measure, it accounts for all possibilities in a nighttime attack.

If, however, one fails to ward off such an assault, the next set of remedies offers cures for elf disease (III:lxii). The four complex remedies found in this section involve a great deal of herb preparation, specific masses, and various prayers as well as special ritual actions (I have numbered them 1–4, with number 4 broken into separate parts labeled alphabetically). These elf prescriptions represent probably the best synthesis of Anglo-Saxon and Christian knowledge on how to combat these pernicious beings, and they make fascinating reading (*Leechbook* III:lxii).

> [1] Against elf disease [*ælfadle*]. Take bishopwort, fennel, lupin, the lower part of *ælfthone*, and lichen from the holy sign of Christ [cross], and incense; a handful of each. Bind all the herbs in a cloth, dip in hallowed font water thrice. Let three masses be sung over it, one "Omnibus sanctis," a second "Contra tribulationem," a third "Pro infirmis." Put then coals in a coal pan, and lay the herbs on it. Smoke the man with the herbs before *undern* [9 A.M.] and at night; and sing a litany, the Creed, and the Pater noster; and write on him Christ's mark on each limb. And take a little handful of the same kind of herbs, similarly sanctified, and boil in milk; drip holy water in it thrice. And let him sip it before his meal. It will soon be well with him.

The familiar herbs, so common in these exorcistic remedies for elves, are combined in equal measure with Christian medicinal powders, lichen, and incense. The virtues the lichen receives from growing on a cross border on the miraculous, echoing the kinds of cures in saints' lives through the power resident in things they have touched (Storms was more interested in noting the possible substitution here of the cross for a Germanic prescription of lichen from a hazel tree).[66] The ritual actions balance equally between traditional lore and the literate Christian tradition, in fumigation to drive the elf out and masses to exorcise it. These specific masses combine the spiritual and physical aspects of the ailment: masses for miraculous saintly intervention, for spiritual troubles and physical hardships, and for illness. References to masses by name also imply access to fairly decent liturgical books as found in a minster or monastery setting, as do the time references to monastic hours. The prescription of a litany, in addition to the basic prayers and signing, gives this remedy an overwhelmingly formal Christian flavor. The presence, then, of elements traceable to Germanic pre-Christian lore demonstrates the relatively high level of amalgamation that was possible. The retention of Germanic ritual actions as well as ingredients, here and in the next remedy, indicate that even literate Christians in a monastery or minster did not perceive these rituals as pagan but as acceptable healing practice.

> [2] For the same [*ælfadle*]. Go on Thursday evening when the sun is setting to where you know helenium [*elenan*] stands.[67] Sing then the Benedicite, the Pater noster, and a litany. And stick your knife into

the plant; leave it sticking therein and go away. Go again, when day and night first divide [dawn]; at that same dawn, go first to church, and cross yourself and offer yourself to God. Go then silently; and though you meet on the way some fearful thing coming or a man, you should not speak to him any word, until you come to the plant that you marked on the evening before. Sing then the Benedicite, and the Pater noster and a litany. Dig up the plant; leave the knife sticking in it. Go again as quick as you can to church, and lay it under the altar with the knife. Let it lie until the sun is up. Wash it then; make it into a drink: with bishopwort and lichen from Christ's sign, boil thrice in [different kinds of] milk; and pour holy water thrice on it. And sing on it the Pater noster, and the Creed and the Gloria in excelsis deo; and sing on it a litany. And also write a cross around it with a sword on [each of] four halves. And then let [the patient] drink the drink. It will soon be well with him.

This remedy has as its central ritual a set of actions that undoubtedly predate Christianity but that are nonetheless infused with Christian ritual, forming a seamless whole. The specification of a particular day, Thursday—perhaps a reference to Thor—undoubtedly crosses the line of acceptability for purists such as Ælfric, and yet immediately the instructions specify the singing of Christian prayers. The careful actions for gathering the herb are designed to protect the herb from any degeneration of its inherent virtues as well as to enhance those virtues; hence its placement under the altar is both a protection and a blessing (if morning services were sung over it). Thus the use of a variety of Christian prayers, the timing of the actions in the morning linked to going to church, and the silence indicate a monastic rather than a pagan setting. Whatever pagan meaning the original ritual for gathering this herb may have had, here it is completely subsumed under a monastic, meditative mood. An alternative, less monastic remedy follows that offers a specifically elf-related herb to smoke out the elf through the patient's sweat.

[3] Again for that. Lay under the altar these herbs, let nine masses be sung over them: incense, holy salt, three heads of cropleek, ælfthone's lower part, and helenium. Take in the morning a cup full of milk; drip thrice some holy water in it. Let him sip it as hot as he can. Eat with it three bits of ælfthone. When he wants to rest, have coals there inside. Lay incense and ælfthone on the coals, and smoke him with that until he sweats; and smoke the house throughout; and eagerly sign the man. And when he goes to rest, let him eat three bits of helenium, and three of cropleek, and three of salt. And let him have a cup full of ale and

drip thrice holy water in it. Let him eat each bit; then let him rest. Do this for nine mornings and nine nights. It will soon be well with him.

This third remedy returns to the idea, found in the first remedy, of exorcising the elf through smoke. The herb ælfthone plays a prominent role here, its prefix employing sympathetic medicine to drive the elf out. Smoking this herb seems to function in tandem with the sign of the cross to accomplish the cure. The Germanic number nine dominates this remedy, which on the whole seems much less liturgical than the first two remedies in this set. The masses and the blessed ingredients add Christian power to an essentially Germanic medicinal formula in a much less monastic way than the previous one (number 2). What follows in the fourth remedy is actually a long, complex set of instructions full of useful information in treating elf-related problems; clearly this affliction was varied and required experimental treatment that nonetheless employed a similar combination of herbal and ritual elements.

> [4a] If he has elf-heartburn [ælfsogotha, lit., "elf-juices"], his eyes are yellow where they should be red. If you want to cure this person, consider his bearing, and know of which sex he is. If it is a male [wæpned man], and he looks up when you first see him, and his appearance is yellow black, then that man you may cure completely, if he has not been therein too long. If it is a woman [wif] and she looks down when you first see her, and her appearance is dark red, this you might also cure. If it is on him a day's space longer than twelve months, and his visage be such, then you might better him for awhile, but may not however completely cure him.[68]

This rare instance of diagnostic measurements for elf affliction is not particularly helpful, not only because the descriptions are hard for us to identify with a particular ailment but also because these symptoms do not seem to match notions associated with elves in other remedies, such as sores or wounds or evidence of fever or madness. The broadest connection is the idea of internal illness, evident in the association of elf affliction with bowel disorders, discussed above. The sex differentiation is unusual in a remedy that is not specific to sex-related ailments. All of the other remedies against elves use neutral nouns and pronouns (mann refers to either sex or to both). Looking up or down and the reference to bearing hint at the possibility of a mental disturbance that alters the patient's normal demeanor. The instructions that follow invoke Latin and Greek Christian formulas in response to this internal and perhaps depression-causing ailment.

[4b] Write this writing: "Scriptum est, rex regum et dominus dominan-
tium. byrnice. beronice. Lurlure. Iehe. aius, aius, aius, sanctus, sanctus,
sanctus, sanctus, dominus, deus sabaoth, amen, alleluiah."
[It is written, king of kings and lord of lords. Veronica, Veronica. Lurlure? Yahweh? holy, holy, holy (Greek *agios*? and then repeated in Latin).
Lord, God of Hosts. Amen, Alleluia.]

Sing this over the drink and the writing: "Deus omnipotens, pater
domini nostri Iesu Christi, per impositionem huius scriptura expelle a
famulo tuo, ———, omnem impetum castalidum de capite, de capillis,
de cerebro, de fronte, de lingua, de sublingua, de guttore, de fauci-
bus, de dentibus, de oculis, de naribus, de auribus, de manibus, de
collo, de brachiis, de corde, de anima, de genibus, de coxis, de pedibus,
de compaginibus omnium membrorum intus et foris. Amen."
[God Almighty, father of our lord Jesus Christ, through the imposition of this writing expel from your servant, (name), all attacks of
muses/fairies (possibly down elves, *dun elfen*) from the head, from the
hair, from the brain, from the forehead, from the tongue, from the epiglottis, from the throat, from the pharynx, from the teeth, from the
eyes, from the nostrils, from the ears, from the hands, from the neck,
from the arms, from the heart, from the breath, from the knees, from
the hips, from the feet, from the connections of all body members
within and without. Amen.]

Writing and the languages of the literate place this remedy in the clerical-
monastic realm. The use of written words as forms of power has, as discussed in Chapter 4, both Christian roots and origins in Germanic, Celtic,
and Scandinavian cultures, where, for example, runes had great power. The
remedy transposes the Greek and even Hebrew words (Sabaoth) retained
in the Latin liturgy of the West into a new context of Germanic words
of power. The exorcism that follows is one of the most interesting amalgamations having to do with elves. Despite its Latin exorcistic formulation,
Storms called it non-Christian.[69] However, this prayer exorcising the various body parts exists in several places and is traceable to the Lorica of
Gildas. For example, an Anglo-Saxon version of Bede has such a formula in
a marginalia exorcism.[70] The most significant parallel, however, is an almost
identical exorcism of body parts found in the *Leofric Missal*.[71] Clearly this
formula is liturgical, and hence Christian. The use of Latin *castalis* (muse,
fairy) to define the elfish attacker referenced in the description of symptoms
(4a, *ælfsogotha*) shows the transformation occurring in the textualization of

this oral tradition as elves are Latinized, demonized, and Christianized.[72] In the same vein, another exorcism follows, this one in conjunction with an herbal drink.

[4c] Work then a drink: font water, rue, sage, hassock, dragonzan, of the smooth waybread the lower part, feverfue, a head of dill,[73] three cloves of garlic, fennel, wormwood, lovage, lupin; an equal amount of each. Write thrice a cross with oil of unction [*oleum infirmorum*] and say "Pax tibi." Take then the writing, write a cross with it over the drink, and sing this there over it: "Deus omnipotens, pater domini nostri Iesu Christi, per inpositionem huius scriptura et per gustum huius expelle diabolum a famulo tuo, ——," [God Almighty, father of our lord Jesus Christ, through the imposition of this writing and through this medicine expel the Devil from your servant, (name)] and the Creed and the Pater noster. Wet the writing in the drink, write a cross with it on each limb, and say "Signum crucis Christi conserva te in vitam aeternam. Amen." [May the sign of the cross of Christ conserve you in life eternal, Amen.] If you prefer not, tell [the patient] himself or whatever relative he has nearest related to him, and sign as best he can. This craft is mighty against every temptation of the fiend.

The drink that accompanies this elaborate exorcism of an elf is made from the usual ingredients with the added virtue of writing and the cross. The Latin formula to be sung empowers both the writing and the drink to expel the Devil, who is troublesome because of the temptations he offers. Storms questions the priest/doctor's reluctance to sign the cross in the manner described. He wonders whether ecclesiastical law was causing him to have qualms about using hallowed church items in such a remedy with "secular charms" (he means the Latin exorcism of body parts) and "magical writings" (the Latin and Greek formula invoking God).[74] This line of reasoning does not make sense in this context. The things that Storms takes for magical and not Christian meet much of the criteria needed in the early Middle Ages for Christian ritual. The language is literate, the prayers pertain to God, and the masses perform a liturgical function (exorcism). The reluctance in this remedy seems to pertain only to making the sign of the cross with the wet writing. If the priest had qualms about this, why would he make the writing in the first place? The priest's repugnance probably stems from some aspect of performing this rite on the sick man, since the prescription suggests that others closely related to the patient might be able to carry it out.

This set of four interrelated remedies in III:lxii has many features demonstrating the amalgamation of different traditions. All of the remedies are for elf disease but are clearly linked to demonic forces and temptation as a spiritual affliction. They do not contain, compared with other elf remedies, much association with fevers or poisons. One significant element running through these four remedies that distinguishes them from other elf remedies is the consistent use of the cross, as in lichen from the cross and signing the cross in particular ways. The cross is the simplest and most accessible symbol of the central truth of Christian belief, the power of Christ's death and resurrection. It was the first and sometimes only symbol many rural Anglo-Saxons experienced. Monumental crosses dotted the Anglo-Saxon landscape, and they may have provided lichen and other healing properties in areas remote from the central churches. Yet this set of remedies, by virtue of its highly literate use of Latin liturgy, reflects a minster environment. Thus the synthesis of traditions seen here is very sophisticated but probably still indicates a general trend of accommodation occurring elsewhere as well. Whoever compiled this set of remedies paid less attention to the different strands and their origins than to the confluence of traditions.

Even though there is little sense here of conflict between the Christian elements and ancient pre-Christian rites, it is odd to find the extremes in the two remedies following after this highly integrated set. The first (III:lxiii), for water elf disease, is free of Christian elements, and the second (III:lxiv), against demonic afflictions, is liturgical. The remedy for water elf disease (III:lxiii) is a charm of mana, sung over herbs in holy water.

If a man is in the water elf disease [wæter ælfadle], then the nails of his hand are dark and the eyes teary, and he will look down. Give him this as medicine [læcedome]: everthroat, hassock, the lower part of fane, yewberry, lupin, helenium, marshmallow head, fen mint, dill, lily, attorlathe, pulegium, marrubium, dock, elder, fel terre, wormwood, strawberry leaves, consolde.[75] Soak with ale; add holy water to it. Sing this gealdor over it thrice:

I have bound on the wounds the best of war bandages, so the wounds neither burn nor burst, nor go further, nor spread, nor jump, nor the wounds increase [waco sian?], nor sores deepen. But may he himself keep in a healthy way [halewæge?]. May it not ache you more than it aches earth in ear [eare?].

Sing this many times, "May earth bear on you with all her might and main." These galdor a man may sing over a wound.[76]

This form of elf disease has visible sores caused by an invisible source. This affliction has led to an imbalance in the humors, an excess of water or other liquid that manifests itself in dark nails and tearfulness as well as running sores. The looking down symptom is similar to ælfsogotha's description above. Storms guesses that this is chicken pox, citing similarities with other Germanic cultures where a "Puck-like" figure maliciously or mischievously causes liquid and burning sores that seem to appear, disappear, or move around.[77] In addition to the more typical herbal drink, this elf charm has a unique emphasis on earth counterbalancing the water. While the words spoken in the charm are mysterious, they nonetheless contain power to inhibit the sores.

The absence of any Christian references, except holy water, does lead scholars to classify this example as a clear case of pagan survival, a remnant of untouched, "pure" Germanic folklore.[78] The "magic" of its use of words of power without prayers oversteps the legal limits and would undoubtedly cause it to fall outside the bounds for a purist such as Ælfric. Yet its continued viability as an acceptable remedy as shown by its inclusion in this Christian context also indicates that the Christian compilers and users did not consider such galdra with statements of mana as in and of themselves "pagan"; rather, they perceived the ailment and its cure as not needing Christianization by adding liturgy.

These words of power operated in the same fashion as the Christian words in the previous remedy (III:lxii)—to bring out the natural potency of the herbs. The difference is that here the leech himself addresses the herbs, not their Creator, a distinction between magic and prayer that anthropologists identified as manipulation versus supplication. On the other hand, the Leofric Missal contains similarly "manipulative" exorcisms of salt and oil that use the "I" formula, Exorcizo te.[79] Whether the Anglo-Saxon compiler or public recognized the modern distinction between manipulation and supplication is therefore questionable.

The immediate return to Christian liturgical medicine for devilish ailments in III:lxiv, right after this "un-Christian" charm, reinforces the lack of distinction in the compiler's thinking between categories we take for granted.

Against the Devil and against madness [ungemynde], a strong drink. Put in ale hassock, lupin roots, fennel, ontre, betony, hind heolothe, marche, rue, wormwood, nepeta (catmint), helenium, ælfthone, wolfs comb. Sing twelve masses over the drink; and let him drink. It will soon be well with him.

A drink against the Devil's temptations: thefanthorn, cropleek, lupin, ontre, bishopwort, fennel, hassock, betony. Sanctify these herbs; put holy water into ale. And let the drink be there in where the sick man is. And continually before he drinks sing thrice over the drink, "Deus! In nomine tuo saluum me fac." [God, in your name make me whole (save me).]

This remedy seems to go to the opposite end of the spectrum in being mostly a Christian remedy for spiritual ailments caused by demonic forces, but it has incorporated elements and ingredients from elf remedies (such as ælfthone). Unlike the previous charm, the words sung here clearly fall within the parameters of the canons concerning the use of prayers that pertain to God and sound to the modern ear supplicative rather than manipulative. The implication here is that spiritual remedies for demonic attacks can benefit from the addition of herbal treatments. To those who might think the twelve masses should be sufficient to get rid of the Devil, the answer is in the closing sung or chanted lines, "God, in your name save me," or literally, "make me safe or well." The inherently dual meaning of saluum me fac echoes Ælfric's discussion of divine medicine in which he argues that God is the source of healing for both body and soul.[80] The individual patient needs a personal cure, and the indivisibility of body and soul while in this life means that physical and spiritual health must be obtained in concrete ways from the supreme deity.

Conclusions: Shifting Views

Interestingly, an early thirteenth-century hand commented beside this remedy, in Latin, on the use of Christian material. The commentator's remarks reflect the same concerns of modern readers about the need to use Christian elements in such remedies.

Nota quod in omni potu et omni medicina maleficorum et demoniacorum ammiscenda est aqua benedicta. et psalmis et orationibus uacandum est sicut in hoc capitulo plene docetur.

[Note that holy water is mixed into all drinks and all medicine for evil-doing and demonic things; and there is time for psalms and prayers just as we are fully taught in this chapter.][81]

This comment validates the unspoken association of liturgical elements in demonic cures visible in all the remedies analyzed here. Any time an illness had potential demonic associations, the remedy included holy water with the regular herbal medicine. The curious thing about this later comment is that it seems to point out the Christian elements of this second remedy without commenting on the lack of the same in the previous one, unless perhaps obliquely. Holy water is the only Christian element in the previous charm for the water elf disease, and the comment mentions holy water here as a significant item for counteracting anything evil or demonic. Also, the commentator's idea that "there is time" for psalms and prayers could refer to both remedies in which the instructions indicate numerous repetitions of a set of verses. This is the only marginalia commentary of this kind in the entire manuscript, placed intriguingly at this point where two such different remedies are so closely linked, and right after the remedy with the least amount of Christianization.[82]

This thirteenth-century reader's comment reflects in some ways the beginning of a shift in views of magic, in which natural and supernatural means were gradually separated from one another and evaluated according to different rationalities, human reason and spiritual insight. But the text the thirteenth-century reader was examining came from an earlier period with a more holistic worldview, in which natural and supernatural elements in remedies functioned together and thus were categorized according to their interconnection with one another. Because supernatural forces manifested themselves in natural phenomena and natural ingredients had supernatural potential, the distinction between natural and supernatural was irrelevant in these cures. What mattered was how to invoke the hidden virtues of natural ingredients to counteract the visible and invisible causes of a patient's complaint and to alleviate the symptoms of both physical and mental-spiritual distress.

CONCLUSION.
RELIGION AND CULTURE
RETHINKING EARLY MEDIEVAL
WORLDVIEWS

The last two chapters brought this study to the point of greatest specificity by examining in detail a set of texts and by proposing a meaningful context for them based on the general principles and background established in the first three chapters. What remains here is to work back from the specific to the general, to suggest ways that this study of elf charms offers new insights on late Saxon Christianity, on popular religion in the early Middle Ages, and on religion and culture in general.

Elf Charms as Folk Liturgical Medicine

What united all of these diverse remedies analyzed in Chapter 5 was the notion that these afflictions—elf attack, Devil sickness, poisons, fevers, various forms of madness, and certain internal ailments—could benefit from treatment with herbs blessed by rituals that were predominantly Christian. The authors, compilers, and scribes involved in the production of the *Leechbook* and the *Lacnunga*, undoubtedly members of clerical communities, were nonetheless Anglo-Saxons and therefore reflect their heritage and culture. The creators and the users of these texts were Anglo-Saxon Christians who saw the world, and the individual's relationship to the world, in a holistic way, a view that led them to combine what seems to us a very diverse group of ideas that sprang from the Graeco-Roman, Christian, and Germanic traditions. For them, the concept of Christianized folklore, or vice versa, popularized Christianity, would not be meaningful, however handy it may be for us to use those labels as a way of reaching some understanding of these practices.

Thus, although it may be of interest to the modern scholar to trace the pagan, Anglo-Saxon, and Christian origins of these remedies, we need to recognize that the remedies existed in their own time as integrated wholes, without any self-consciousness of a conflict of traditions or beliefs. They operated simultaneously as folklore, medicine, and liturgy, the three strands analyzed in Chapter 4. The invisible powers associated with the Devil afflicted people with physical as well as spiritual ailments; hence Christian words of power made herbal medicine handed down through classical and Germanic lore efficacious against these forces. The diverse origins of these practices, as we understand them, did not concern late Saxon Christians because the accompanying Christian words sanctified and validated the practice. These remedies suggest that, in the tenth and eleventh centuries, elf disease was treatable but only with the use of a church and the help of a priest who could exorcise the evil being through the power of his words and actions.

Late Saxon Christianity

The remedies as we have them, in manuscripts produced within the textual communities of religious institutions, show us the practical side of the Germanic-Augustinian worldview, a view expounded formally by Ælfric and Wulfstan, as discussed in Chapter 3. All of the remedies show the conjunction of good forces against evil forces without a necessary distinction between physical and spiritual, natural and supernatural. In Ælfric's eyes, body and soul, within and without, were interconnected. Any material phenomenon had a potential spiritual meaning, whether it be a demonic illness or temptation testing the resistance of a Christian or a weakness of body designed to demonstrate God's miraculous power. In any case, Christians should seek remedies from the Creator. The charm remedies put this same principle into practice. Evil beings—whether elves or demons—attacked humans and cattle in mysterious ways, leaving physical marks and distressing the spirit. All creation was connected in one unending continuum through the mind of the Creator, from microcosmic organisms to the macrocosm of the heavens; therefore, any cure involved invoking the forces of good found in nature to rebalance the body. The medical remedies represent a practical expression of this emerging cosmology articulated by Ælfric.

In addition, the similarity in worldview between late Antique Christianity and pre-Christian Anglo-Saxon culture enhanced this acculturation process. Germanic animism, with its sacred trees, wells, and stones, and early Christianity, with its Neoplatonic world and cult of dead saints, shared a common outlook on the intimate connection between the spiritual and the material. Saints' relics, churches, and crosses sanctified the landscape, displacing or transforming pagan sites. Likewise in the charm remedies, holy water, prayers, the sign of the cross, and written liturgical formulas brought out the hidden virtues of herbs long known to have curative powers if properly prepared. The Christian charms were a logical product of the meeting of these two traditions, as part of the process of Christianization. The sheer range of remedies combining folk and liturgical traditions in such variable ways, all in one manuscript, is evidence of a widespread process of amalgamation outside the textual centers producing these manuscripts.

Between, then, the extremes of magic and miracle that exemplify the conflict between pagan and Christian beliefs, stand these middle practices, remedies that meet the practical, everyday needs of a rural population with a new synthetic tradition mediated by the growing body of local clergy.

Popular Religion

The presence of these middle practices in the texts of the formal church offer us a glimpse of popular religion in late Saxon England. They hint at a more diverse amalgamation occurring in oral culture and in rural areas remote from the textual centers that produced these manuscripts. The remedies for mind-altering afflictions stand at the point of contact between textual and oral, clergy and laity, popular and formal. Rather than treating these texts as the outer and lowest boundaries of the formal intellectual tradition, as early scholars have done, or as the upper end of a still-pagan culture, as more recent scholars have done, this book places them in the center of a dynamic interchange between Anglo-Saxon folklore and Christian ritual. From this interaction emerged a vibrant Christian tradition in late Saxon England.

Moreover, as discussed in Chapter 2, this amalgamation was part of a larger dynamic of cultural transformation in the early Middle Ages, as Roman, Celtic, Anglo-Saxon, and Scandinavian traditions interacted. This type of crosscultural contact, with the related phenomena of religious conversion and the development of literacy, caused rapid transformations throughout early medieval European cultures. The crosscurrents of new and old ideas, in the context of migrating peoples, developing land settlement, and emerging kingdoms, created an environment in the early Middle Ages that produced phenomena such as elf charms. In particular, the dynamics in the early history of the British Isles of displaced Romano-Celtic culture supplanted by converting Anglo-Saxon culture, itself disrupted by Scandinavian incursions, contributed to the tension in late Saxon England between diversifying and centralizing forces.

The conflict between centrifugal and centripetal forces in the tenth and eleventh centuries is exemplified, on the one hand, in the growth of proprietary churches and, on the other, in the reform efforts of leading churchmen. The upheavals and tensions caused by the Scandinavian presence in the Danelaw weighed in on the side of the diversifying forces, impeding even further the centralizing efforts in the minds of reformers. Interestingly, the explosive cultural conflicts encoded in the labels "pagan Viking" versus "Christian Anglo-Saxons" were mitigated by the conversion of the Viking settlers, their intermarriage with Anglo-Saxons, and the subsequent refounding of monasteries and the building of local churches. This grassroots acculturation fostered a gradual religious conversion that tempered the vehemence of Wulfstan and the controlled reform of Ælfric.

The charms are a product of both forces, the diversifying, burgeoning lay piety and the centralizing, codifying formal religion. In the variety of ways that they combined folk practice and Christian ritual, the elf charms represent the literate edge of an ongoing acculturation process occurring in oral culture among rural churches. As a consequence of the increase in the number of small, local churches, more native clergy established closer relationships with the needs of a rural population, meeting their day-today hardships with the power of Christian ritual and yet still utilizing the familiar folkways, as seen in the blessings of fields and in various liturgical remedies for Germanic afflictions such as elf attack. Yet, by their existence in the written, textual tradition of the church, the charms also represent the formal effort to systematize and regularize these emerging practices. These medical texts have a clear connection with classical medical theories and with written liturgical practice. They even, to a certain extent, reflect the same cosmological principles established by Ælfric in his sermons, emphasizing the spiritual meaning in material life.

Thus these medical texts incorporating middle practices stand at the center of the interaction between clerical culture and lay practice. This negotiated territory, with all of its conflicts and problematic interpretations, reveals the heart of popular religion as practiced in the tenth and eleventh centuries. The construct popular religion functions as a useful frame for redefining Christianity in terms of overlapping and interacting spheres rather than exclusive categories of elite and popular. It allows us to see a spectrum of middle practices stretching between magic and religion. Most of all, popular religion validates the importance of assimilation and acculturation as competing traditions interact.

Religion and Culture

The richness and complexity of this merger of traditions in the early Middle Ages suggest new ways for us to think about religion and culture and crosscultural dialogue. Late Saxon popular religion gives us a sense of the diversity in the way religion adapts to culture and vice versa. The religion may control and dominate, but it also melts and shifts; it is always becoming, as is the culture.

The dynamic nature of this meeting of religion and culture produced both conflict and a new synthesis. Traditionally the conflicts between paganism and Christianity, magic and religion, attract more attention as the main force behind conversion and "progress" toward some higher standard of civilization. As our view of religion broadens, however, to incorporate the popular as well as the formal, another dynamic emerges, that of acculturation as the basis for a new cultural matrix. The resulting synthesis was a product of the old and the new, as past and future collided.

Early medieval culture, highly traditional and yet evolving in a rapidly changing world, was adept at this art of looking both backward and forward at the same time. The Anglo-Saxon charms reveal the creativity involved in allowing traditions to do what they must to stay alive—adapt. That adaptation was not passive, imposed from without by a monolithic church; rather, the adaptations that made Christianity a viable religion in Anglo-Saxon culture were initiated from within, in the daily lives of ordinary people. In the midst of the often violent conflict between pagan culture and Christian culture in these centuries, a more subtle process was at work: as liturgy got into the charms, and elves got into the liturgy, Christianity prospered and Anglo-Saxon traditions survived.

Likewise the dialogue between the modern and the medieval, the historian and the past, can be a fruitful, if sometimes difficult, interchange. The modern medieval historian lives in a global, heterodox, relativist world dominated by scientific expansion, while studying an isolated and distant realm that favored orthodoxy and tradition and that believed the natural world was alive with spiritual agencies. Ælfric said in his Midlent sermon on Christ feeding the five thousand with five loaves that "it is not enough that we wonder at the miraculous sign, or through it praise God, unless we also understand its spiritual sense."[1] Likewise, it is not enough to wonder at medieval practices such as elf charms and field blessings unless we also seek to understand what these rituals signified to the participants. The benefit of engaging in this historical dialogue with a different worldview comes not from trying to reject or explain away these older perspectives but from the process of attempting to be in two worlds simultaneously, a kind of stereoscopic vision that can add depth to our understanding of the human condition.

NOTES

Abbreviations

The following abbreviations appear in the notes and bibliography.

ASPR   *The Anglo-Saxon Poetic Records.*
6 vols. Edited by George Philip
Krapp and Elliott Van Kirk
Dobbie. New York: Columbia
University Press, 1931–42.

EETS   *Early English Text Society,* original
series (o.s.), new series (n.s.),
and supplementary series (s.s.).
London: Trubner, 1864– .
Oxford: Oxford University
Press, 1920– .

EH   Bede. *Ecclesiastical History.* Cited
by book and chapter. See
bibliography for different
editions.

EHD   *English Historical Documents.* Vol. 1,
500–1042. Edited and translated
by Dorothy Whitelock.
London: Methuen, 1955. Vol. 2,
1042–1189. 2nd ed. Edited and
translated by David C. Douglas
and G. W. Greenaway. London:
Methuen, 1981.

HF   Gregory of Tours. *The History of
the Franks.* Translated by Lewis
Thorpe. London: Penguin,
1974. Cited by book and
chapter.

PG   *Patrologiae Cursus Completus, Series
Graeca.* Edited by Jacques-Paul
Migne. 161 vols. Paris: 1857–66.

PL   *Patrologiae Cursus Completus, Series
Latina.* Edited by Jacques-Paul
Migne. 221 vols. Paris: 1844–64.

VCH   *The Victoria History of the Counties
of England,* edited by H. Arthur
Doubleday, William Page,
Louis F. Salzman, and Ralph B.
Pugh. London and Westmin-
ster: A. Constable, 1900–1934.
London: University of London,
Institute of Historical Research,
1935– . General introduction
by Ralph B. Pugh, London:
Oxford University Press, 1970.

Introduction

1 *Leechbook,* Book I, lxxxviii.2–3 (MS Royal 12. D. XVII, British Library, fols. 58a–
b); translated from Cockayne, *Leechdoms,* 2:156, and Wright facsimile, fols. 58a–
b. These two prescriptions occur in a series of veterinary remedies at the end

of Book I. The same ointment remedy also appears in the eleventh-century *Lacnunga* CXVIII (60). Cockayne translates *ofscoten* as "elfshot," with a note that it is "the Scottish phrase for this disease." Most scholars generally accept the identification of such "shot" with elves (see discussion of elves in Chapter 5, below).

2 Christian historiography manifests these dualities from Augustine's *Two Cities* to the histories of Orosius, Gregory of Tours, and Bede, and on throughout the Middle Ages. The dualities of Christian versus pagan, civilized versus barbaric, and magic versus religion or science played a significant role in European expansion and in colonial discourse about non-European peoples and carried over into anthropology in the seminal works of Edward Tylor, J. G. Frazer, and Bronislaw Malinowski, among others. For a succinct deconstruction of the changing concepts of magic, religion, and science, see Tambiah, *Magic, Science, Religion*; see also discussion of magic in Chapter 1, below.

3 The editions consulted in the translation of the medical material include Cockayne's three-volume *Leechdoms*; Leonhardi's edition of the medical manuscripts in *Kleinere angelsächsische Denkmäler*; Wright's facsimile of *Bald's Leechbook*; Grattan and Singer's edition of the *Lacnunga* in *Anglo-Saxon Magic*; Grendon, "Anglo-Saxon Charms"; Storms's selection of charms in *Anglo-Saxon Magic*; and the verse charms in *ASPR*, vol. 6.

Chapter One

1 MS Cotton Caligula, British Library A. VII, fol. 176a–178a, late tenth or early eleventh century; these folios were bound here with the *Heliand* poem in the seventeenth century. Translated from two editions: Storms, *Anglo-Saxon Magic*, pp. 172–87, and *ASPR*, 6:116–18.

2 These terms are difficult to translate without evoking later meanings and contexts concerning magic and witchcraft. *Dry*, related to *druid*, has been translated as "magician," "sorcerer," or "witch." *Lyblace* means literally "drug-leech," but in the surviving texts most of the uses imply a malicious intent rather than a curative function, although conceivably the same individual carried out both types of tasks in an earlier period. In both cases, these roles have taken on a negative meaning under the influence of Christianity.

3 Most editors assume these exclusions are, first, for "sacred" hardwoods such as oak and beech and, second, for burdock as a guess at the Anglo-Saxon *glappan*. An alternative interpretation, suggested by my colleague in the English department Kathleen Falvey, is that the remedy specifies using light branches and leaves of trees, rather than pieces of wood, in order to sprinkle the holy water as prescribed in the next line. The exclusion of burdock, with its prickly burrs, would make sense.

4 The Latin titles indicate specific prayers from the liturgy: the Sanctus (Holy),

Benedicite (Blessed be), Magnificat (My soul magnifies the Lord), and Pater noster (Our Father, the Lord's Prayer).

5 The word is untranslatable but appears to be a pre-Christian invocative phrase appealing to Mother Earth by this name. Alternatively, it could be a corrupt version of *ecce* (behold). See Niles, "Æcerbot Ritual," p. 55 and n. 14.

6 As with *dry* and *lyblac*, these two types of people are difficult to place. A *cwidol wif* or "speaking-woman" implies a woman skilled in charms; a *cræftig man* likewise indicates a man skilled in lore and remedies. They seem to be male and female counterparts in the pre-Christian folk medicinal trade.

7 See Mircea Eliade's call for more study of folk religious experience in "History of Religions and 'Popular Cultures,'" p. 2. Much of the most distinguished work done on the medieval church until recently was concerned with issues of church and state, scholasticism, heresy, the Crusades, and related subjects of institutional, intellectual, or political history. In the last fifteen years, more work has been done on the cultural aspects of medieval Christianity, as discussed below.

8 For ease of use in the text, I am using the now-problematic designation "Germanic" to reference the various cultures of similar extraction and belief that migrated into and settled throughout western Europe. To some degree Germanic cultural characteristics are consonant with Celtic and Scandinavian cultures even though these deserve separate treatment. My primary interest is in the coalescing group in England known as the Anglo-Saxons and the general traits of this group as Saxons, their shared Scandinavian characteristics, and the Celtic influence on their development.

9 For discussion of the context and meanings of this ritual, see the following articles: Jolly, "Father God and Mother Earth"; Thomas D. Hill, "Æcerbot Charm"; and Niles, "Æcerbot Ritual."

10 See discussion in Chapters 4 and 5 of Cockayne, Grendon, and Storms for the earlier view of degraded forms of Christianity, and below for discussion of the new de-Christianizing view evident in Keith Thomas and Valerie Flint, and reviewed by Van Engen, "Christian Middle Ages," pp. 521, 528–29. A good example of the negative approach to popular religion is Walter de Bont, "La psychologie devant la religion populaire," pp. 19–22. See Frantzen, *Desire for Origins*, pp. 73, 89, for discussion of the valuation of Latin sources over vernacular on a sliding scale, and Davis, "Some Tasks and Themes in the Study of Popular Religion," pp. 307–8, 311–12, on approved and disapproved categories of religion. On the failure of Christianization and the emphasis on a non-Christian folk religion, see Le Goff, *La civilisation de l'occident médiévale*, pp. 18–19, and also Schmitt, "Les traditions folkloriques," who, on p. 9, has a good critique of the type of approach taken by de Bont.

11 The "Age of Faith" view is rooted in nineteenth-century Romanticism and a desire for a unifying European culture, evident in Novalis and Chateaubriand.

On the de-Christianization view, see Delumeau, "Déchristianisation," pp. 3–20. For a survey of both views, see John Van Engen, who defines the problem well in his landmark 1986 article, "Christian Middle Ages," pp. 532, 549, 551–52.

12 See Gurevich, *Medieval Popular Culture*, pp. 218–21.

13 See Bharati, "Anthropological Approaches," pp. 232–33.

14 For an excellent survey of trends in cultural history, see Lynn Hunt, *New Cultural History*, and Hutton, "History of Mentalities." For analogous developments in the study of folklore, which also suffered from nineteenth-century romanticism, see Dorson, *Folklore and Fakelore*; Rosenberg, "Folkloristes et médiévistes," p. 945; and Burke, *Popular Culture*, pp. 1–87, for a survey of popular culture.

15 Gurevich, *Medieval Popular Culture*; Van Engen, "Christian Middle Ages"; Murray, *Reason and Society*; Kieckhefer, *Magic in the Middle Ages*; discussed below.

16 Manselli, *La religion populaire au moyen âge*; Vovelle, "La religion populaire"; Delaruelle, *La piété populaire au moyen âge*.

17 On *religion savante* and *religion populaire*, see Manselli, *La religion populaire*, pp. 16–17; official and unofficial, Burke, *Popular Culture*, p. xi, who also uses little tradition (pp. 23–24), unofficial, nonelite, and subordinate to describe popular culture; great and little tradition, reflective and unreflective, Redfield, *Peasant Society and Culture*, p. 70; literate and illiterate, Congar, "Clercs et laïcs."

18 Manselli, *La religion populaire*, pp. 17–18, for definitions; pp. 20, 218, for the idea of dialectical rapport.

19 Brooke and Brooke, *Popular Religion*, p. 9, where they simply refer to ordinary lay people as the defining element of popular religion.

20 Gurevich, *Medieval Popular Culture*, p. 179.

21 Frantzen, *Desire for Origins*, p. 57, discussing John Kemble.

22 See Hodges, "Parachutists and Trufflehunters: At the Frontiers of Archaeology and History," in Aston, *Rural Settlements*, pp. 287–88.

23 Ruth Karras, "Pagan Survivals and Syncretism," takes this approach to the conversion of Saxony, arguing that the subtle traces of pagan practices are not the remnants of paganism but "popular expressions of Christian belief" (p. 553). On ethnography, see in particular the work of James Clifford in Clifford and Marcus, *Writing Culture*, p. 2, where he describes ethnography as sitting on the boundaries, decoding and recoding; the work of Clifford Geertz, *Interpretation of Culture*, discussing his "webs of significance" view of culture and his method of "thick description"; and Greg Dening's *Islands and Beaches*, which models the idea of crossing boundaries graphically for the Marquesan Islands.

24 Russell's BAVB as "belief-attitude-value-behavior" is explained only, but not substantiated as a model, in a note (*Germanization*, p. 11). The more historically oriented, culture-specific approach that I prefer starts with the culture and looks for patterns and constructs that work. Rather than Russell's "Germanization," I use "Germanicization," adding an extra syllable, in order to avoid the implication of some monolithic German culture. "Germanic" as an adjective describes the practices and beliefs of a variety of related peoples.

25 The term *modes of rationality* as "ways of knowing," no matter how clumsy, is a little more friendly and less exclusive than *epistemology*. On modes of thought and rationalities, see the edited collection by Neusner et al., *Religion, Science, and Magic*. See especially Jacob Neusner's introduction (pp. 3–7) and Hans Penner's statement of the question, "Rationality, Ritual, and Science" (pp. 11–24).

26 For my purposes, religion is a system of belief, practice, and organization relative to sacred things, which shapes an ethic manifested in the behavior of its adherents. Hence, the beliefs and practices of the body of believers as a whole are as significant as the doctrine and structure established by the leaders or intellectuals. For definitions of religion, see Birnbaum, "Religion"; also, Durkheim, *Elementary Forms of the Religious Life*, p. 47.

27 See Murray, *Reason and Society*, pp. 1–22, and discussion of the Augustinian view of magic, religion, and science in Chapter 3, below.

28 See discussion of miracles and magic in Chapter 3, below. In addition to avoiding the term *magic* in relation to Christian practice, I have also eschewed the use of *syncretism* on the grounds that it invokes a number of confusing meanings that are incompatible with some of the main theological positions held by the dominant forms of Christianity. Syncretism refers to the attempt to reconcile different religious systems in one or more domains (in doctrine, myth, ritual, social, ethical, or experiential, to invoke Ninian Smart's six worldview dimensions [*Worldviews*, pp. 6–9]); the -ism implies a systematic approach or a consistent pattern or policy of accepting other religions. In many ways, formal Christianity, with its emphasis on monotheism and exclusivity, resists doctrinal and mythological syncretism. The denial of other gods or any merger with other pantheons is evident, for example, in the martyrs under Roman persecution. Further, in their conversion efforts Christian missionaries preferred to displace or dominate existing rituals and sites. Comparatively, Christianity is at the opposite end of the spectrum from other religions that are syncretic in nature; for a brief discussion of Christian conversion versus syncretism, see Capps, *Ways of Understanding*, pp. 275–79. Christianity manifests syncretic behaviors in the social, experiential, and ritual domains, so in a few instances I use the adjective to describe these; but I have refrained from using *syncretism* to describe a systematic way of thinking in Christianity. See, however, Ruth Karras's careful use of the term to elucidate Saxon conversion, in "Pagan Survivals and Syncretism."

29 Culture, as described by Edward Tylor (*Primitive Culture*, 1:1), is "that complex whole which includes knowledge, belief, art, morals, law, custom, and any other capabilities and habits acquired by man as a member of society"; or, as Margaret Mead puts it (in her introduction to Benedict, *Patterns of Culture*, p. vii), culture is "the systematic body of learned behavior which is transmitted from parents to children." Culture is a social, that is, a public, phenomenon; it is, however, observed solely through representations, whether oral, textual, or ritual (see Chartier, *Cultural History*, pp. 13–14).

30 Or, as Francis Rapp asserts, "le christianisme populaire, c'est le christianisme de tout le monde," in "Reflexions sur la religion populaire au môyen age," in Plongeron, *La Religion populaire*, p. 54. See also Jacques Duquesne, "Un debat actuel: 'La religion populaire,'" in Dye and Hameline, *Religion populaire*, pp. 8–10, on the ambiguity of the term *popular religion*.

31 Ariès, "Religion populaire et reformes religieuses," in Dye and Hameline, *Religion populaire*, p. 95, has a series of diagrams showing the changing relationship from the Middle Ages, the seventeenth and eighteenth centuries, and the nineteenth and twentieth centuries of what he calls *para-religion* and *vrai christianisme*. Schmitt, "Les traditions folkloriques," pp. 12–14, uses line diagrams to show the interaction of two poles of religion. My own circles are drawn and described in "Magic, Miracle, and Popular Practice in the Early Medieval West: Anglo-Saxon England," in Neusner et al., *Religion, Science, and Magic*, pp. 177–78.

32 One later instance of rituals purposely kept secret from uninitiated laity occurs with the Knights Templars, and this secrecy in part contributed to accusations of heresy against them.

33 Ladurie's *Montaillou* and Ginzburg's *The Cheese and the Worms*, for example, explore the localized religious adaptations revealed in inquisition records. Microhistory, of which Ginzburg is a proponent, advocates exploring precisely the particular anomalies in local culture in order to emphasize the discontinuities and changes in history that are either ignored or irrelevant to the present, in contrast to the unmoving history or *longue durée* of the Annales school (see Muir and Ruggiero, *Microhistory*, p. xii).

34 Manselli, *La religion populaire*, pp. 17, 40, identifies *religion savante* with *la parole*, and *religion populaire* with emotive and practical values, stressing everyday experiences.

35 On the "professionals of culture," see Chartier, *Cultural History*, p. 5.

36 For similar discussions of the interaction between popular and formal, see Gurevich, *Medieval Popular Culture*, pp. 180, 222–23; Charles Halperin, review of Gurevich, *Speculum* 58 (1983): 472, 474–75; Vovelle, "La religion populaire," pp. 9, 29; Manselli, *La religion populaire*, pp. 216–18; Schmitt, "Les traditions folkloriques," p. 12; and Wormald, "Uses of Literacy," p. 100.

37 Derek Baker, "Vir Dei: Secular Sanctity in the Early Tenth Century," in Cuming and Baker, *Popular Belief and Practice*, pp. 42–43, and Davis, "Tasks and Themes," p. 309, both make this point about priests versus laity as a false distinction in popular religion. See also Congar, "Clercs et laïcs."

38 Andre Varagnac, *Definition du Folklore* (Paris, 1938), p. 18, defines folklore as collective beliefs without doctrine, collective practices without theory, as cited and discussed in Courtas and Isambert, "Ethnologues et sociologues," p. 29.

39 Stock, *Implications of Literacy*, p. 522; see also Schmitt, "Les traditions folkloriques," p. 5.

40 Gurevich, *Medieval Popular Culture*, pp. 223–24, suggests that this writing down ended the life of the oral folklore, changing its existence; the ability of oral

culture to oppose learned culture lies in its orality. We have lost, as in the case of the charms, the performance aspect of the oral tradition (see Darnton, *Great Cat Massacre*, pp. 17–18). This ambiguity is evident as well in literary studies such as those concerned with *Beowulf*.

41 The distinction at work here is popular versus popularized, as pointed out by Pietro Boglioni, "La religion populaire au moyen âge," in Lacroix and Boglioni, *Les religions populaires*, pp. 53–63, and by Gennep, *Le folklore*, pp. 42–43, as discussed by Courtas and Isambert in "Ethnologues et sociologues," pp. 26–28.

42 Perhaps the postmodern experience of the media and advertising has led to a greater awareness of the power of images and the influence of ritual behaviors.

43 On "thinking with things," see Darnton, *Great Cat Massacre*, p. 189.

44 This valuation of abstract over concrete thinking is in part a product of the evolutionary models of Tylor, Frazer, Durkheim, and Weber in which "rationality" is seen as the highest result of progress, in opposition to earlier expressions of thought through ritual (see Bharati, "Anthropological Approaches," pp. 232–33). This bias is also evident in Anglo-Saxon studies in the higher value placed on Latin writings and culture (Frantzen, *Desire for Origins*, pp. 73, 89).

45 Rosenberg, "Folkloristes et médiévistes," p. 945.

46 EH, 1:30.

47 *Leofric Missal*, pp. 187, 224–28.

48 The effect of later reforms (for example, the eleventh-century Gregorian reform) was to eliminate popular religion from the formal definition of Christianity, that is, to change the standard of what was Christian. See Ariès, "Religion populaire," p. 88, and Gurevich, *Medieval Popular Culture*, pp. 218–20.

49 See Jacques Maître, "La religion populaire," *Encyclopaedia Universalis*, 14 (1972), p. 35, as cited in Courtas and Isambert, "Ethnologues et sociologues," p. 40. See also Le Goff, "Culture cléricale," pp. 785–87.

50 Peter Brown's seminal work, *The Cult of the Saints*, has inspired a new line of studies on sainthood, examining the meaning of relics in the medieval mind. See, for example, Van Dam's *Saints and Their Miracles in Late Antique Gaul*, Rollason's *Saints and Relics*, Kieckhefer's *Unquiet Souls*, and Bynum's *Resurrection*.

51 Modern reconstructions of pagan beliefs for the most part come from archaeological sources (runes and burial practices) and from mostly post-Christian written sources from Celtic, Anglo-Saxon, and Scandinavian peoples. These written sources are problematic because they are so removed in time and because the amount of Christian influence is indeterminate. Likewise, our knowledge of pagan practices among Anglo-Saxons is largely gleaned from Christian sources, such as the laws and sermons condemning them, the charms themselves, and poems such as *Beowulf*. The richest vein of Scandinavian material, albeit post-Christian, is found in the Old Icelandic Eddas and the work of Snorri Sturluson. The Hávamál, one of the Eddic poems, recites a series of charm powers attributed to Woden (see Storms, *Anglo-Saxon Magic*, pp. 2–5, for an excerpt). Snorri Sturluson's *Prose Edda* recites the stories from Norse mythology

about the various deities and includes quotes from the Poetic Edda. Some aspects of the diverse Celtic material are evident in the Irish tales of the Táin bo Cúailgne and the Welsh tales of the Mabinogion. For surveys of pagan beliefs, see Anne Ross, Pagan Celtic Britain; Wilson, Anglo-Saxon Paganism; Gale R. Owen, Rites and Religions; and Davidson, Myths and Symbols in Pagan Europe.

52 Rollason's book, Saints and Relics, is focused on the growth of the cult of the saints in the Anglo-Saxon period. Rodwell, Archaeology of Religious Places, p. 154, gives an overview of church foundations at natural springs or "holy wells," citing relevant site studies; "Wells" is consequently a common name associated with such sites. See also Morris, Church in British Archaeology, pp. 19–48. For a bibliography of studies on wells in England and Ireland and a cogent but brief explanation of them, see Gribben, Holy Wells, pp. 15–20.

53 Christ II, l. 457, in the Exeter Book, in ASPR, 3:17.

54 Franks Casket, London, British Museum.

55 Bradley, Anglo-Saxon Poetry, p. 250.

56 Guthlac, ll. 170–81a, in the Exeter Book, in ASPR, 3:54. See also Karras, "Pagan Survivals and Syncretism," pp. 568–70, on the heroic in the Heliand.

57 The Dream of the Rood, ll. 35–37a, in the Vercelli Book, in ASPR, 2:62.

58 Dream of the Rood, ll. 39–41.

59 See the British archaeological report edited by Addyman and Morris, Archaeological Study, in particular the reports by J. G. Hurst on St. Martin's Church at Wharram Percy, Yorkshire (pp. 36–39), P. A. Rahtz on churchyard archaeology (pp. 41–45), and Martin Biddle on structural continuity (pp. 65–71). For surveys of these church buildings and other finds at Barton-on-Humber, Rivenhall, and Asheldham, see Richard Morris, Church in British Archaeology, pp. 5, 33, 40, 62; Rodwell, Archaeology of the English Church, pp. 32, 36, 109, and Archaeology of Religious Places, pp. 156, 165, 169.

60 The evidence for gradual use of Christian memorial sculpture, such as stone or wooden crosses, on graves, although fragmentary earlier in the seventh to ninth centuries, indicates the increasing influence of Christian beliefs in the burial of the dead. Rodwell, Archaeology of Religious Places, p. 173.

Chapter Two

1 Asser, Alfred the Great, pp. 84–85. The Anglo-Saxon Chronicle also records this event in the year 878. The treaty proper, formulated in or after 886, spelled out the boundaries and some regulations (see pp. 171–72).

2 Malcolm Godden, "Apocalypse and Invasion," discusses the fear of invasion among Anglo-Saxon reformers. For an example of this traditional view of the Vikings as heathens, see Smyth, Warlords, p. 146. Hollister, Making of England, p. 57 n. 10, quotes Wallace-Hadrill's observation regarding the new minimization of the Viking impact, that they are not easily dismissed as "long-haired tourists

who occasionally roughed up the natives." See discussion below under "Differences in the Danelaw" for debates on the Viking impact evident in the Danelaw and in Normandy.

3 Hart, *Danelaw*, pp. vii, 24.

4 On the idea of conversion, see Morrison, *Understanding Conversion, Conversion and Text*, and Sullivan, *Christian Missionary Activity*.

5 For Constantine, see Eusebius, *Life of Constantine*, chaps. 27–31; for Benedict, see Gregory the Great, *Dialogues*, 2:8–10; for Clovis see *HF*, 2:30, p. 143.

6 *EH*, 3:1–3, 6, 9–13. King of Northumbria from 633 to 641, Oswald had a dream-vision on the model of Constantine in which he was promised victory. His people were baptized after the victory that made the Christian Oswald overlord of all Britain (*Adomnan's Life of St. Columba*, in *EHD*, 1:751–52). He was considered a martyr because of his death at the hands of the pagan King Penda (*Historia Brittonum*, in *EHD*, 1:263). His subsequent miracles earned him sainthood, so that his deeds after death had the effect of establishing his kingdom even more firmly in and through the Christian religion.

7 The story of Rollo is in Dudo of St. Quentin, *Dudonis sancti Quintini de moribus et actis primorum Normanniae Ducum*. For a discussion of the possible connections between the Eastern Danelaw and Rollo, see Hart, *Danelaw*, pp. 34–37. Similar negotiations with Vikings occurred throughout the ninth century in the context of competing alliances, the giving of hostages, and becoming Christian. See, for example, the years 862 and 873 in *Annals of St-Bertin*, pp. 98–99, 184–85.

8 *Exodus* is in the Junius MS, *ASPR* 1:89–107; *The Wanderer* and *The Seafarer* are in the Exeter MS, *ASPR* 3:134–40, 143–47.

9 *EH*, 5:8. See Stancliffe, "Kings Who Opted Out," and Ridyard, "Monk-Kings."

10 See Hollis, *Anglo-Saxon Women and the Church*, esp. chap. 7, "Queen Converters and the Conversion of the Queen."

11 *EH*, 1:25.

12 In *EH*, 2:9, Bede attributes the conversion of the Northumbrian people to the king's alliance with Kent through his marriage to Ethelberga, a marriage conditional on his openness to the Christian faith. *EH*, 2:11 (trans. Sherley-Price, pp. 118–19), records the following letter from the pope to the Northumbrian queen:

> To his illustrious daughter, Queen Ethelberga, from Bishop Boniface, servant of the servants of God.
>
> In His great providence, our loving Redeemer has offered a saving remedy to the human race, which He has saved from the Devil's enslaving tyranny by the shedding of His own precious Blood. Christ has made His Name known to the nations in various ways, so that they may acknowledge their Creator by accepting the mysteries of the Christian Faith. God in His mercy has revealed this truth to Your Majesty's own mind in your own mystical cleansing and regeneration. We have been greatly encouraged by God's

goodness in granting you, through your own conversion, an opportunity to kindle a spark of the true religion in your husband, for in this way He will more swiftly inspire not only the mind of your illustrious Consort to love of Him, but the minds of your subjects as well.

13 EH, 2:11 (trans. Sherley-Price, pp. 119–20):

But how can it be called a true union between you, so long as he remains alienated from your glorious Faith by the barrier of dark and lamentable error?

Let it therefore be your constant prayer that God of His mercy will bless and enlighten the King, so that you, who are united in earthly marriage, may after this life remain united for ever in the bond of faith. My illustrious daughter, persevere in using every effort to soften his heart by teaching him the laws of God. Help him to understand the excellence of the mystery which you have accepted and believe, and the wonderful reward that you have been accounted worthy to receive in this new birth. Melt the coldness of his heart by teaching him about the Holy Spirit, so that the warmth of divine faith may enlighten his mind through your constant encouragement, and remove the chilling and ruinous errors of paganism.

14 Nuns and abbesses play a major role in Bede's narrative. See, for example, EH, 4:7–10, on Barking Abbey; 4:18–20, on the virginal Queen Etheldreda as abbess; and 5:23, on Abbess Hilda. As evidenced in Boniface's biography and letters, abbesses and nuns were his colleagues, correspondents, and friends in a sisterly fashion. At one point Boniface took English nuns with him into Germany as coworkers in a monastic foundation there, Tauberbischofsheim, presided over by the charismatic Abbess Leoba. On Boniface's relationship with these women, and the role of other such women, see Boniface, *Letters of St. Boniface*, letters VI–VII, XIX, LXXVII for Abbess Bugga; letters XXI, LXXIX for Abbess Lioba; and letters XXII, XXVI, LIII for Abbess Eadburga; Duckett, *Saints and Scholars*, pp. 61, 207, 361, 400, 444; Deanesly, *Pre-Conquest Church*, p. 243; and Mayr-Harting, *Coming of Christianity*, pp. 267–68.

15 See Hart, *Danelaw*, pp. 145–46, for a discussion of Anglo-Scandinavian relations in Northampton. Hart (p. 29) interprets the lack of any evidence suggesting Guthrum denied the faith as positive evidence of his continued support. On pp. 29–31 he also chronicles the story of the Danish aristocratic family of Oda as prominent churchmen and details the Danish reverence for the cult of King Edmund the Martyr.

16 Barlow, *English Church*, uses such a combination of evidence admirably to give the most comprehensive view of this topic thus far.

17 The statistics in Domesday Book are unreliable for a number of reasons: the investigators asked different questions between and within different circuits,

the survey was done rapidly, two stages of returns are visible in Domesday and Little Domesday, and the types of values used vary and are hard to interpret. See Darby, *Domesday England*, pp. 13–14; Morris, *Church in British Archaeology*, p. 69; and Lennard, "Economic Position of Villani," p. 245. Other useful volumes on Domesday are Hallam's *Domesday Book through Nine Centuries*, a good introduction for the nonspecialist, and Bates's *Bibliography of Domesday Book*, a partially annotated bibliography of books and articles, comprehensive from 1886 through 1984.

18 For example, Kent, where Domesday Book records 186 churches out of 347 places, has numerous other churches contained in the *Domesday Monachorum* and the *White Book of St. Augustine*: see *VCH*, 3:253–69, for the *Domesday Monachorum*; see also Darby, *Domesday England*, pp. 52, 75. The lack of a universal formula for churches and priests means that some counties recorded priests, others recorded churches, and some recorded both. Generally, unless the entry indicates otherwise, one can assume that the presence of one implies the other; see Darby, *Domesday England*, pp. 52–53, and William Page, "Some Remarks," p. 63. The exceptions to this rule are generally cases where it is obvious that the priest named was the landholder and not the priest of the church.

19 Morris, *Church in British Archaeology*, pp. 72, 75; Blair, "Local Churches," p. 266.

20 The recent work by Rodwell (*Archaeology of the English Church*), Addyman and Morris (*Archaeological Study*), and Morris (*Church in British Archaeology*) in updating the classic work of Taylor and Taylor (*Anglo-Saxon Architecture*) is changing our views on pre-Conquest church building in dating, workmanship, and the relationship of church and vill. See also Nigel Baker, "Churches, Parishes."

21 On pre- and post-Conquest church building, see Platt, *Parish Churches*, pp. 3–6, and Loyn, *Anglo-Saxon England*, pp. 257–63, 284, 332. Franklin, "Identification of Minsters," p. 76, suggests reinterpreting the criteria used for identifying Anglo-Saxon buildings. See also L. A. S. Butler, "Documentary Evidence and the Church Fabric," pp. 18–21, and J. G. Hurst, "Wharram Percy: St. Martin's Church," p. 39, in Addyman and Morris, *Archaeological Study*; also, Rodwell, *Archaeology of Religious Places*, p. 33.

22 See Reynolds, *Kingdoms and Communities*, pp. 1–38, 101–54, on collective activity and rural society, and Reynolds, *Fiefs and Vassals*, pp. 324–42, on late Saxon land tenure.

23 Stenton, *Anglo-Saxon England*, pp. 451–52; Loyn, *Anglo-Saxon England*, pp. 251–52; John, *Orbis Brittaniae*; Hart, *Danelaw*, pp. 135, 149, 153 (map of fenland monastery holdings). See also the monastic rule established in Edgar's reign, Æthelwold, *Regularis Concordia*.

24 For a succinct summary of some of these dynamics for ealdormen in the Danelaw, see Hart, *Danelaw*, pp. 126–35.

25 Wainwright, "Æthelflæd, Lady of the Mercians," in Wainwright, *Scandinavian England*, pp. 305–24. On Athelstan "Half-King," see Hart, *Danelaw*, p. 576, and

Whitelock, "Conversion." For the will of Ælfgar, see Sawyer, Charters, nos. 1483, 1494, and Whitelock, Anglo-Saxon Wills, pp. 6–9 (no. 2). Fisher, "Anti-Monastic Reaction" and John, "War and Society."

26 The term Danelaw is a convenient one to describe the eastern areas of England that fell under Viking control, even though the word does not appear in any documents until 1008. Even though the term does not indicate the diversity of rule and custom within the Danelaw itself, between the Northern Danelaw, the Five Boroughs, and the Eastern Danelaw, it nonetheless serves to indicate the cultural separation between the laws and customs of the Danes in these territories, as opposed to the Engla lage of the West Saxons and the Myrcna lage of Mercia. See Hart, Danelaw, pp. 5–24, for a discussion of "What is the Danelaw?"

27 On Æthelred's reign, see Keynes, Diplomas and "The Declining Reputation," as well as Hart's summary judgment on Keynes's attempts to rehabilitate the ill-fated king, Danelaw, p. 533, n. 1. See also Niles and Amodio, Anglo-Scandinavian England, for debates on Æthelred and his Viking policies by Theodore Andersson and Phyllis Brown.

28 See Anglo-Saxon Chronicle for 1018 and Whitelock et al., Councils and Synods, 1:431–34. For a general biography of Cnut and study of sources, see Lawson, Cnut, and Rumble, Reign of Cnut.

29 Hart, Danelaw, p. 140.

30 For a complete picture of this tension between local churches and minsters, see Blair, Minsters and Parish Churches.

31 For discussion of these forces, see Brooke, "Rural Ecclesiastical Institutions"; John, "Social and Political Problems," pp. 53–54, 56; Loyn, Anglo-Saxon England, pp. 256–57; Morris, Church in British Archaeology, p. 75; and Böhmer, "Das Eigen-kirchentum." For general histories of the parochial system, see Addleshaw, Development of the Parochial System and Beginnings of the Parochial System, and Gaudemet, "La paroisse," p. 8.

32 Many early churches were founded on older Roman and pagan religious sites or graveyards; others were built at the site of a cross originally established as a preaching station. See Barlow, English Church, p. 184; Godfrey, "Emergence," p. 131; Campbell, "Church in Anglo-Saxon Towns," p. 121; Martin Biddle, "The Archaeology of the Church: A Widening Horizon," in Addyman and Morris, Archaeological Study, p. 67; Franklin, "Identification of Minsters," pp. 69–71; Varah, "Minsters"; and Morris, Church in British Archaeology, pp. 40–45, 62. Historians of Frankish church development refer to these two types of churches being founded either in vici by the bishop as a mission church or in villae as private churches (see Wallace-Hadrill, Frankish Church, pp. 286–87).

33 Fouracre, "Work of Audoenus," and Wood, "Early Merovingian Devotion."

34 Blair, "Local Churches," p. 267.

35 Pope Gregory I and Theodore of Tarsus apparently attempted to develop a planned diocesan organization, which never reached fruition, in the eighth

century. John, "Social and Political Problems," pp. 53–56; Campbell, "Church in Anglo-Saxon Towns," p. 120; Stenton, *Anglo-Saxon England*, p. 146.

36 EH, 3:5; see Bede, *Old English Version*, p. 161, and Campbell, "Church in Anglo-Saxon Towns," p. 121. Aidan was a monk-bishop who traveled throughout his territory rather than staying in a central seat (see Mayr-Harting, *Coming of Christianity*, pp. 94–99).

37 A true parish church not only is part of a network of churches hierarchically organized but is defined by a clear area of jurisdiction or territory, a definite congregation under a leader, and certain well-defined rights to perform baptism and burial and to collect tithes, all of which appear only from the mid-twelfth century. Brooke and Keir, *London*, p. 129; Gaudemet, "La paroisse," p. 10.

38 Norfolk Domesday, in *Domesday Book*, ed. Farley and Ellis, Little Domesday (ii), fols. 133a–b. Campbell, "Church in Anglo-Saxon Towns," pp. 133–34; Wood, "Early Merovingian Devotion," p. 62; Gaudemet, "La paroisse," pp. 10–11; Brooke and Keir, *London*, pp. 126, 142–43.

39 Stutz, "Proprietary Church," pp. 35–70.

40 Stenton, *Anglo-Saxon England*, pp. 148–49; Brooke and Keir, *London*, pp. 127, 131; Morris, *Church in British Archaeology*, p. 64. The size of a lay manor with a church in Domesday Book varies from one virgate to ninety hides, indicating a wide range in the wealth, and hence rank, of the owner. While some places were large enough to have several churches, many records indicate a fraction of a church, showing a church shared by several manors but perhaps one vill.

41 Barlow, *English Church*, pp. 193–94.

42 Gethynctho, c. 2, and VII Æthelred 2.5, in Liebermann, *Gesetze*; Preamble to the Ely Inquest, *VCH*, Cambridgeshire, 1 (1938): 400–427; Barlow, *English Church*, p. 194.

43 Richard Morris, "The Church in the Countryside: Two Lines of Inquiry," in Hooke, *Medieval Villages*, p. 47.

44 Darby, *Domesday England*, appendix 4, p. 346; see also Morris, *Church in British Archaeology*, table 7, p. 69, for similar statistics.

45 In a number of instances it is clear that the church listed was a minster—where it is named, or several clergy served it, or its landownership indicates its status. In other cases the priest named in the entry is obviously the proprietor of the manor on which the church is recorded.

46 See Sawyer, *From Roman Britain and Kings and Vikings*, and Brook, "England in the Ninth Century." A similar debate occurs over the Viking impact in Normandy. See, for example, Bates, *Normandy before 1066*, pp. 238, 247, on Frankish continuity in Norman institutions, and Searle, *Predatory Kinship*, p. 5, on Norman hostility toward Frankish ideas and the resilience of Viking identity.

47 Hart, *Danelaw*, pp. 231–79, for a discussion of sokes and Stenton's thesis on manorial structure in the Northern Danelaw, and pp. 70–100, for the unique

conditions in the Eastern Danelaw. For an examination of similar phenomena in the rapid reestablishment of monasteries in Normandy, see Potts, "Revival of Monasticism."

48 Platt, *Parish Churches*, pp. 1–3; Franklin, "Identification of Minsters," p. 72; Campbell, "Church in Anglo-Saxon Towns," pp. 125–29; Hart, *Danelaw*, pp. 30–33. See also Brooke and Keir, *London*, pp. 142–43, Gaudemet, "La paroisse," p. 15, and Addleshaw, *Development of the Parochial System*, p. 5.

49 David Hill, *Atlas*, p. 148. For a graphical view of the gradual reconquest in the tenth century, see Hill's maps 83–102, pp. 56–60.

50 Stenton, *Anglo-Saxon England*, pp. 451–52, on Æthelwold; Hart, *Danelaw*, appendix 21.1, considers the problem of monasticism in East Anglia (pp. 598–600).

51 David Hill, *Atlas*, pp. 155–64.

52 For the *Domesday Monachorum*, see the Kent *VCH*, 3:253–69; *Domesday Monachorum*; Gordon Ward, "Lists of Saxon Churches in the Domesday Monachorum," and "List of Saxon Churches in the Textus Roffensis"; William Page, "Some Remarks," pp. 66, 69–77, on Wessex in general and the counties of Somerset, Hampshire, and Berkshire in particular, where strong minsters are visible in these counties' Domesday Book entries. In Sussex, Page, pp. 79–81, also notes the difference between the older, settled districts of the south, which had strong minsters, and the forests of the north, which had strong manorial churches. Also, some charters show certain minsters exerting authority over other churches; for example, no. 1478 in Sawyer, *Charters*, and no. 115 in Robertson, *Charters*; see also Robertson's appendix 1-v.

53 See Hart, *Danelaw*, pp. 233–59, with detailed maps showing these networks.

54 Barlow, *English Church*, pp. 200–203; Warner, "Shared Churchyards." William Page, "Some Remarks," p. 63, discusses how the parish developed further in these regions; *VCH*, Suffolk, 1:419, 431. Page, pp. 85–87, also notes that Norfolk and Suffolk show more ownership by groups of freedmen; one example occurs in the Suffolk *Domesday Book*, ed. Farley and Ellis, Little Domesday (ii), fol. 281-2. There were also different agrarian patterns here (see Loyn, *Anglo-Saxon England*, p. 195, and Hart, *Danelaw*, pp. 70–100). For a discussion of the urban centers in the Danish areas, see Hall, "Five Boroughs of the Danelaw."

55 Æthelred 8.5 and Cnut 1.2, in Liebermann, *Gesetze*.

56 See Barlow, *English Church*, p. 187; Franklin, "Identification of Minsters," pp. 69–72; and Morris, *Church in British Archaeology*, p. 64. A single priest would not have been able to sing the daily routine of the office as done by a collegiate body of clergy in a minster; also, he was prohibited from saying mass alone and would thus have to make sure he had some kind of helper or deacon present.

57 Addleshaw, *Development of the Parochial System*, p. 6.

58 Barlow, *English Church*, p. 159, defines *ecclesia* as an economic entity, that is, as an individual physical church with its lands, rights, privileges, and jurisdiction. Brooke and Keir, *London*, pp. 129–31, define churches in this legal way and see the tithe as central to identifying a parish.

59 II Edgar 2 and I Cnut 11, in Liebermann, *Gesetze*; see also Franklin, "Identification of Minsters," p. 72. Hart, *Danelaw*, p. 5, argues that Edgar's laws are the earliest evidence of church dues reintroduced into the Danelaw.

60 See Morris, *Church in British Archaeology*, p. 62.

61 Ibid., p. 66; Ælfric, Brief I, 43, and Brief II, 177, in *Die Hirtenbriefe Ælfrics*; see below for yearly visitation.

62 II Edgar 2.2, in Liebermann, *Gesetze*; see also Barlow, *English Church*, p. 195.

63 See, for example, VIII Æthelræd 7–15, in Liebermann, *Gesetze*; also Barlow, *English Church*, p. 196.

64 See Addleshaw, *Development of the Parochial System*, pp. 7–8, on commendation.

65 Addleshaw, *Beginnings of the Parochial System*, pp. 3, 10, for continental comparisons. See *The Dialogue of Egbert*, in Hadden and Stubbs, *Councils and Ecclesiastical Documents*, pp. 403–13, on the need for episcopal consent for a priest to serve in a lay-owned church. See Morris, *Church in British Archaeology*, p. 66, on the initiation of the priest by the bishop; on the continent, see Fouracre, "Work of Audoenus," p. 79.

66 On investiture, see Addleshaw, *Development of the Parochial System*, p. 8; on ordination, see the eleventh-century ordination instructions, attributed to Wulfstan, in Whitelock et al., *Councils and Synods*, 1:422–27.

67 Ælfric, Brief I, 73, and Brief II, 207–10, in *Die Hirtenbriefe Ælfrics*; also *The Dialogue of Egbert* in Hadden and Stubbs, *Councils and Ecclesiastical Documents*.

68 One Anglo-Saxon will specifically grants the church to the priest and his issue (*bearntem*): Whitelock, *Anglo-Saxon Wills*, p. 37.

69 Ælfric, *Homilies of Ælfric*, ed. Thorpe, 2:593–95; IV Æthelred 10, in Liebermann, *Gesetze*, on church oppression and simony.

70 An example of this kind of conflict is in the letter of Lanfranc to Stigand, bishop of Chichester, in which he disputes the right of Chichester to direct priests on Lanfranc's lands in Chichester's diocese, except to give them chrism; Lanfranc, *Letters of Lanfranc*, item 30, pp. 116–19. See also Barlow, *English Church*, pp. 249–54.

71 See also the chrism lists of Kent cited above. Dorothy M. Owen, "Episcopal Visitation Books," pp. 185–88, talks about episcopal visitation in the fifteenth to seventeenth centuries, noting that these visits became common in the thirteenth century.

72 William of Malmesbury's *Life of Saint Wulstan*, p. 78, and St. Swithun in Malmesbury's *De Gesta Pontificum Anglorum*, pp. 161–62. Aidan, as noted above, was a migratory bishop in Bede's account of him. Fouracre, "Work of Audoenus," pp. 90–91, also notes how exemplary some of the continental bishops were in this respect.

73 Ayer, "Church Councils," pp. 101–3. See Ælfric, Brief III, 1–10, in *Die Hirtenbriefe Ælfrics*, where he links synods and the chrism; and Canons of Edgar, 3–6, in Wulfstan, *Wulfstan's Canons*.

74 Also, there is an increasing tendency for lay persons to donate churches to a minster that would then take charge of its priest: Sawyer, *Charters*, no. 1234,

printed in Robertson, Charters, no. 116; see also Dorothy Owen, "Documentary Sources for the Building History of Churches in the Middle Ages," in Addyman and Morris, Archaeological Study, pp. 21–25.

75 Whitelock et al., Councils and Synods, 1:424–25.

76 Ælfric, Brief III, 78–82, in Die Hirtenbriefe Ælfrics, indicates that a priest should take on someone to train—not a son unrightly begotten. See Ælfric, Brief III, 182, 190–92, in Die Hirtenbriefe Ælfrics, on helping teach one another.

77 On the seven levels, see Ælfric, Brief I, 29–45, and Brief II, 99–116, in Die Hirtenbriefe Ælfrics. The prohibition against saying mass alone is in Brief III, 78–84.

78 Barlow, English Church, pp. 189–90, 199–200.

79 Canons of Edgar, 32 (in Wulfstan, Wulfstan's Canons); Deanesly, Sidelights, pp. 61–62. See some of the lists of books in Sawyer, Charters, no. 1448, printed in Robertson, Charters, no. 39, and see also no. 109 in Robertson (no Sawyer no.); see Lapidge, "Surviving Booklists." Ælfric, Brief I, 52–53, and Brief II, 157, list the books every priest should have; Brief I, 54–60, lists the proper utensils and their care (in Die Hirtenbriefe Ælfrics).

80 See Wulfstan's Institutes of Polity, 102–3, in Wulfstan, Die "Institutes," p. 85; and Ælfric, Homilies of Ælfric, ed. Thorpe, 1:207.

81 Ælfric, Homilies of Ælfric, ed. Thorpe, 2:533.

82 Whitelock et al., Councils and Synods, 1:422–27; Ælfric, Brief III, 182, 190–92, in Die Hirtenbriefe Ælfrics.

83 Moore, "Family, Community, and Cult," p. 68; note the prevalence of the term cleanliness in Ælfric and Wulfstan's writings about priests and celibacy.

84 Ælfric, Brief I, 74–82; Brief II, 183–205; and Brief III, 187–188, in Die Hirtenbriefe Ælfrics; Canons of Edgar, 14–20, 59, 65, in Wulfstan, Wulfstan's Canons; William of Malmesbury, Life of Saint Wulstan, p. 81.

85 Canons of Edgar, 61, 68, in Wulfstan, Wulfstan's Canons; VI Æthelræd 5, VIII Æthelræd 28, and following, in Liebermann, Gesetze.

86 For Ælfric's letters to Wulfgeat, Sigeweard, and Sigefyrth, see Ælfric, Angelsachsische Homilien und Heiligenleben. For Wulfstan, see the prologues to the laws of Æthelræd and Cnut, in Liebermann, Gesetze.

87 IV Æthelred 10; VI Æthelred 42; VIII Æthelred 1, 35; and I Cnut 2, in Liebermann, Gesetze.

88 Canons of Edgar, 56, in Wulfstan, Wulfstan's Canons; Ælfric, Brief I, 68, in Die Hirtenbriefe Ælfrics. See Barlow, English Church, pp. 200–205, on the proprietor's use of church revenues.

89 Sawyer, Charters, no. 566, printed in Robertson, Charters, no. 30.

90 Barlow, English Church, pp. 186–87, 206.

91 Darby, Domesday England, p. 75; Lennard, Rural England, p. 329; Stenton, Anglo-Saxon England, p. 152; Lennard, "Economic Position of Villani."

92 See the Rectitudines in Thorpe, Ancient Laws and Institutes, p. 185; Loyn, Anglo-Saxon England, pp. 266–67. Addleshaw, Development of the Parochial System, p. 15, claims that

the rent was usually monetary, although sometimes services. On variation in the glebe, see Darby, *Domesday England*, pp. 74–75; Stenton, *Anglo-Saxon England*, p. 152; and Campbell, "Church in Anglo-Saxon Towns," p. 130.

93 VI Æthelred 42, I Cnut 21, in Liebermann, *Gesetze*.

94 Canons of Edgar, 6, in Wulfstan, *Wulfstan's Canons*; also, see *Blickling Homilies*, pp. 42–43.

95 See Wulfstan's Institutes of Polity, in Wulfstan, *Die "Institutes"* VII; Thorpe, *Ancient Laws and Institutes*, 2:426–27. Barlow, *English Church*, p. 207, notes that the reformers were much more interested in rebuking lazy priests than oppressive proprietors.

96 On village churches, see Lennard, *Rural England*, pp. 288–338.

97 Moore, "Family, Community, and Cult," p. 65; Ælfric, *Homilies of Ælfric*, ed. Thorpe, 1:371. On the power of the mass because it joins heaven and earth, see also *EH*, 4:22, in which Bede repeats a popular story about a prisoner's chains falling off whenever mass is sung for him. See also Gregory the Great's *Dialogues*, for example 2:24, where the consecrated host keeps a young monk's body safely interred.

98 See Ælfric, Brief I, Brief II, and Brief III, in *Die Hirtenbriefe Ælfrics*, and Wulfstan, *Wulfstan's Canons of Edgar* and his Institutes of Polity in *Die "Institutes,"* all of which emphasize liturgical etiquette—they feel compelled to stress the fine details of caring for the Eucharist.

99 I Cnut 4, in Liebermann, *Gesetze*.

100 Ælfric, Brief I, 40–41, and Brief II, 109, in *Die Hirtenbriefe Ælfrics*.

101 On the local church as central, see Moore, "Family, Community, and Cult," pp. 56–57, and Rodwell, *Archaeology*, p. 43. On the strength of communal bonds, see the arguments of Reynolds, *Kingdoms and Communities*, and Blair, *Minsters and Parish Churches*.

102 Rodwell, *Archaeology*, pp. 140, 142. In one case the lord's hall moved to a new building, leaving the older building to the church.

103 See Bettey, *Community*, pp. 12–13, citing an early life of St. Dunstan. *Vita Dunstani*, a Saxon priest wrote c. 1000; see *Memorials of St. Dunstan*.

104 Barlow, *English Church*, p. 186.

105 Illustrations based on Rodwell, *Archaeology*, pp. 62, 109, and Taylor, "Position of the Altar." See also Taylor and Taylor, *Anglo-Saxon Architecture*, 3:970, and Platt, *Parish Churches*, pp. 13–19.

106 Rodwell, *Archaeology*, pp. 123–24, discusses reclamation of original wall paintings.

107 Platt, *Parish Churches*, p. 13. Brooke and Keir, *London*, p. 141, have noticed that the many parishes in London in late Anglo-Saxon England were mostly dedicated to English and Viking saints, showing the direction of popular devotion.

108 For example, St. Ninian's well in Northumbria predates Christianity. See *The Anglo-Saxons* (CD-Rom); Gribben, *Holy Wells*, pp. 15–20.

109 Ælfric, Brief III, 115, in *Die Hirtenbriefe Ælfrics*; Canons of Edgar, 26–27, 42, in

Wulfstan, *Wulfstan's Canons*; Morris, Church in British Archaeology, p. 5, discusses archaeological evidence for such uses; Campbell, "Church in Anglo-Saxon Towns," pp. 128–29.

110 Moore, "Family, Community, and Cult," p. 61; Canons of Edgar, 55–57, in Wulfstan, *Wulfstan's Canons*.

111 Ælfric, Brief I, Brief II, and Brief III, in Die Hirtenbriefe Ælfrics.

112 Ælfric, Brief III, 110, in ibid.

113 Ælfric, Brief III, 2–10, in ibid., and Canons of Edgar, 69, in Wulfstan, *Wulfstan's Canons*.

114 Ælfric, Brief I, 133–49, and Brief III, 86–92, in Die Hirtenbriefe Ælfrics; Canons of Edgar, 38, in Wulfstan, *Wulfstan's Canons*.

115 See Ælfric, Brief I, 84–92, and Brief II, 178–82, in Die Hirtenbriefe Ælfrics.

116 See Frantzen, Literature of Penance.

117 Ælfric, Homilies of Ælfric, ed. Thorpe, 1:3–9, 2:315, 343, 531. Gatch, Preaching and Theology, pp. 119–20, sees this preaching emphasis for clergy as unique to Ælfric.

118 Ælfric, Brief I, 61, in Die Hirtenbriefe Ælfrics; Blickling Homilies, pp. 44–47; Canons of Edgar, 52, in Wulfstan, *Wulfstan's Canons*.

119 Canons of Edgar, 17, in Wulfstan, *Wulfstan's Canons*; Ælfric, Homilies of Ælfric, ed. Thorpe, 2:605, on Pater noster and Creed.

Chapter Three

1 For a survey of this period, see P. A. Stafford, "Church and Society in the Age of Ælfric," in Szarmach and Huppe, Old English Homily, pp. 11–42.

2 In Miracles and the Medieval Mind, pp. 3–19, Benedicta Ward demonstrated that an Augustinian worldview, essentially Platonic, prevailed in western Christendom until the emergence of scholastic philosophy. For a succinct and penetrating insight on the early medieval mindset as opposed to that which emerged in the twelfth century, see Bynum, Jesus as Mother, p. 12; see also Erickson's Medieval Vison for a perceptive study of the medieval mentality. For a discussion of Augustine's views on magic and the supernatural, primarily in The City of God, as a basis for the Anglo-Saxon views, see Flint, Rise of Magic, pp. 31–34.

3 In his review in Speculum 65 (April 1990): 393, Raymond van Dam used this apt phrase to describe the approach of Giselle de Nie in her book on Gregory of Tours, Views from a Many-Windowed Tower.

4 For a discussion of this model, see Lees, "Working with Patristic Sources," pp. 157–80, esp. p. 163, and Gatch, Preaching and Theology, on Ælfric and Wulfstan.

5 See Gatch, Preaching and Theology, p. 7.

6 Aronstam, "Blickling Homilies."

7 Sermon X, in Blickling Homilies, 1:106–15.

8 For discussion of concepts of apocalypse and millenium, see Landes, "Millenarismus absconditus" and "Sur les traces du Millennium."

9 Blickling Homilies, 1:5–6.

10 Ibid., 1:59–60.

11 See Szarmach, "Vercelli Homilies," and Szarmach's Vercelli Homilies ix–xxiii.

12 For a full analysis of Ælfric and Wulfstan as homilists, see Gatch, Preaching and Theology.

13 On reform, see Darlington, "Ecclesiastical Reform," and Loyn, "Church and State," pp. 94–102.

14 See Wormald, "Uses of Literacy," pp. 108–9.

15 Ælfric, Homilies of Ælfric, ed. Thorpe, 1:3, 2:3, 343, 371.

16 Stanley Greenfield, Critical History, pp. 46–49, and Milton McC. Gatch, "The Achievement of Ælfric and His Colleagues in European Perspective," in Szarmach and Huppe, Old English Homily, p. 60, discuss how Ælfric saw his homilies as catechetical rather than exegetical.

17 Ælfric's letters are available in Ælfric, Angelsachsische Homilien und Heiligenleben; see also James Hurt's biography, Ælfric, pp. 38–40.

18 Ælfric, Homilies of Ælfric, ed. Thorpe, 2:315, 371.

19 Godden, "Ælfric and the Vernacular Prose Tradition," p. 110.

20 Ælfric, Homilies of Ælfric, ed. Thorpe, 2:460; see also 2:520.

21 Ibid., 2:446. Preceding this statement he notes that the story of Job, the subject of the sermon, is deep even for him and thus more so for the unlearned. See also 2:2, 314, 320, 456, 460, 466, for other qualifications he makes about his audience.

22 Ibid., preface, 1:2. Again, in 2:444, he warns about the availability of heretical teachings to ignorant men and warns them to stick to orthodox teachings. According to Godden, "Ælfric and the Vernacular Prose Tradition," pp. 99–102, Ælfric probably was thinking of the Blickling Homilies, and perhaps even the Vercelli.

23 For a discussion of Ælfric's radicalism (in response to Gatch's Preaching and Theology), see John, "World of Abbot Ælfric."

24 For Wulfstan's sermons, see Wulfstan, Homilies of Wulfstan. On Wulfstan's experience in the north, see Whitelock, "Wulfstan at York," "Archbishop Wulfstan," and "Wulfstan and the So-Called Laws." On the relation of Wulfstan's homilies to royal laws, see M. K. Lawson, "Archbishop Wulfstan and the Homiletic Element in the Laws of Æthelred II and Cnut," in Rumble, Reign of Cnut, pp. 141–64. On the impact of the Vikings, see Loyn, Vikings in Britain. See Chapter 2, above, for discussion of the priestly instructions in the Canons of Edgar, attributed to Wulfstan.

25 VII Æthelred, in Whitelock et al., Councils and Synods, 1:379.

26 Wulfstan, Sermo Lupi ad Anglos, ll. 53–62 (pp. 53–54).

27 See Whitelock, "Wulfstan and the Laws of Cnut."

28 Ælfric's three main sources were Gregory the Great's homilies, Bede, and Augustine. See Förster, "Uber de quellen," and White, Ælfric, pp. 185–88. Malcolm Godden (in "Ælfric and the Vernacular Prose Tradition," pp. 102–5) has shown

that he was familiar with Alfred's works, Bede's *Ecclesiastical History*, the Rule of St. Benedict, and the Pseudo-Egberti Penitential as well as the other homilies of which he disapproved. For other sources Ælfric used in particular sermons, see Reinsma's bibliography, *Ælfric*, and the ongoing Sources of Anglo-Saxon Literary Culture project, from which a preliminary study has been issued, Biggs, *Sources of Anglo-Saxon Literary Culture*.

29 Ælfric, Homilies of Ælfric, ed. Thorpe, 1:236. See Bynum, *Resurrection*, pp. 23, 39, 130, for seed metaphors.

30 Vercelli homily XVI also uses a homely Anglo-Saxon analogy to explain the Trinity; see Szarmach, "Vercelli Homilies," pp. 255–56.

31 For a similar view in Africa, see Lienhardt, *Divinity and Experience*, p. 28.

32 Quote from Ælfric, Homilies of Ælfric, ed. Thorpe, 2:232. On within and without, see ibid., 2:268. On *ungesewenlice* and *gesewenlice* and *lichaman* and *gastas*, see ibid., 1:160, 272–76, and Blickling Homilies, 1:20–21. See also Le Goff, "Culture cléricale," p. 785.

33 Ælfric, Homilies of Ælfric, ed. Thorpe, 1:262, 280. See also Blickling Homilies, 1:18–19, 22–23, 50–51, and Die Vercelli Homilen, p. 20.

34 Ælfric, Homilies of Ælfric, ed. Thorpe, 1:102, 276, 286. See Augustine, *Against the Manichees*, 1:16.

35 For examples of this hand of God, see The Canterbury Psalter facsimile, fol. 39b, 44b, 23, 72b, and throughout.

36 Ælfric, Homilies of Ælfric, ed. Thorpe, 1:302, 276. See also Die Vercelli Homilen, pp. 80–81.

37 Ælfric, Homilies of Ælfric, ed. Thorpe, 1:470–72.

38 See especially Augustine, *De civitate dei*, books 21–22. For discussion of Augustine and miracles, see Benedicta Ward, *Miracles and the Medieval Mind*, p. 3; Brown, *Augustine of Hippo*, pp. 413–18; and Van der Meer, *Augustine the Bishop*, pp. 529–57.

39 Caesarius of Heisterbach, Dialogus Miraculorum 10.1: *Miraculum dicimus quicquid fit contra solitum cursum naturae, unde miramur. Secundum causas superiores miraculum nihil est.* See also Gurevich, *Medieval Popular Culture*, p. 205.

40 Benedicta Ward, *Miracles and the Medieval Mind*, pp. 4, 8–9.

41 Ælfric, Homilies of Ælfric, ed. Thorpe, 1:306.

42 Ibid., 1:122, 184–86, 230, 292, 406–8, 2:20–22, 72, 376, 378.

43 Ibid., 1:186. See also examples of *wundor* and *tacn* in Blickling Homilies, 1:16–17 and 2:160–61, where the heavenly mystery is betokened (*tacnath*) in the miracle.

44 Ælfric, Lives of Saints, 1:433, 439, 469.

45 Ælfric, Homilies of Ælfric, ed. Thorpe, 1:184–86. See also Augustine, In Johannes Evangelium, 24.1, in PL 35:1379, and Sermon 130, in PL 38:725–28. Ironically, the discussion that follows of how the five loaves Christ multiplied signified the five books of Moses was marked for omission in a margin note in Ælfric's hand as too tiresome in both books. Thus the miracle as an extended metaphor for Ælfric's hermeneutics was omitted (see Gatch, *Preaching and Theology*, p. 179 n. 32).

See Bynum, *Resurrection*, pp. 101, 126, for discussion of loaves and fishes story in Augustine, Hugh of St. Victor, and Peter Lombard.

46 The analogy of written characters is an interesting insight into medieval illiteracy. For an exploration of changing attitudes toward texts, see Stock, *Implications of Literacy*. For another example of this kind of allegorical reading of miracles as natural, see *Blickling Homilies*, 1:6–7, the description of the miracle of virgin birth as an expansion of the natural process of birth.

47 Ælfric, *Homilies of Ælfric*, ed. Thorpe, 1:292; see also 1:304.

48 Ælfric, *Lives of Saints*, 2:332–35.

49 Ælfric, *Homilies of Ælfric*, ed. Thorpe, 2:130–32; see EH, 1:31.

50 See Douglas's discussion of the similarity and difference between magic and miracle, in *Purity and Danger*, pp. 58–72, and Flint's discussion of Augustine of Hippo's concessions, in *Rise of Magic*, pp. 31–32.

51 For a survey of magic in the Christian worldview of late Antiquity and the Middle Ages, see Kieckhefer, *Magic in the Middle Ages*. On the history of the concept of the Devil, see Jeffrey B. Russell's four-volume series, *The Devil*, *Satan*, *Lucifer*, and *Mephistopheles*.

52 See Augustine, *De civitate dei*, books 8–10, esp. 10:8. The line of writers developing this notion of magic includes Caesarius of Arles, Martin of Braga, Pirmin of Reichenau, Isidore of Seville, Rabanus Maurus, and Gregory the Great. See Flint, *Rise of Magic*, pp. 42–58, for a discussion of these sources.

53 See Meaney, "Ælfric and Idolatry."

54 Ælfric, *Homilies of Ælfric*, ed. Thorpe, 1:556; also 1:342, 348, 540.

55 Ibid., 1:4; see also *Blickling Homilies*, 1:60–61.

56 Ælfric, *Lives of Saints*, 1:470–71. St. Benedict also dissolves such delusions of the Devil, in Gregory the Great, *Dialogues*, 2:10.

57 Ælfric, *Lives of Saints*, 1:373–75 ("On Auguries," based on Augustine's *De auguriis*). Numerous other instances of this argument appear in Christian writings. See, for example, Ambrose's response to Symmachus in the Altar of Victory dispute (in Ambrose, *Letters*, pp. 414–22), and Gregory of Tours's account of Clotild's speech to Clovis about his ineffectual gods (*History of the Franks*, 2:29). See also Ælfric's "De Falsis Diis," in Ælfric, *Homilies of Ælfric*, ed. Pope, 2:676–724.

58 *Prica*, point, can refer to time, perhaps a quarter or a fifth of an hour.

59 Ælfric, *Homilies of Ælfric*, ed. Thorpe, 1:100–102.

60 For a similar section as a source for Ælfric's discussion of the moon and forbidden practices, see Bede, *De Temporibus* 8 (De Saltu Lunae), in Cockayne, *Leechdoms*, 3:210–13.

61 Ælfric, *Homilies of Ælfric*, ed. Thorpe, 1:110.

62 Ælfric, *Lives of Saints*, 1:375; *Blickling Homilies*, 1:46–47, 2:242–43.

63 Valerie Flint refers to "neutral practices" and "a no-man's land" between magic and science (*Rise of Magic*, pp. 321, 323–24); she sees this space a bit more narrowly than described here.

64 *Blickling Homilies*, 1:126–27.

65 Matt. 9:1–8.

66 Ælfric, *Homilies of Ælfric*, ed. Thorpe, 1:470–72.

67 See Kroll and Bachrach, "Sin and the Etiology of Disease" and "Sin and Mental Illness," for persuasive arguments on the complex understanding of disease in early medieval thought. The former article uses a statistical survey of chronicles and saints' lives looking for instances of illness attributed to sin; the authors find only 19 percent fall into this category, implying a recognition of natural causes in the other 81 percent.

68 Ælfric, "Passion of St. Bartholomew," in Ælfric, *Homilies of Ælfric*, ed. Thorpe, 1:474–75, in which he cites the example of Jesus healing the man who was born blind not through sin but to demonstrate Christ's healing power.

69 Ælfric, "On Auguries," in *Lives of Saints*, 1:376–77; see also Ælfric, *Homilies of Ælfric*, ed. Thorpe, 1:474.

70 Ælfric, *Lives of Saints*, 1:378–79; see also 1:368–69.

71 Ælfric, *Homilies of Ælfric*, ed. Thorpe, 1:474–76. See also Augustine, *De doctrina christiana*, 2:29, in PL 34:15, and Flint, *Rise of Magic*, pp. 301, 309.

72 Thorpe, *Ancient Laws and Institutes*, p. 371, translated from the Anglo-Saxon and the Latin. The most notable extremists against charms are the sixth-century Saint Eligius (see Grendon, "Anglo-Saxon Charms," p. 143) and Burchard of Worms in his Decretum (see Penitentials, *Medieval Handbooks of Penance*, pp. 41–42).

73 Ælfric, *Lives of Saints*, 1:369.

74 Ælfric, *Homilies of Ælfric*, ed. Thorpe, 1:304.

75 Ibid., 2:268–72.

76 Ibid., 2:356–58.

77 Ibid., 2:268–70.

Chapter Four

1 See below under "Historiography" for a discussion of Grendon, Storms, and Grattan and Singer.

2 For *galdor*, see Bosworth and Toller, *Anglo-Saxon Dictionary* and *The Dictionary of Old English*, currently under production at Toronto's Centre for Medieval Studies. One hint that the text retains its orality is in the lay "With Færstice," below. The scribe wrote without poetic breaks; however, lines breaking the text have been inserted, although not always according to our sense of Anglo-Saxon poetic rules. Nonetheless, the fact that someone marked the text in this way indicates some thought for oral use (Storms, *Anglo-Saxon Magic*, pp. 141–44). On runes, see Gale R. Owen, *Rites and Religions*, pp. 52–58, and R. I. Page, *Introduction to English Runes*.

3 On speech acts, see Noth, "Semiotics," p. 62; Nelson, "Woman's Charm," p. 4; and Nelson, " 'Wordsige and Worcsige,' " p. 57.

4 Grendon, "Anglo-Saxon Charms," pp. 110, 123–24.

5 Storms, *Anglo-Saxon Magic*, p. 129.

6 Cameron, *Anglo-Saxon Medicine*, pp. 130–31, 158.

7 On defining the concept behind the word *superstition*, see Jeffrey B. Russell, *History of Witchcraft*, p. 12.

8 See discussion in Chapter 1, above, of work by Gurevich, Neusner, Tambiah, and Kieckhefer.

9 The exceptions are Woden, who is named in one charm, *Lacnunga* LXXX (45), and the Æsir (as the evil attackers) in *Lacnunga* CXXXIV–V (75–76), "With Færstice," both discussed below.

10 Noth, "Semiotics," pp. 75, 79 n. 24, in which he notes that the laws condemn only magic of the symbolic (with heathen references) type, not the indexical or iconic types.

11 On the eight Anglo-Saxon physicians, see Kealey, *Medieval Medicus*, pp. 31–33; also Talbot and Hammond, *Medical Practitioners*, and Stanley Rubin, "Anglo-Saxon Physician," in Deegan and Scragg, *Medicine in Early Medieval England*, pp. 7–15. On women, medicine, and magic, see Meaney, "Women, Witchcraft, and Magic," and Anthony Davies, "Witches in Anglo-Saxon England," in Scragg, *Superstition*, pp. 41–56; see also Fell, *Women in Anglo-Saxon England*, pp. 29–30. On evidence of monastic medicine in the early Middle Ages, see Pinto, "Medical Science and Superstition," and Kroll and Bachrach, "Monastic Medicine."

12 Major studies in this field include Cameron, *Anglo-Saxon Medicine*; Rubin, *Medieval English Medicine*; Grattan and Singer, *Anglo-Saxon Magic*; Talbot, *Medicine in Medieval England*; Bonser, *Medical Background*; Singer, *From Magic to Science*; and Payne, *English Medicine*. For a survey text on medieval medicine, see Siraisi, *Medieval and Early Renaissance Medicine*. Recent reinterpretation of Anglo-Saxon medicine indicates a knowledge of skills predating the famous Salnertian school (Kealey, *Medieval Medicus*, p. 4, and Rubin, *Medieval English Medicine*, pp. 58–59). While scholars such as Rubin (*Medieval English Medicine*, pp. 46–47) assert that the herbal illustrations were merely drawing exercises with no relationship to actual herbs, Voigts ("Anglo-Saxon Plant Remedies") and Cameron (*Anglo-Saxon Medicine*, p. 64) persuasively demonstrate that the medical texts were for practical use and that the practitioners understood and used the herbal information.

13 See Charles Singer's introduction to the 1961 edition of Cockayne, *Leechdoms*, pp. xlv–xlvi, and Grattan and Singer, *Anglo-Saxon Magic*, pp. 6, 93, on the degradation of classical science into superstition, and religion into magic; see also Kitson, "From Eastern Learning," p. 58, on popular and learned categories.

14 The *Anglo Saxon Herbal* or *The Herbarium of Apuleius Platonicus*, MS Cotton Vitellius C. III, London; MS Hatton 76, Oxford, is a Christian translation of the fifth-century Latin *Herbarium of Apuleius* and is dated around 1000 (Rubin, *Medieval English Medicine*, pp. 45–46). A supplement to the herbal, the *Medicina de Quadrupedibus*, is another translation from a Latin text, this one attributed to Sextus Placitus (Rubin, *Medieval English Medicine*, p. 50). Both texts are available in an edi-

tion by de Vriend, *The Old English Herbarium and Medicina de Quadrupedibus* (EETS, o.s. 286).

15 Also called *Schools of Medicine*, found in MS Harley 6258, London (Rubin, *Medieval English Medicine*, p. 45).

16 Grattan and Singer, *Anglo-Saxon Magic*, pp. 39–40; see also Singer and Singer, "Unrecognized Anglo-Saxon Medical Text." The *Handbook of Byrhtferth* (Oxford, St. John's College MS 17) is printed in Cockayne, *Leechdoms*, and in a critical edition, *Byrhtferth's Manual*, edited by Crawford.

17 See Kitson, "From Eastern Learning," for an analysis of how classical traditions might have entered Anglo-Saxon medical knowledge. See Lapidge, "Surviving Booklists," pp. 118–19, 147–48, for vague references to medical books in the collections at Winchester and Bury St. Edmunds.

18 Both texts with parallel translation can be found conveniently in Cockayne's three-volume *Leechdoms*, but his edition is out of date. Günther Leonhardi issued a critical edition of the *Leechbook*, *Lacnunga*, and the *Loricas* in 1905. The *Leechbook* is available in facsimile, *Bald's Leechbook* edited by Wright. Marilyn Deegan at Oxford is currently working on a computer edition of the *Leechbook*. Grattan and Singer produced a critical edition of the *Lacnunga* in *Anglo-Saxon Magic*. The *Lacnunga* will hereafter be cited in the text followed by the Roman numeral used by Grattan and Singer (with Cockayne's Arabic number in parentheses). The *Leechbook* will hereafter be cited in the text followed by the book number in Roman numerals and the remedy number (e.g., I:lv), sometimes followed by an Arabic numeral showing further subdivisions of the text.

19 For discussions of *Leechbook* composition, see *Bald's Leechbook*, ed. Wright, pp. 14–15; Cameron, "Sources," p. 147, and *Anglo-Saxon Medicine*, pp. 35–45, 74–99; Singer, *From Magic to Science*, p. 137; Ker, *Catalogue*, pp. 332–33; Meaney, "Variant Versions," pp. 250–51; and Adams and Deegan, "Bald's Leechbook," pp. 87–89. Flint, *Rise of Magic*, p. 313 n. 167, suggests "pastoral use" for the *Leechbook*. The dedication at the end of Book II says *Bald habet hunc librum cild quem conscribere jussit*.

20 Grattan and Singer, *Anglo-Saxon Magic*, p. 15.

21 Ibid., pp. 15–21. See also Meaney, "Variant Versions," pp. 255–56, on a single scribal hand.

22 See Meaney, "Variant Versions," pp. 255–64, for a discussion of the compilation of these two works and for parallel remedies.

23 On this scale, see Grattan and Singer, *Anglo-Saxon Magic*, p. 92, and Singer, *From Magic to Science*, p. 135, who put the *Lacnunga* at the opposite pole from the scholarly texts. Talbot, *Medicine in Medieval England*, pp. 18–23, touts the too-neglected *Leechbook* as representing the height of medical knowledge and regards the *Lacnunga* as atypical of Anglo-Saxon scholarship and learning, attributing its degeneracy to the effects of the Danish invasions.

24 See Kroll and Bachrach, "Sin and the Etiology of Disease" and "Sin and Mental Illness," for discussions of disease causation. For different categories of how such medicine or magic works, see Grattan and Singer, *Anglo-Saxon Magic*, p. 3;

Noth, "Semiotics," p. 66; Grendon, "Anglo-Saxon Charms," p. 110; and Bonser, *Medical Background*, pp. 213–54.

25 Grattan and Singer, *Anglo-Saxon Magic*, pp. 196–97.

26 For stanching blood, see Leechbook I:ix. For the herb *ælfthone*, see elf remedies in Chapter 5, below.

27 Pliny, *Naturalis Historia*, 1:xxii.1, cited in Grattan and Singer, *Anglo-Saxon Magic*, p. 55.

28 Melitta Weiss-Amer (Modern Languages and Literatures, University of Western Ontario), "*Cibus Medicinalis*: The Link between Food and Drugs in the Middle Ages" (paper given at the Medieval Association of the Pacific annual conference, Davis, Calif., March 1–3, 1991).

29 See Singer and Singer, "Unrecognized Anglo-Saxon Medical Text," pp. 141, 148; Noth, "Semiotics," pp. 67–68; and Nelson, "Sound as Meaning," pp. 122–24.

30 For example, *Lacnunga* XXIX (11), discussed below. See also Grattan and Singer, *Anglo-Saxon Magic*, pp. 31–34.

31 *Lacnunga* CLXIX (103). See below for a discussion of "I" formulas as a kind of mana.

32 Leechbook I:lxviii.

33 See Grendon, "Anglo-Saxon Charms," pp. 157–59, for a discussion of narrative charms with examples.

34 Cross, "Aspects of Microcosm and Macrocosm."

35 Grattan and Singer, *Anglo-Saxon Magic*, pp. 39–40, and figs. 9, 14–16. See Singer and Singer, "Unrecognized Anglo-Saxon Medical Text," for an analysis of the Byrhtferth diagram, and Grattan and Singer, *Anglo-Saxon Magic*, p. 55, for the classical seven spheres.

36 See Cross, "Aspects of Microcosm and Macrocosm," pp. 1–2; Gregory the Great, *Moralium Libri*, VI.c.xvi, in PL 75:740; and Ælfric, *Homilies of Ælfric*, ed. Thorpe, 1:302.

37 The full title is *De Observation Lunae et quid cavendum sit, de somniorum eventu*, with the original in Anglo-Saxon, printed by Cockayne, *Leechdoms*, 3:152–54; see comments by Singer in his introduction to Cockayne, *Leechdoms*, 1:xxiv–xxv. The document also includes information on moon phases related to dream interpretation and birthdays.

38 *Lacnunga* CLXXXIX (117–18), specifying the last Monday in April and the first Mondays of August and January. References to such computations can be found throughout the *Lacnunga* and in the *Handbook of Byrhtferth*. See also Rubin, *Medieval English Medicine*, p. 64.

39 Computational skills and the development of calendars constitute another field of study, manifested here in the connection between medicine and liturgy. Astronomical observations, the computation of Easter and other holidays seen in Bede, Ælfric's discussion of the moon's effects on the earth, and the computation of days for bloodletting were all interrelated skills of the literate. For a discussion of early medieval numeracy, see Murray, *Reason and Society*, pp. 141–61.

40 See, for example, the Irish *Stowe Missal* (early ninth century), which influenced English practice.

41 For a survey of medieval liturgical history, see Vogel, *Medieval Liturgy*.

42 On Anglo-Saxon liturgical texts, see Gneuss, "Liturgical Books in Anglo-Saxon England," and Dumville, *Liturgy*.

43 For a discussion of instructions and other records in the margins, see Gatch, "Old English Literature and the Liturgy," and Dumville, *Liturgy*, pp. 119–23, 127–32.

44 For discussions of these manuscripts, see R. I. Page, "Old English Liturgical Rubrics"; Grant, *Cambridge, Corpus Christi College 41*; Conner, *Anglo-Saxon Exeter*, p. 3 (on the Exeter origins of MS 41, Corpus Christi College); Dumville, *Liturgy*, pp. 70, 72; and Flint, *Rise of Magic*, p. 319.

45 MS Bodley 579, Oxford; critical edition is *Leofric Missal*, ed. Warren. See Conner, *Anglo-Saxon Exeter*, pp. 18–19, and Dumville, *Liturgy*, p. 82, for a discussion of its complex history. See Chapter 5, below, for examples of *Leofric Missal* similarities to medical manuscripts.

46 See "The Liturgy and Ritual of the Anglo-Saxon Church" for an outdated response to the "objectionable" additions in the form of exorcisms and prayers to saints, and Hohler, "Some Service Books of the Later Saxon Church," pp. 71–72, for some rude remarks on the state of late Saxon clergy and the liturgy.

47 See Dumville's remarks, *Liturgy*, pp. 136–38, for a different way of looking at these texts.

48 For the Augustinian background to this practice, see Van der Meer, *Augustine the Bishop*, pp. 527–30; see also Flint's discussion, *Rise of Magic*, pp. 303–4.

49 See Grattan and Singer, *Anglo-Saxon Magic*, p. 7, on the *Lacnunga*, and p. 9 and Singer, *From Magic to Science*, p. 135, on the survivability of magic as opposed to religion.

50 *Lacnunga* LXXXI (45) for "I blow this poison away"; *Leofric Missal*, ed. Warren, esp. p. 235, for exorcisms of salt and oil, anomalies of English liturgy noted by the missal's editor.

51 See Douglas, *Purity and Danger*, pp. 59–60, on magic, miracle, and mana; on mana in Anglo-Saxon culture, see Magoun, "Survivals of Pagan Belief," and Glosecki, *Shamanism*. The use of *mana* to describe certain European practices, in comparison to the imposition of European notions of magic on Polynesian and other societies, reflects the aphorism "turnabout is fair play."

52 Grattan and Singer, *Anglo-Saxon Magic*, p. 197, label this remedy "a Semi-Pagan-Christianized Rite for Heartache." The gender is unclear here, as virgin (*mæden man*) could refer to a celibate man or woman who knew the Creed and Pater noster.

53 See Grattan and Singer, *Anglo-Saxon Magic*, pp. 184–85, for comments on this charm. A blank space after "Nine were" was filled in by a later hand with "for churnels." Grattan and Singer speculate that some, perhaps pagan, words

were omitted in that half-line. Some scholars treat "node" as a proper name ("Nothe"), an unsubstaniated speculation.

54 According to the *Oxford English Dictionary*, the word *gibberish* and its root, *gibber*, first appear in the sixteenth century as a type of onomatopoeia. See also Cameron, *Anglo-Saxon Medicine*, p. 139.

55 John Chrysostom, *From the Exposition of Psalm XLI* (PG, 55:155–59); translation in Strunk, *Source Readings in Music History*, p. 69: "Even though the meaning of the words be unknown to you, teach your mouth to utter them meanwhile. For the tongue is made holy by the words when they are uttered with a ready and eager mind."

56 See *Lacnunga* LXIII (29), XC (53), and *Leechbook* I:xlv.5. Cockayne, *Leechdoms*, 3:10 n. 1, gives a similar passage from MS Bodley 163, f. 227 (also cited by Grattan and Singer, *Anglo-Saxon Medicine*, p. 106 n. 5).

57 Storms, *Anglo-Saxon Magic*, p. 302.

58 For an example of the use of the Trinity reference, see *Lacnunga* XXV (9).

59 Cockayne and Leonhardi write these as three capital letters, alpha, C, and D; Storms, *Anglo-Saxon Magic*, pp. 258–59, has alpha and omega. Given the context of the passage quoted, and the way the so-called C is half-formed and connected closely to the supposed D, I think Storms is right. In the next two remedies (*Leechbook* I:lxiv and lxv, both discussed in Chapter 5, below) garbled Greek writing also appears, including an alpha and an O representing, presumably, omega. Thus it is unclear whether the W-shaped omega was known to the scribe. See the facsimile by Wright, fols. 51a and 52b. Alpha and omega (W) appear in the *Lacnunga* LXXXVII–III. Also, Grattan and Singer, *Anglo-Saxon Magic*, pp. 49–50, mention an instance of mistranscribed Greek in which *co* was used for omega.

60 John 1:1–3. *Hoc* (He) is neuter, referring to *verbum*.

61 See Chapter 3, above, and Ælfric, *Homilies of Ælfric*, ed. Thorpe, 2:269–73.

62 Grattan and Singer, *Anglo-Saxon Magic*, pp. 202–5.

63 Ibid., pp. 45, 203 n. 2.

64 See Cockayne, *Leechdoms*, 3:79 n. 1.

65 Studies in anthropology, religion, and folklore since the 1950s question the identification of magic with manipulation and prayer with supplication prominent in the work of Tylor, Frazer, and other nineteenth century theorists (see criticism of this model by Wax and Wax, "Magical World View," pp. 179–88, and Pettersson, "Magic-Religion," pp. 109–19, and Tambiah, *Magic, Science, Religion*, pp. 42–64, who gives a fascinating survey of Ludwig Wittgenstein's reading of Frazer). Keith Thomas notes the distinction, its rejection by modern anthropologists, but then proceeds to use it as a way of showing how the medieval church weakened the distinction, already blurry in the popular mind, between prayer and charm (Thomas, *Religion*, pp. 41–42). Certainly Christian theology viewed prayer as a request, not a coercive demand; however, at the

same time, Christian ritual asserted that the prayers of the priest in his official capacity had the power to transform bread and wine. Likewise, the ritual of exorcism is "coercive" in calling on God's divine power to drive out demons before baptizing a person or sanctifying an object. The same is true of prayers of blessing said over food. How are these prayers, where divine answer is assumed, different from liturgical cures, in which the illness is perceived to be caused by invisible agencies who can be commanded through the power of God? Did not the disciples exhibit the same coercive power as Jesus in driving out demons?

66 Peter Brown, "Sorcery, Demons, and the Rise of Christianity: From Late Antiquity into the Middle Ages," in his *Religion and Society.*

67 See *Lacnunga* LXXI–LXXVII (37–43) for a series of *theor* or dry disease remedies (bronchial trouble?). *Lacnunga* CLXXVIII (111), "The Prescription of Arestolobius," contains a cure for a long list of ailments including dry disease and "for every infirmity and every temptation of the fiend." See *Lacnunga* CXXXIII and *Leechbook* II:lxiv for flying venom. For the association of fever with delusions, see *Leechbook* II:lxiv.

68 Cattle theft charms were popular. See, for example, MS CCC 41 marginalia, in Cockayne, *Leechdoms,* 1:385, 391–93, and *Lacnunga* CLVIII (91).

69 In their analysis of the layers in the *Lacnunga,* Grattan and Singer conclude that the more "pagan" charms (those without Christian elements) indicate an ignorant, possibly not quite Christian compiler (*Anglo-Saxon Magic,* pp. 7, 15–22).

70 On the four Germanic or "Teutonic" elements, see Grattan and Singer, *Anglo-Saxon Magic,* p. 52; Singer, *From Magic to Science,* p. 149; and Bonser, *Medical Background,* p. 43.

71 Cockayne, *Leechdoms,* has the two lays as one remedy (45); Grattan and Singer's critical edition in *Anglo-Saxon Magic* splits the two, unnecessarily putting the word *Pagan* in the title of the first.

72 It occurs after a series of charms for "dry" diseases; immediately preceding and following it are remedies for "fig" swellings—i.e., hemorrhoids. The fig remedy following the lay is also for worms, *Lacnunga* LXXXIII (47).

73 As Grattan and Singer (*Anglo-Saxon Magic*) note, these two herbs, missing from the lay above, are the only two listed in Latin and the only two with Christian elements. Clearly, this remedy was still in a process of transformation.

74 This line (fol. 162a, l. 43) is problematic; see Grattan and Singer, *Anglo-Saxon Magic,* p. 154.

75 Grattan and Singer, *Anglo-Saxon Magic,* separate the following section into yet another lay, entitled "Pagan Lay of the Magic Blasts" (p. 155).

76 *Crist stod ofer alde / ængan cundes.* Editors propose widely variant readings of this line, emending *alde* (old) to *adle* (poison) and reading *ængan cundes* as "of every kind" (Grendon) or "in a way that is unique" (Bosworth and Toller, *Anglo-Saxon Dictionary, Supplement*). Thus it is unclear whether Christ stood over various

poisons, over some old malicious beings, or in some unique fashion over everything.

77 See *Leechbook* I:xlv.5, lxxii, II:lxiv.

78 Grattan and Singer, *Anglo-Saxon Magic*, p. 173 n. 1.

79 See Chapter 3, above, for a discussion of this rule from the *Penitential of Egbert*.

80 *Leechbook* III:lxii uses *draconzan* (discussed in Chapter 5, below); the *Anglo-Saxon Herbal* XV (Cockayne, *Leechdoms*, 1:107) identifies this gem as *dracentse* or *dracontea*, linked to dragon's blood and effective against snake wounds and for broken bones. Pliny's *Natural History* (*Naturalis Historia*, xxxvii, 57) recounts how the gem is taken from a live dragon's brain (see Thorndike, *History of Magic*, 1:75).

81 The context of these remedies in the *Lacnunga* indicates a number of associations: scrofula, hemorrhoids, insects, toothache, migraine headaches, and demon possession. See Bonser, *Medical Background*, pp. 277–81, for a discussion of the worm, and Pinto, "Medical Science and Superstition," for migraine. For toothache, see *Lacnunga* XXII (8) and Storms, *Anglo-Saxon Magic*, pp. 297–99. Herbs used for treating worms are discussed by Brian Moffat, "Investigations into Medieval Medical Practice: The Remnants of Some Herbal Treatments, on Archaeological Sites and in Archives," in Deegan and Scragg, *Medicine in Early Medieval England*, pp. 33–40.

Chapter Five

1 Stuart, "Anglo-Saxon Elf," pp. 314, 316; Grattan and Singer, *Anglo-Saxon Magic*, pp. 59–60. On the positive meaning of *ælf*, see Stuart, "Meaning of Old English Ælfsciene." See also Peters, "OE Ælf, -Ælf, Ælfen, -Ælfen."

2 See Bosworth and Toller, *Anglo-Saxon Dictionary*, p. 14, under *ælf*. These compounds are akin to, or translations of, the various kinds of nymphs found in classical literature, according to Somner's *Dictionarium*.

3 Davidson, *Myths and Symbols in Pagan Europe*, pp. 105–6.

4 Snorri Sturluson, *Prose Edda*, p. 44.

5 Ibid., p. 46.

6 See also Flint's speculations on elfshot as airborne disease, in *Rise of Magic*, pp. 115, 165.

7 *Leechbook* III:lxii–lxiii.

8 Singer, *From Magic to Science*, pp. 153–54; Stuart, "Anglo-Saxon Elf," p. 313; Bonser, *Medical Background*, p. 164. Dwarves are a related phenomenon (see Grattan and Singer, *Anglo-Saxon Magic*, p. 61). For revisions on the identification of spiders and dwarves, see Nelson, "An Old English Charm against Nightmare," and Stuart, "Spider in Old English."

9 *Heahhiolothe* is glossed by Cockayne, *Leechdoms*, and Bosworth and Toller, *Anglo-Saxon Dictionary*, as elecampane, or *hinnula helenium* in the *Anglo-Saxon Herbal*, where

it is translated as Anglo-Saxon *spere wyrte* or spearwort; see also Bierbaumer, *Der botanische*, 1:79, 83–84. The Latin *helenium* also appears as an herb in several preparations. See Grattan and Singer, *Anglo-Saxon Magic*, pp. 85–86, for the difficulties in identifying *ælfthone* and their rejection of Cockayne's "romantic" translation of it as "enchanter's nightshade." See Bierbaumer, *Der botanische*, 1:9–10, for the etymology of *ælfthone*. See Grattan and Singer, *Anglo-Saxon Magic*, pp. 90–91, for a discussion of the confusions associated with these generally fruitless attempts to identify herbs.

10 Ælfric, *Ælfric's Grammatik und Glossar*, includes feverfew, waybread, fennel, lupin, bishopwort, pennyroyal, rue, mugwort, and wormwood. The *Anglo-Saxon Herbal* or *Herbarium Apuleius*, in Cockayne, *Leechdoms*, vol. 1, includes feverfew, waybread, fennel, bishopwort, attorlathe, pennyroyal, rue, mugwort, wormwood, and elecampane, among other less prominent herbs, in these remedies.

11 I have used bishopwort for Anglo-Saxon *bisceopwyrt* and betony for Latin *betonica*. For all fifty-three instances of *bisceopwyrt* in the *Leechbook*, see Bierbaumer, *Der botanische*, 1:19.

12 Cockayne, *Leechdoms*, 1:70.

13 On libcorn, see Grattan and Singer, *Anglo-Saxon Magic*, p. 117; on dill, see pp. 89–90.

14 See Storms, *Anglo-Saxon Magic*, p. 246, on the two ways of getting rid of elves. Other useful studies of elf remedies include Thun, "Malignant Elves"; Bonser, "Magical Practices against Elves"; and Remly, "Magic, Myth, and Medicine," which connects elf attacks on animals with colic.

15 Jeffrey B. Russell, *Lucifer*, pp. 62–158.

16 For a discussion of this manuscript, see Gibson et al., *Eadwine Psalter*. For the manuscript facsimile, see *Canterbury Psalter*. For a description of the manuscript's provenance, see Kauffmann, *Romanesque Manuscripts*, item 68.

17 See Ohlgren, *Insular and Anglo-Saxon Illuminated Manuscripts*, and his iconographic index (also available electronically in a hypertext version as *Corpus*).

18 See fol. 5b for the black, monstrous demons.

19 For comparable pictures, none quite so clear as this one, see the following folios with illustrations representing demons: 10, 11b, 43b, 46b, 235b, and 244b. For similar-looking angels, see fol. 14b. For uglier demons, see fols. 152, 246, 251b, and 263. Neither the Utrecht Psalter nor the early eleventh-century Harley 603 version shows these beings in the same way the Canterbury Psalter does. In MS Harley 603, fol. 22, the figures appear as seminaked winged demons with few if any facial features. For a facsimile of the Utrecht, see *Utrecht-Psalter*, ed. Horst and Engelbregt. For the Harley manuscript, see descriptions in Ohlgren, *Insular and Anglo-Saxon Illuminated Manuscripts*, p. 169, and Temple, *Anglo-Saxon Manuscripts*, pp. 81–83.

20 Grattan and Singer, *Anglo-Saxon Magic*, p. 60 and frontispiece illustration; Cameron, *Anglo-Saxon Medicine*, p. 142.

21 References to the *Lacnunga* are from Grattan and Singer's critical edition, with Roman numerals; the Arabic numbers in parentheses refer to Cockayne's edition in his *Leechdoms*, vol. 3.

22 Storms, *Anglo-Saxon Magic*, pp. 141–43, calls it "Against Rheumatism"; Grendon, "Anglo-Saxon Charms," p. 165, like Grattan and Singer, *Anglo-Saxon Magic*, p. 173, translates it as a "sudden stitch." Grattan and Singer assign the lay to their Teutonic Pagan stratum (as opposed to their Latin Christian stratum). See Cameron, *Anglo-Saxon Medicine*, pp. 140–44, for analysis of this charm's problematic translation.

23 *Stod* is unclear, whether it is "he stood," invoking a heroic story sympathetically, or "I stood," the speaker of the charm who uses his own voice below to fight the attackers.

24 "Screaming" can go with the subject, the mighty women, or with the spears "whizzing" through the air, as Grattan and Singer prefer (*Anglo-Saxon Magic*, p. 175).

25 See ibid., pp. 176–77, for possible emendations to this line.

26 For a discussion of hags (*hægtesse*) and witches, see Meaney, "Women, Witchcraft, and Magic," pp. 15–17.

27 These Latin descriptions refer to sections of the gospels, psalms, or litanies with liturgical connections: John 1:1–5 near the end of the Ordinary in the mass; Matthew 4:23–25, used for disease in early missals; Psalm 54 (53) used in exorcism; opening of Litanies of the Saints; Psalm 60 (59), also in the litanies (See Grattan and Singer, *Anglo-Saxon Magic*, pp. 108–9).

28 The *unmælne* person could indicate a virgin, which would make sense in a monastic setting, or the term could refer to an older conception of a spotless person, someone without deformities or physical marks. The instructions here are comparable to *Lacnunga* CLXXXIII (114) discussed in Chapter 4, above, which specifies a virgin (*mæden man*) fetching water from a stream in silence.

29 The first mass is All Saints, the second is against tribulation, and the third is for St. Mary. Grattan and Singer, *Anglo-Saxon Magic* (p. 108 n. 12), note that these three collects are in the usual office: *Ne despicas*, *Suscipe Domine*, and *Tribulationem nostram*.

30 Psalms 51, 54, 67, 88, 86 (see Grattan and Singer, *Anglo-Saxon Magic*, p. 108 n. 13).

31 Storms, *Anglo-Saxon Magic*, pp. 234–35. Grattan and Singer, *Anglo-Saxon Magic*, p. 109 n. 2, comment that "it is remarkable" that the housel dish could have been used in this fashion, apparently with the priest's consent.

32 Storms, *Anglo-Saxon Magic*, p. 235. The Black Mass does not appear before the seventeenth century (Jeffrey B. Russell, *Mephistopheles*, pp. 89–91).

33 Flint refers to this charm as a "Christian curative incantation," ambiguous terminology that nonetheless suggests the existence of a Christian magic (*Rise of Magic*, pp. 311–13).

34 *Leechbook* I:lxxxviii.3, in a veterinary section; see also *Leechbook* II:lxv, below.

35 Remly, "Magic, Myth, and Medicine," pp. 203–9, describes how pricking just the right spot through the ribs would release the buildup of gases caused by colic, producing a stream of "foul green slime" (p. 207).

36 Grattan and Singer, *Anglo-Saxon Magic*, p. 185; see also p. 18.

37 Similar to *Lacnunga* CLXII (95) in Chapter 4, above, the title for this remedy was added in a different but contemporary hand in a different ink (Grattan and Singer, *Anglo-Saxon Magic*, p. 184 n. 8).

38 For similar exorcisms using the formula *et extinguatur per impositionem manuum nostrarum*, see *Leofric Missal*, ed. Warren, pp. 232–33.

39 Grattan and Singer note the scriptural references as Romans 8:35 ("who can separate us from the love of Christ"), Psalm 3:1 ("Lord, wherefore they are increased"), and Jeremiah 40:4 ("Rejoice, loose their chains, Lord").

40 For *a Christo*, Singer, *History of Medicine*, p. 31, has *aepistolam*; Storms, *Anglo-Saxon Magic*, p. 294, suggests *a Chrysostomo*, St. Chrysostom, as an alternative.

41 MS Royal 2. A. XX., fol. 45b, London, eleventh century; see Storms, *Anglo-Saxon Magic*, p. 294, and Grattan and Singer, *Anglo-Saxon Magic*, p. 50.

42 The declension of *aelfae* is unclear, since the ending *ae* (or *æ*?) does not correspond to any known Anglo-Saxon inflection; it could be either nominative or genitive, matching either *Devil* or *Satan*. However, given the inflection of the latter, *Satanae* (gen.), it could be argued that *aelfae* is meant to gloss *Satan*.

43 Lent or Spring disease (*Lencten adle*) with a fever may refer to typhus.

44 Psalms 119, 68, 69.

45 *Brœcseoc* literally means "break" or "breech"-sick, indicating either a physical collapse or a mental breakdown or both; it is associated with epilepsy and frenzy (Lat. *phreneticus*).

46 See also the similar recipe in *Leechbook* III:lxviii, below.

47 *Leodrunan*, literally, "people counselor," feminine. Cockayne has "rune lay" while Storms, Grendon, and Bosworth and Toller identify this with a female person. See Meaney, "Women, Witchcraft, and Magic," pp. 14–15.

48 These are Storms's guesses; Cockayne suggests IESUM instead of *huios* and *ichthus*. Both refer to the legend of St. Veronica's kerchief, with the miraculous portrait of Christ imprinted on it when she wiped the sweat from his brow on the way to Calvary.

49 Grendon, "Anglo-Saxon Charms," p. 199.

50 Hebrew origin, "you may be established for nights as our guardian spirit" (see Storms, *Anglo-Saxon Magic*, p. 270).

51 Storms, *Anglo-Saxon Magic*, p. 271, suggests this practice.

52 *Leechbook* I:lxv.5 reads, "Against elf and against a strange [unknown] charm, rub myrrh in wine and equal part of white frankincense, and shave off a part of the stone [called] agate into the wine; let him drink this three mornings after fasting at night, or for nine, or for twelve." Cockayne, *Leechdoms*, 2:297, translates *uncuthum sidran* as "strange visitor," noting that it is perhaps miswritten. Grendon,

"Anglo-Saxon Charms," p. 213, uses "strange charm-magic" and notes, p. 237, the lack of Christian elements in comparison with similar thaumaturgic drinks.

53 Cockayne replaces some of the missing folios by adding a parallel section of remedies (all but the gynecological set) from another manuscript, MS Harley 55 (ca. 1040).

54 This entire section is preceded, as in the Book II section, by gynecological remedies (xxxvii for infertility and other childbirth matters; xxxviii for menstrual problems). Cockayne delicately translates the Anglo-Saxon language for these afflictions into Latin rather than English.

55 Note the presence of both the Latin betony and the Anglo-Saxon bishopwort side by side, even though they are supposedly the same herb (as glossed in Ælfric and in the *Anglo-Saxon Herbal*), a fact that seems to have escaped the notice of the author, compiler, or scribe of this remedy.

56 Cockayne translates *hocces* as "hollyhock"; see Bierbaumer, *Der botanische*, 1:85. Grattan and Singer, *Anglo-Saxon Magic*, p. 88, in their short list of safely identifiable herbs, translate *ellenwyrt* as "dwarf elder" (*Sambucus ebulus*); see Bierbaumer, *Der botanische*, 1:53, for identification as *Sambucus nigra* or elder.

57 See Chapter 4 discussion of the manuscript.

58 *Leechbook* III:lxvi for the dry disease or *theor*, discussed above; *Leechbook* III:lxviii for a "wood heart."

59 Fols. 109a–111a. Book III's table of contents begins right after the closing dedication words in Latin referring to Bald and Cild, at the top of fol. 109a.

60. *Leechbook* III:lv, "If a man's head pan be *gehlenced* [bound? ridged?], lay the man upward. Drive two stakes at the shoulders. Lay then a board across over the feet [?]. Strike then thrice on [it] with a sledge hammer. It [the skull?] will come right soon."

61 Cockayne, *Leechdoms*, 2:343; Grendon, "Anglo-Saxon Charms," p. 213. Also, the verb *gemathel* is used as a description of the devil's talk (see Bosworth and Toller, *Anglo-Saxon Dictionary*, p. 414).

62 Cockayne and Leonhardi emend *molin* (mullein) in the manuscript to "niolin."

63 On those ones (*mannum*) who have intercourse with the devil: *mannum* can refer to either men or women or both. Most translations of this text use "women," but since the text does not use a gender-specific word, I use "people."

64 Cockayne, *Leechdoms*, and Bosworth and Toller, *Anglo-Saxon Dictionary*, identify *eowohumelan* as "the ewe hop plant" (*humulus femina*); Bierbaumer, *Der botanische*, 1:57–58, explains the etymology. See Grattan and Singer, *Anglo-Saxon Magic*, p. 89, for a discussion of *beolone* or henbane, and its identification problems.

65 Storms, *Anglo-Saxon Magic*, pp. 246–47.

66 Ibid., p. 230. A similar case is the story discussed in Chapter 4, above, of mold taken from foot imprints and used to heal.

67 See discussion of this herb in Grattan and Singer, *Anglo-Saxon Magic*, p. 90, and of this remedy on p. 34.

68 Rather than struggle with awkward "he/she" or "him/her" constructions, I have chosen in this translation to stay with the masculine pronoun forms, which in Anglo-Saxon usage could refer to either a man or a woman.

69 Storms, *Anglo-Saxon Magic*, p. 245.

70 Grattan and Singer, *Anglo-Saxon Magic*, pp. 69–70, discuss the manuscripts containing these popular body-naming formulas traced to the Lorica of Gildas (found in *Lacnunga* 152a–157a, where it is a glossed version, Latin and Anglo-Saxon; see Leonhardi, *Kleinere*, pp. 181–91). The marginalia exorcism in the Bede (MS 41, Corpus Christi, Cambridge, p. 272, margin) is printed in Cockayne, *Leechdoms*, 1:386, and is quoted by Grattan and Singer, p. 70.

71 *Leofric Missal*, ed. Warren, p. 235 and n. 1, where he cites other liturgical texts with this formula, such as the *Stowe Missal*. The later *Leofric Missal* version reads,

Domine, sancte pater, omnipotens aeterne deus, per impositionem scripture huius et gustum aquae expelle diabolum ab homine isto, de capite, de capillis, de uertice, de cerebro, de fronte, de oculis, de auribus, de naribus, de ore, de lingua, de sublingua, de guttore, de collo, de corpore toto, de omnibus membris, de compaginibus membrorum suorum, intus et foris, de ossibus, de uenis, de neruis, de sanguine, de sensu, de cogitationibus, de omni conuersatione, et operetur in te uirtus christi, in eo qui pro te passus est, ut uitam aeternam merearis.

[Lord, holy Father, omnipotent eternal God, through the imposition of this scripture and taste of this water expel the devil from this man, from the head, from the hair, from the crown, from the brain, from the forehead, from the eyes, from the ears, from the nostrils, from the mouth, from the tongue, from the epiglottis, from the throat, from the neck, from the whole body, from all limbs, from the connections of his members, within and without, from the bones, from the veins, from the nerves, from the blood, from the perception, from the thoughts, from all conversation, and may the power of Christ work in you, in him who for you has died, so that you may merit eternal life.]

Although the introductory formula is similar to the *Leechbook* remedy, this exorcism has a different order of parts and continues after the phrase "within and without" with internal body parts and mental capacities, concluding with a benediction.

72 The identification of Latin *castalidas* (*nymphas*) with down-elves (*dunylfa*) occurs in Byrhtferth's *Manual*, fol. 151 (ed. Crawford, p. 148, l. 17), an association carried further in Somner's seventeenth-century *Dictionarium Saxonico-Latino-Anglicum* (p. 79) to include other kinds of elves (mountain, field, etc.) as translations for various classical beings such as nymphs, dryads, etc. See Storms, *Anglo-Saxon Magic*,

p. 229, and Grendon, "Anglo-Saxon Charms," p. 225, for a discussion of this identification; see also Bosworth and Toller, *dunelfen.*

73 See Grattan and Singer, *Anglo-Saxon Magic,* pp. 89–90, for a discussion of dill and its possible gas-reducing effects.

74 Storms, *Anglo-Saxon Magic,* p. 233; see also Cameron, *Anglo-Saxon Medicine,* p. 140.

75 I have left Latin *fel terre* and *consolde* as in the text, even though other texts (Ælfric's glossary, for example) identify them as Anglo-Saxon earthgall and daisy. See Bierbaumer, *Der botanische,* 1:60, for *fel terre* as *centaurium,* and 1:38, for *consolde* as comfrey.

76 This *galdor* is problematic in translation. Cockayne's, Grendon's, and Storms's translations differ markedly, and their points of divergence occur at words for which we can find no clear sense. For example, *waco sian* is virtually unintelligible; Dobbie, in *ASPR,* vol. 6, reads the apparent *co* double circles as *x* for *waxsian,* as does Storms, who renders it as *weacsan* (increase), which makes the most sense. However, Cockayne and Grendon translate it as "be wicked or filthy wounds." In the phrase "himself keep healthy" it is unclear grammatically whether the speaker of the charm is asserting "I" keep the patient healthy or whether the patient does so by this remedy. Likewise, Cockayne translates *halewæge* as "way to health," probably a false etymology for *wæge,* while Storms and Grendon translate it as "water" from the meaning "wave," and Dobbie suggests "holy cup." *Eare* in this last phrase could be "ear," "sea," or even the rune for the letters *ea,* which means ground or earth, giving a nice play on the use of earth in this passage. Storms, *Anglo-Saxon Magic,* pp. 161–63, gives a word-by-word analysis.

77 Storms, *Anglo-Saxon Magic,* p. 162; Cameron, *Anglo-Saxon Medicine,* pp. 154–55.

78 Grendon, "Anglo-Saxon Charms," pp. 128, 194–95, classifies this remedy as a heathen vernacular herbal charm (B5 in his system). Storms, *Anglo-Saxon Magic,* p. 129, puts the purest Germanic charms first; this one is number 5 in his collection.

79 *Leofric Missal,* ed. Warren, p. 235.

80 *Saluum me fac* in later ages is usually read as "spiritual salvation," but the idea of physical rescue in this phrase is clearly present in the Psalms and is arguably present in this early medieval context.

81 *Bald's Leechbook,* ed. Wright, p. 25 and fol. 125b.

82 There is one earlier addition of a remedy in the margins in Anglo-Saxon; there are also several *Nota* or *Nota totum* in the margins from the same thirteenth-century hand, but without comment.

Conclusion

1 Ælfric, *Homilies of Ælfric,* ed. Thorpe, 1:186.

BIBLIOGRAPHY

Primary Sources

COLLECTIONS

Attenborough, F. L., ed. *The Laws of the Earliest English Kings*. New York: Russell and Russell, 1963.

Cockayne, Oswald, ed. and trans. *Leechdoms, Wortcunning, and Starcraft of Early England*. 3 vols. Rolls series. London, 1864–66. Reprint, London: Holland Press, 1961.

Corpus Christianorum Series Latina. Turnhout: Brepols, 1954– .

Gee, Henry, ed. *Documents Illustrative of English Church History*. London: Macmillan, 1910. Reprint, New York: Kraus, 1966.

Grattan, J. H. G., and Charles Singer. *Anglo-Saxon Magic and Medicine*. Publications of the Wellcome Historical Medical Museum. London: Oxford University Press, 1952. Reprint, Folcroft, Pa.: Folcroft Library Editions, 1971.

Grendon, Felix, ed. and trans. "The Anglo-Saxon Charms." *Journal of American Folklore* 22 (1909): 105–237.

Hadden, Arthur West, and William Stubbs, eds. *Councils and Ecclesiastical Documents Relating to Great Britain and Ireland*. Vol. 3. Oxford: Clarendon, 1871. Reprint, 1964.

Leonhardi, Günther. *Kleinere angelsächsische Denkmäler*. Bibliothek der angelsachsischen Prosa 6. Hamburg: Henri Grand, 1905.

Liebermann, F., ed. *Die Gesetze der Angelsachsen*. 3 vols. Halle: Niermeyer, 1906–16. Aalen: Scientia, 1960.

Robertson, A. J., ed. and trans. *Anglo-Saxon Charters*. Cambridge: Cambridge University Press, 1956.

Robertson, A. J., ed. and trans. *The Laws of the Kings of England from Edmund to Henry I*. Cambridge: Cambridge University Press, 1925.

Sawyer, Peter H. *Anglo-Saxon Charters: An Annotated List and Bibliography*. London: Royal Historical Society, 1968.

Storms, Godfrid, ed. and trans. *Anglo-Saxon Magic*. Halle: Nijhoff, 1948. Reprint, Folcroft, Pa.: Folcroft Library Editions, 1975.

Thorpe, Benjamin, ed. and trans. *Ancient Laws and Institutes of England*. Public Records Commission. London: Eyre and Spottiswoode, 1840.

Whitelock, Dorothy, ed. *Anglo-Saxon Wills*. Cambridge: Cambridge University Press, 1930. Reprint, New York: AMS, 1973.

Whitelock, Dorothy, M. Brett, and C. N. L. Brooke, eds. *Councils and Synods with Other Documents Relating to the English Church.* Vol. 1, *A.D. 871–1204.* Part 1, 871–1066. Oxford: Clarendon, 1981.

REFERENCE WORKS

Bates, David, ed. *A Bibliography of Domesday Book.* Royal Historical Society. Woodbridge: Boydell, 1986.

Bierbaumer, Peter. *Der botanische Wortschatz des Alt-englischen.* 4 vols. Frankfurt: Peter Lang, 1975.

Bosworth, Joseph, and T. Northcote Toller, eds. *An Anglo-Saxon Dictionary.* Oxford: Oxford University Press, 1898. Reprint, 1929. *Supplement with Addenda.* Edited by T. Northcote Toller. Revised by Alistair Campbell. Oxford: Oxford University Press, 1921. Reprint, 1955.

Darby, Henry C. *The Domesday Geography of Eastern England.* Cambridge: Cambridge University Press, 1952.

Darby, Henry C., and E. M. J. Campbell. *The Domesday Geography of South-east England.* Cambridge: Cambridge University Press, 1962.

Darby, Henry C., and R. W. Finn. *The Domesday Geography of South-west England.* Cambridge: Cambridge University Press, 1967.

Darby, Henry C., and I. S. Maxwell. *The Domesday Geography of Northern England.* Cambridge: Cambridge University Press, 1962.

Darby, Henry C., and I. B. Terrett. *The Domesday Geography of Midland England.* Cambridge: Cambridge University Press, 1954.

Kauffmann, C. M. *Romanesque Manuscripts, 1066–1190.* Vol. 3 of *A Survey of Manuscripts Illuminated in the British Isles,* edited by J. J. G. Alexander. London: Harvey Miller, 1975.

Ker, N. R. *Catalogue of Manuscripts Containing Anglo-Saxon.* Oxford: Clarendon, 1957.

Lendinara, Patrizia. "Gli incantesimi del periodo anglosassone: Una ricerca bibliografica." *Annali del Istituto Universitario Orientale, filologia germanica* 21 (1978): 299–362. A bibliography of manuscripts with charms, listed by individual charms, and with references to editions and translations.

Ohlgren, Thomas H. *Insular and Anglo-Saxon Illuminated Manuscripts: An Iconographic Catalogue c. A.D. 625 to 1100.* New York: Garland, 1986.

Somner, William. *Dictionarium Saxonico-Latino-Anglicum.* Oxford, 1659. Facsimile ed., Menston, England: Scolar, 1970.

Temple, Elzbieta. *Anglo-Saxon Manuscripts, 900–1066.* Vol. 2 of *A Survey of Manuscripts Illuminated in the British Isles,* edited by J. J. G. Alexander. London: Harvey Miller, 1976.

Ælfric. *Ælfric's Catholic Homilies*. Edited by Malcolm Godden. EETS n.s. 5 (1979).

——. *Ælfrics Grammatik und Glossar: Text und Varianten*. Edited by Julius Zupitza.
Berlin: Max Niehans, 1966.

——. *Homilies of Ælfric: A Supplementary Collection*. 2 vols. Edited by J. C. Pope. EETS
259–60 (1967–68).

——. *Ælfric's Lives of Saints*. 2 vols. Edited by Walter Skeat. EETS o.s. 76, 82, 94, 114
(1881–1900). London: Oxford University Press, 1966.

——. *Angelsachsische Homilien und Heiligenleben*. Edited by Bruno Assmann. Kassel:
G. H. Wigand, 1889. Reprint with supplement, Darmstadt: Wissenschaftlich
Buchgesellschaft, 1964.

——. *First Series of Catholic Homilies*. Edited by Norman Eliason and Peter Clemoes.
Early English Manuscript in Facsimile 13. Copenhagen: Rosenkilde and Bagger, 1966.

——. *Die Hirtenbriefe Ælfrics*. Edited by Bernard Fehr. Hamburg: H. Grand, 1914.
Reprint, Darmstadt: Wissenschaftlich Buchgesellschaft, 1966.

——. *The Homilies of the Anglo-Saxon Church: The Homilies of Ælfric*. 2 vols. Edited by
Benjamin Thorpe. London: Ælfric Society, 1844, 1846. Reprint, New York:
Johnson, 1971.

Æthelwold. *Regularis Concordia Anglicae Nationis Monachorum Sanctimonialumque: The
Monastic Agreement of the Monks and Nuns of the English Nation*. Edited by Thomas
Symons. New York: Oxford University Press, 1953.

Ambrose. *Letters of St. Ambrose*. Edited and translated by H. De Romestin. Vol. 10 of
A Select Library of Nicene and Post-Nicene Fathers of the Church. 2nd series. New York:
Christian Literature, 1896. Reprint, Grand Rapids, Mich.: Eerdmans, 1955.

Anglo-Saxon Chronicle. *Two of the Saxon Chronicles Parallel with supplementary extracts from the
others*. 2 vols. Edited by Charles Plummer. Revised by Dorothy Whitelock.
Oxford: Oxford University Press, 1892, 1899. Rev. ed., 1952.

The Annals of St-Bertin: Ninth-Century Histories. Vol. 1. Translated and annotated by
Janet L. Nelson. Manchester: Manchester University Press, 1991.

Asser. *Alfred the Great*. Translated by Simon Keynes and Michael Lapidge. London:
Penguin, 1984.

Augustine. *Against the Manichees*. In PL 34:173–220. Translated by Roland J. Teske,
Saint Augustine on Genesis. The Fathers of the Church 84. Washington, D.C.:
Catholic University of America Press, 1991.

——. *De catechezandis rudibus*. In PL 40:309. *The First Catechetical Instruction*. Translated
and annotated by Joseph P. Christopher. Ancient Christian Writers 2. London,
1946. Westminster, Md.: Newman, 1962.

——. *De civitate dei*. In PL 41. *Concerning the City of God against the Pagans*. Translated by
Henry Bettenson. Harmondsworth: Penguin, 1972.

——. *Confessio*. In PL 32. *Confessions*. Translated by R. S. Pine-Coffin.
Harmondsworth: Penguin, 1961.

Bald's Leechbook. Edited by C. E. Wright. Early English Manuscript in Facsimile 15. Copenhagen: Rosenkilde and Bagger, 1955.

Bede. Ecclesiastical History. Edited by Bertram Colgrave and R. A. B. Mynors. Oxford: Clarendon, 1969.

——. A History of the English Church and People. Translated by Leo Sherley-Price. Baltimore: Penguin, 1955.

——. The Old English Version of Bede's Ecclesiastical History of the English People. Edited by Thomas Miller. EETS o.s. 95 (1890). Reprint, Oxford: Oxford University Press, 1959.

The Blickling Homilies of the Tenth Century. Edited by R. Morris. Part 1, EETS o.s. 58 (1874). Part 2, EETS o.s. 63 (1876). Part 3, EETS o.s. 73 (1880). Paginated continuously.

Boniface. The Letters of Saint Boniface. Translated by Ephraim Emerton. New York: Columbia University Press, 1940. New York: Octagon Books, 1973.

Byrhtferth's Manual. Edited by Samuel J. Crawford. EETS 177 (1929).

Caesarius of Heisterbach. Dialogus Miraculorum. Edited by J. Strange. 2 vols. Cologne: Heberle, 1851. Printed in English as Caesarius of Heisterbach: The Dialogue of Miracles. Translated by H. von E. Scott and C. C. Swinton Bland. New York: Harcourt Brace, 1929. Reprint, Ridgewood, N.J.: Gregg, 1966.

The Canterbury Psalter. Facsimile with introduction by M. R. James. Friends of Canterbury Cathedral. London: Percy Lund, Humphries & Co, Ltd., 1935.

Chronicon Monasterii de Abingdon. Vol. 2. Part 2. Rolls series. Edited by Joseph Stevenson. London: Public Record Office, 1858.

Chrysostom, John. The Exposition of Psalm XLI. In PG 55:155–59.

Domesday Book. 4 vols. Edited by Abraham Farley and Henry Ellis. London: Record Commission, 1783–1816.

Domesday Book. 38 vols. Edited and translated by J. Morris. Chichester: Phillimore, 1975–92.

The Domesday Monachorum of Christ Church Canterbury. Edited by David C. Douglas. London: Offices of the Royal Historical Society, 1944.

Dudo of St. Quentin. Dudonis sancti Quintini de moribus et actis primorum Normanniae Ducum. Edited by M. J. Lair. Caen: F. Le Blanc-Hardel, 1865. See also J. Lair, "Dudo de St. Quentin: De moribus et actis primum Normannorum ducum." Memoirs de la Société des Antiquaires de Normandie 23 (Caen, 1895).

Einhard and Notker the Stammerer. Two Lives of Charlemagne. Translated by Lewis Thorpe. London: Penguin, 1969.

Eusebius. Life of Constantine. 2nd series, vol. 1. Translated by Arthur Cushman McGiffert. A Select Library of Nicene and Post-Nicene Fathers of the Christian Church. New York: Christian Literature, 1890.

Exameron Anglice. Edited by S. J. Crawford. Bibliothek der angelsachsischen Prosa 10. Hamburg: H. Grand, 1921. Reprint, Darmstadt: Wissenschaftlich Buchgesellschaft, 1968.

Great Domesday Book: Facsimile. Edited by R. W. H. Erskine. London: Alecto Historical Editions, 1986. In 2 cases.

Great Domesday Book: Translation and Maps. London: Alecto, 1988. In 3 cases.

Gregory of Tours. Life of the Fathers. Translated by Edward James. Liverpool: Liverpool University Press, 1985.

Gregory the Great. Forty Gospel Homilies. Translated by David Hurst. Kalamazoo, Mich.: Cistercian Publications, 1990.

————. The Dialogues of Gregory the Great. Book Two: St. Benedict. Translated by Myra L. Uhlfelder. Indianapolis: Bobbs-Merrill, 1967.

Hippolytus. The Apostolic Tradition of Hippolytus. Translated by Burton Scott Easton. Cambridge: Cambridge University Press, 1934.

Lanfranc. The Letters of Lanfranc, Archbishop of Canterbury. Edited and translated by Helen Clover and Margaret Gibson. Oxford: Clarendon, 1979.

The Leofric Missal. Edited by W. L. Warren. Oxford: Clarendon, 1883.

Liber Eliensis. Edited by E. O. Blake. London: Royal Historical Society, 1962.

Memorials of St. Dunstan. Rolls series. Edited by William Stubbs. London: Longman, 1874.

The Missal of Robert of Jumièges. Edited by H. A. Wilson. Henry Bradshaw Society 11. London: Henry Bradshaw Society, 1896.

The Old English Herbarium and Medicina de Quadrupedibus. Edited by Hubert Jan De Vriend. EETS o.s. 286 (1984).

Orosius, Paulus. Historiarum adversus paganos. In Anglo Saxon: The Old English Orosius, edited by Janet Bately. EETS s.s. 6 (1980).

Penitentials. Medieval Handbooks of Penance. Edited by John T. McNeill and Helena M. Gamer. Reprint, New York: Octagon Books, 1965.

Pliny. Naturalis historia. Natural History, with an English Translation. 10 vols. Cambridge, Mass.: Harvard University Press, 1938–63.

Snorri Sturluson. The Prose Edda: Tales from Norse Mythology. Translated by Jean I. Young. Berkeley: University of California Press, 1954.

Utrecht-Psalter. 2 vols. Facsimile. Edited by R. van der Horst and J. H. A. Engelbregt. Codices Selecti 75. Graz, 1984.

Die Vercelli Homilen. Edited by Max Forster. Bibliothek der Angelsachsischen Prosa 12. Hamburg, 1932. Reprint, Darmstadt: Wissenschaftlich Buchgesellschaft, 1964.

Vercelli Homilies ix–xxiii. Edited by Paul Szarmach. Toronto: University of Toronto Press, 1981.

William of Malmesbury. De Gestis Pontificum Anglorum. Rolls series 52. London: Public Records Office, 1870. Reprint, Wiesbaden: Kraus, 1969.

————. Life of Saint Wulstan: Bishop of Worcester. Translated by J. H. F. Peile. Oxford: Blackwell, 1934.

Willibald. The Life of Saint Boniface. Translated by George W. Robinson. Cambridge, Mass.: Harvard University Press, 1916.

Wulfstan. The Homilies of Wulfstan. Edited by Dorothy Bethurum. Oxford: Clarendon, 1957.

————. Die "Institutes of Polity, Civil and Ecclesiastical." Edited by Karl Jost. Bern: Francke, 1959.

————. Sermo Lupi ad Anglos. 3rd ed., revised. Edited by Dorothy Whitelock. London: Methuen, 1963.

————. A Wulfstan Manuscript Containing Institutes, Laws, and Homilies: British Museum Cotton Nero A.I. Early English Manuscript in Facsimile 17. Copenhagen: Rosenkilde and Bagger, 1971.

————. Wulfstan's Canons of Edgar. Edited by Roger Fowler. EETS 266 (1972).

Secondary Sources

Abels, Richard. "King Alfred's Peace-Making Strategies." Haskins Society Journal 3 (1991): 23–34.

Adams, J. N., and Marilyn Deegan. "Bald's Leechbook and the Physica Plinii." Anglo-Saxon England 21 (1992): 87–114.

Addleshaw, G. W. O. The Beginnings of the Parochial System. St. Anthony's Hall Publication 3. London: St. Anthony's Press, 1954.

————. The Development of the Parochial System from Charlemagne (768–814) to Urban II (1088–1099). St. Anthony's Hall Publications 6. London: St. Anthony's Press, 1954.

Addyman, Peter, and Richard Morris, eds. The Archaeological Study of Churches. CBA Research Report 13. London: Council for British Archaeology, 1976.

Andersson, Theodore M. "The Viking Policy of Ethelred the Unready." Scandinavian Studies 59 (1987): 284–95.

The Anglo-Saxons: An Exploration of their Art, Literature, and Way of Life. CD-ROM. Developed by R M Learning Resources and the British Museum. Oxford: Research Machines, plc; Woodland Hills, Calif.: Cambrix, 1993.

Aronstam, Robin Ann. "The Blickling Homilies: A Reflection of Popular Anglo-Saxon Belief." In Law, Church, and Society: Essays in Honor of Stephan Kuttner, edited by Kenneth Pennington and Robert Somerville, pp. 271–80. Philadelphia: University of Pennsylvania Press, 1977.

Aston, Michael, David Austin, and Christopher Dyer. The Rural Settlements of Medieval England. Cambridge, Mass.: Blackwell, 1989.

Aston, T. H., ed. Landlords, Peasants, and Politics in Medieval England. Past and Present Publications. Cambridge: Cambridge University Press, 1987.

Ayer, Joseph C. "Church Councils of the Anglo-Saxons." American Society of Church History, 2nd ser., 7 (1923): 91–107.

Baker, Derek, ed. The Church in Town and Countryside. Studies in Church History 16. Oxford: Blackwell, 1979.

Baker, Nigel. "Churches, Parishes, and Early Medieval Topography." Worcestershire Archaeological Society, transactions, 3rd ser., 7 (1980): 31–38.

Barley, Nigel. "Anglo-Saxon Magico-Medicine." *Journal of Anthropological Society of Oxford* 3 (1972): 67–77.

Barlow, Frank. *The English Church, 1000–1066.* 2nd ed. London: Longman, 1979.

Barraclough, Geoffrey. *The Crucible of Europe: The Ninth and Tenth Centuries in European History.* Berkeley: University of California Press, 1976.

Barrow, G. W. S. *Kingship and Unity: Scotland, 1000–1306.* Toronto: University of Toronto Press, 1981.

Bates, David. *Normandy before 1066.* New York: Longman, 1982.

Benedict, Ruth. *Patterns of Culture.* 1934. With preface by Margaret Mead, Boston: Houghton Mifflin, 1959.

Benson, John, and Giles Constable, eds. *Renaissance and Renewal in the Twelfth Century.* Cambridge, Mass.: Harvard University Press, 1982.

Bettey, J. H. *Church and Community: The Parish Church in English Life.* New York: Barnes and Noble, 1979.

Bharati, Agehananda. "Anthropological Approaches to the Study of Religion: Ritual and Belief Systems." In *Biennial Review of Anthropology 1971*, edited by Bernard J. Siegel, pp. 230–63. Stanford: Stanford University Press, 1971.

Biggs, Frederic M., Thomas D. Hill, and Paul E. Szarmach, eds. *Sources of Anglo-Saxon Literary Culture: A Trial Version.* Binghamton, N.Y.: Center for Medieval and Early Renaissance Studies, SUNY, 1990.

Birnbaum, N. "Religion." In *A Dictionary of the Social Sciences*, edited by Julius Gould and William L. Kolb. New York: Free Press, 1964.

Blair, John. "Local Churches in Domesday Book and Before." In *Domesday Studies: Papers Read at the Novocentenary Conference of the Royal Historical Society and the Institute of British Geographers*, edited by J. C. Holt, pp. 265–78. Woodbridge: Boydell, 1987.

———. "Parish Churches in the Eleventh Century." In *Domesday Book: Studies*, edited by Ann Williams and R. W. H. Erskine, pp. 65–68. London: Alecto Historical Editions, 1987.

———, ed. *Minsters and Parish Churches: The Local.Church in Transition, 950–1200.* Oxford: Oxford University Committee for Archaeology, 1988.

Böhmer, Heinrich. "Das Eigenkirchentum in England." In *Texte und Forshungen zur Englischen Kulturgeschichte, Festgabe fur Felix Liebermann*, pp. 301–53. Halle: Niermeyer, 1921.

Boglioni, P. "Miracle et nature chez Gregoire le Grand." In *Épopées, légendes, miracles: Cahiers d'études médiévales*, 1:11–102. Montreal: Bellarmin, 1974.

Bonser, Wilfrid. *Bibliography of Folklore.* Publications of the Folklore Society. London: W. Glaisher, 1961.

———. "Magical Practices against Elves." *Folklore* 37 (1926): 350–63.

———. *The Medical Background of Anglo-Saxon England: A Study in History, Psychology, and Folklore.* London: Wellcome Historical Medical Library, 1963.

———. "Survivals of Paganism in Anglo-Saxon England." *Transactions of the Birmingham Archaeological Society* 56 (1939): 37–70.

Bont, Walter de, "La psychologie devant la religion populaire." In *Les religions populaires*, edited by Benoit Lacroix and Pietro Boglioni, pp. 19–22. Colloque international 1970. Quebec: Les Presses de l'Universite Laval, 1972.

Bradley, S. A. J., ed. and trans. *Anglo-Saxon Poetry*. London: Dent, 1982.

Brooke, C. N. L. "The Church in the Towns, 1000–1250." *Studies in Church History* 6 (1970): 59–83.

———. "Rural Ecclesiastical Institutions in England: The Search for their Origins." *Settimane di studio* 28 (Spoleto, 1982): 685–711.

Brooke, C. N. L., and G. Keir. *London, 800–1216: The Shaping of a City*. Berkeley: University of California Press, 1975.

Brooke, Rosalind, and Christopher Brooke. *Popular Religion in the Middle Ages*. London: Thames and Hudson, 1984.

Brooks, N. P. "England in the Ninth Century: The Crucible of Defeat." *Transactions of the Royal Historical Society*, 5th ser., 29 (1979): 1–20.

Brown, Peter. *Augustine of Hippo*. Berkeley: University of California Press, 1967.

———. *The Cult of the Saints*. Chicago: University of Chicago Press, 1981.

———. *Relics and Social Status in the Age of Gregory of Tours*. Reading: University of Reading, 1977.

———. *Religion and Society in the Age of St. Augustine*. London: Faber and Faber, 1972.

Brown, Phyllis. "The Viking Policy of Ethelred: A Response." *Scandinavian Studies* 59 (1987): 296–98.

Bullough, Donald. "Burial, Community, and Belief in the Early Medieval West." In *Ideal and Reality in Frankish and Anglo-Saxon Society*, edited by Patrick Wormald, Donald Bullough, and Roger Collins, pp. 177–201. Oxford: Blackwell, 1982.

Burke, Peter. *Popular Culture in Early Modern Europe*. New York: Harper and Row, 1978.

Bynum, Caroline Walker. *Jesus as Mother: Studies in the Spirituality of the High Middle Ages*. Berkeley: University of California Press, 1982.

———. *The Resurrection of the Body in Western Christianity, 200–1336*. New York: Columbia University Press, 1995.

Cameron, M. L. *Anglo-Saxon Medicine*. Cambridge: Cambridge University Press, 1993.

———. "Anglo-Saxon Medicine and Magic." *Anglo-Saxon England* 17 (1988): 191–215.

———. "Bald's *Leechbook* and Cultural Interactions in Anglo-Saxon England." *Anglo-Saxon England* 19 (1991): 5–12.

———. "Bald's *Leechbook*: Its Sources and Their Use in Its Compilation." *Anglo-Saxon England* 12 (1983): 153–82.

———. "The Sources of Medical Knowledge in Anglo-Saxon England." *Anglo-Saxon England* 11 (1982): 135–55.

Campbell, J. "The Church in Anglo-Saxon Towns." In *The Church in Town and Countryside*, edited by Derek Baker, pp. 119–35. Studies in Church History 16. Oxford: Blackwell, 1979.

Capps, Walter. *Ways of Understanding Religion*. New York: Macmillan, 1972.

Caraman, P. G. "The Character of the Late Saxon Clergy." *Downside Review* 63 (1945): 171–89.

Chaney, William A. *The Cult of Kingship in Anglo-Saxon England: The Transition from Paganism to Christianity*. Berkeley: University of California Press, 1970.

———. "Paganism to Christianity in Anglo-Saxon England." *Harvard Theological Review* 53 (1960): 197–217.

Chartier, Roger. *Cultural History: Between Practices and Representations*. Translated by Lydia G. Cochrane. Ithaca: Cornell University Press, 1988.

Clayton, Mary. "Homiliaries and Preaching in Anglo-Saxon England." *Peritia* 4 (1985): 207–42.

Clifford, James, and George E. Marcus, eds. *Writing Culture: The Poetics and Politics of Ethnography*. Berkeley: University of California Press, 1986.

Congar, Yves. "Clercs et laïcs au point de vue de la culture au moyen âge: 'Laicus' = sans lettres." In *Studia medievalia et Mariologia*, edited by P. Carolo Balíc, pp. 309–32. Rome, 1971.

Conner, Patrick. *Anglo-Saxon Exeter: A Tenth-Century Cultural History*. Studies in Anglo-Saxon History 4. Woodbridge: Boydell, 1993.

Courtas, Raymonde and François-A. Isambert, "Ethnologues et sociologues aux prises avec la notion de 'populaire.'" In *Religion populaire et réforme liturgique*, edited by Dominique Dye and Jean-Yves Hameline, pp. 20–42. Paris: Les Editions du Cerf, 1975.

Crawford, Jane. "Evidences for Witchcraft in Anglo-Saxon England." *Medium Ævum* 32 (1963): 99–116.

Cross, J. E. "Aspects of Microcosm and Macrocosm in Old English Literature." In *Studies in Old English Literature in Honor of Arthur G. Brodeur*, edited by Stanley B. Greenfield, pp. 1–22. Eugene: University of Oregon Books, 1963.

Cross, J. E., and S. I. Tucker. "Allegorical Tradition and the Old English Exodus." *Neophilologus* 44 (1960): 122–27.

Crossly-Holland, Kevin, ed. and trans. *The Anglo-Saxon World*. Oxford: Oxford University Press, 1982.

Cuming, G. J., and Derek Baker. *Popular Belief and Practice*. Studies in Church History 8. Cambridge: Cambridge University Press, 1972.

Darby, Henry C. *Domesday England*. Cambridge: Cambridge University Press, 1977.

Darlington, R. R. "Ecclesiastical Reform in the Late Old English Period." *English Historical Review* 51 (1936): 385–428.

Darnton, Robert. *The Great Cat Massacre and Other Episodes in French Cultural History*. New York: Basic Books, 1984.

D'Aronco, Maria Amalia. "The Botanical Lexicon of the Old English Herbarium." *Anglo-Saxon England* 17 (1988): 15–33.

Davidson, H. R. Ellis. *Myths and Symbols in Pagan Europe: Early Scandinavian and Celtic Religions*. Syracuse: Syracuse University Press, 1988.

Davis, Natalie Zemon. "Some Tasks and Themes in the Study of Popular Religion." In *The Pursuit of Holiness in Late Medieval and Renaissance Religion*, edited by Charles Trinkaus and Heiko A. Oberman, pp. 307–36. Leiden: Brill, 1974.

Day, Virginia. "The Influence of the Catechetical Narratio on Old English and Some Other Medieval Literature." *Anglo-Saxon England* 3 (1974): 51–61.

Deanesly, Margaret. *The Pre-Conquest Church in England*. New York: Oxford University Press, 1961. 2nd ed., London: A. and C. Black, 1963.

———. *Sidelights on the Anglo-Saxon Church*. London: A. and C. Black, 1962.

Deegan, Marilyn, and D. G. Scragg, eds. *Medicine in Early Medieval England: Four Papers*. Manchester: Manchester Centre for Anglo-Saxon Studies, 1989.

Delehaye, Hippolyte. *Les légendes hagiographiques*. 4th ed. Brussels: Societé des Bollandistes hagiographiques, 1968. Printed in English as *The Legend of the Saints: An Introduction to Hagiography*. Translated by V. M. Crawford. Notre Dame: University of Notre Dame Press, 1961.

Delaruelle, Etienne. *La piété populaire au moyen âge*. Turin: Bottega d'Erasmo, 1975.

Delumeau, Jean. "Déchristianisation ou nouveau modèle de christianisme?" *Archives de sciences sociales des religions* 40 (1975): 3–20.

De Nie, Giselle. *Views from a Many-Windowed Tower: Studies of Imagination in the Works of Gregory of Tours*. Amsterdam: Rodopi, 1987.

Dening, Greg. *Islands and Beaches, Discourse on a Silent Land: Marquesas, 1774–1880*. Chicago: Dorsey, 1980.

Dewald, E. T. *The Illustrations of the Utrecht Psalter*. Princeton: Princeton University Press, 1933.

Dorson, Richard. *Folklore and Fakelore: Essays towards a Discipline of Folk Studies*. Cambridge, Mass.: Harvard University Press, 1976.

Douglas, Mary. *Purity and Danger: An Analysis of the Concepts of Pollution and Taboo*. New York: Praeger, 1966. Reprint, London: ARK Paperbacks, 1984.

Drake, H. A. *In Praise of Constantine: A Historical Study and New Translation of Eusebius' Tricennial Orations*. Berkeley: University of California Press, 1975.

Duckett, Eleanor. *Anglo-Saxon Saints and Scholars*. New York: Macmillan, 1947. Reprint, Hamden, Conn.: Archon, 1967.

Dudden, Frederick H. *Gregory the Great*. Vol. 2. New York: Russell and Russell, 1905. Reprint, 1967.

Dumville, David. *Liturgy and the Ecclesiastical History of Late Anglo-Saxon England: Four Studies*. Studies in Anglo-Saxon History 5. Woodbridge: Boydell, 1992.

Durkheim, Emile. *The Elementary Forms of the Religious Life: A Study in Religious Sociology*. Translated by Joseph Ward Swain. New York: Macmillan, 1915. Reprint, New York: Free Press, 1965.

Dye, Dominique, and Jean-Yves Hameline, eds. *Religion populaire et réforme liturgique*. Paris: Les Editions du Cerf, 1975.

Eliade, Mircea. "History of Religions and 'Popular' Cultures." *History of Religions* 20 (1980–81): 1–26.

Erickson, Carolly. *The Medieval Vision*. New York: Oxford University Press, 1976.

Faire croire: Modalités de la diffusion et de la réception des messages religieux du XIIe au XVe siecle. Table ronde organisée par l'École Française de Rome, en collaboration avec l'Institut d'Histoire Médiévale de l'Université de Padoue. Coll. de l'École Française de Rome 51. Turin: Bottega d'Erasmo, 1981.

Fell, Christine. *Women in Anglo-Saxon England*. London: British Museum Publications, 1984.

Fichtenau, Heinrich. *Living in the Tenth Century: Mentalities and Social Orders*. Translated by Patrick J. Geary. Chicago: Chicago University Press, 1991. Originally published as *Lebensordnung des 10. Jahrhunderts: Studien über Denkart und Existenz im einstigen Karolingerreich*. Stuttgart: Anton Hiersemann, 1984.

Fisher, D. J. V. "The Anti-Monastic Reaction in the Reign of Edward the Martyr." *Cambridge Historical Journal* 10 (1952): 254–70.

———. "The Church in England between the Death of Bede and the Danish Invasions." *Transactions of the Royal Historical Society*, 5th ser., 2 (1952): 1–19.

Flint, Valerie. *The Rise of Magic in Early Medieval Europe*. Princeton: Princeton University Press, 1991.

Foot, Sarah. "Parochial Ministry in Early Anglo-Saxon England: The Role of Monastic Communities." In *The Ministry: Clerical and Lay*, edited by W. J. Sheils and Diana Wood, pp. 43–54. Studies in Church History 26. Cambridge, Mass.: Blackwell, 1990.

Förster, Max. "Uber de quellen von Ælfric's exegetischen Homiliae catholicae." *Anglia* 16, no. 4 (1894): 1–61.

Fossier, Robert. *Peasant Life in the Medieval West*. Translated by Juliet Vale. New York: Blackwell, 1988.

Foucault, Michel. *Madness and Civilization: A History of Insanity in the Age of Reason*. Translated by Richard Howard. New York: Vintage Books, 1965. Originally published as *Histoire de la folie*. Paris: Librairie Plon, 1961.

———. *The Order of Things: An Archaeology of the Human Sciences*. New York: Vintage, 1970. Originally published as *Les Mots et les choses*. Paris: Editions Gallimard, 1966.

Fouracre, Paul. "The Work of Audoenus of Rouen." In *The Church in Town and Countryside*, edited by Derek Baker, pp. 77–91. Studies in Church History 16. Oxford: Blackwell, 1979.

Franklin, M. J. "The Identification of Minsters in the Midlands." In *Anglo-Norman Studies* 7, edited by R. Allen Brown, pp. 69–89. Woodbridge: Boydell, 1985.

Frantzen, Allen J. *Desire for Origins: New Language, Old English, and Teaching the Tradition*. New Brunswick, N.J.: Rutgers University Press, 1990.

———. *The Literature of Penance in Anglo-Saxon England*. New Brunswick, N.J.: Rutgers University Press, 1983.

Frazer, J. G. *The Golden Bough: A Study in Magic and Religion*. 3rd ed. London: Macmillan, 1911.

Gatch, Milton McC. "Old English Literature and the Liturgy: Problems and Potential." *Anglo-Saxon England* 6 (1977): 237–47.

———. *Preaching and Theology in Anglo-Saxon England: Ælfric and Wulfstan*. Toronto: University of Toronto Press, 1977.

Gaudemet, J. "La paroisse au moyen âge." *Revue d'histoire de l'église de France* 59 (1975): 5–22.

Geertz, Clifford. *The Interpretation of Cultures*. New York: Basic Books, 1973.

Gem, Samuel Harvey. *An Anglo-Saxon Abbot: Ælfric of Eynsham*. Edinburgh: T. and T. Clark, 1912.

Gennep, Arnold van. *Le folklore: Croyances et coutumes populaires françaises*. Paris: Stock, 1924.

Gibson, Margaret, T. A. Heslop, and Ricard W. Pfaff, eds. *The Eadwine Psalter: Text, Image, and Monastic Culture in Twelfth-Century Canterbury*. London: Modern Humanities Research Association. University Park: Pennsylvania State University Press, 1992.

Ginzburg, Carlo. *The Cheese and the Worms: The Cosmos of a Sixteenth-Century Miller*. Translated by John and Anne Tedeschi. Baltimore: Johns Hopkins University Press, 1980. Originally published as *Il formaggio e i vermi*. Turin: G. Einaudi, 1976.

Glosecki, Stephen. *Shamanism and Old English Poetry*. New York: Garland, 1989.

Gneuss, Helmut. "Liturgical Books in Anglo-Saxon England and their Old English Terminology." In *Learning and Literature in Anglo-Saxon England: Studies Presented to Peter Clemoes on the Occasion of His Sixty-Fifth Birthday*, edited by Michael Lapidge and Helmut Gneuss, pp. 91–141. Cambridge: Cambridge University Press.

Godden, Malcolm. "Ælfric and the Vernacular Prose Tradition." In *The Old English Homily and Its Backgrounds*, edited by Paul E. Szarmach and Bernard F. Huppe, pp. 99–117. Albany: SUNY Press, 1978.

———. "Apocalypse and Invasion in Late Anglo-Saxon England." In *From Anglo-Saxon to Early Middle English: Studies Presented to E. G. Stanley*, edited by Douglas Gray, Malcolm Godden, and Terry Hoad. Oxford: Clarendon, 1994.

Godden, Malcolm, and Michael Lapidge, eds. *The Cambridge Companion to Old English Literature*. Cambridge: Cambridge University Press, 1991.

Godfrey, John. "The Emergence of the Village Church in Anglo-Saxon England." In *Anglo-Saxon Settlement and Landscape*, edited by Trevor Rowley, pp. 131–38. British Archeological Report 6. Oxford: BAR, 1974.

———. *The English Parish, 600–1300*. London: S.P.C.K., 1969.

Gollancz, Israel. *The Caedmon Manuscript of Anglo-Saxon Biblical Poetry*. Oxford: Oxford University Press, 1927.

Goody, Jack. "Religion and Ritual: The Definitional Problem." *British Journal of Sociology* 12 (1961): 142–64.

Grant, Raymond J. S. *Cambridge, Corpus Christi College 41: The Loricas and the Missal*. *Costerus*, n.s. 17. Amsterdam: Rodopi, 1979.

Greenfield, Kathleen. "Changing Emphases in English Vernacular Homiletic Literature, 960–1225." *Journal of Medieval History* 7 (1981): 283–97.

Greenfield, Stanley B. *A Critical History of Old English Literature*. New York: New York University Press, 1965.

Gribben, Arthur. *Holy Wells and Sacred Water Sources in Britain and Ireland: An Annotated Bibliography*. New York: Garland, 1992.

Gurevich, Aron. *Medieval Popular Culture: Problems of Belief and Perception.* Translated by János Bak and Paul A. Hollingsworth. Cambridge: Cambridge University Press, 1988. Originally published as *Problemy srednevekovoi narodnoi kul'tury.* Moscow: Iskusstvo, 1981.

Hall, R. A. "The Five Boroughs of the Danelaw: A Review of Present Knowledge." *Anglo-Saxon England* 18 (1989): 149–206.

Hallam, Elizabeth. *Domesday Book through Nine Centuries.* New York: Thames and Hudson, 1986.

Halpin, Patricia. "Women Religious in Late Anglo-Saxon England." *Haskins Society Journal* 6 (1994): 97–110.

Hammer, Carl I., Jr. "Country Churches, Clerical Inventories, and the Carolingian Renaissance in Bavaria." *Church History* 49 (1980): 5–17.

Hardon, John A. "The Concept of Miracle from St. Augustine to Modern Apologetics." *Theological Studies* 15 (1954): 229–57.

Hart, Cyril. *The Danelaw.* London: Hambledon, 1992.

Herbert, Christopher. *Culture and Anomie: Ethnographic Imagination in the Nineteenth Century.* Chicago: Chicago University Press, 1991.

Hill, David. *An Atlas of Anglo-Saxon England.* Toronto: University of Toronto Press, 1981.

Hill, Thomas D. "The Æcerbot Charm and Its Christian User." *Anglo-Saxon England* 6 (1977): 213–21.

Hocart, Arthur Maurice. "The Purpose of Ritual." *Folklore* 46 (1935): 343–49.

Hodges, Richard. *The Anglo-Saxon Achievement: Archaeology and the Beginnings of English Society.* London: Duckworth, 1989.

Hohler, C. E. "Some Service Books of the Later Saxon Church." In *Tenth-Century Studies,* edited by David Parsons, pp. 60–83, 217–27. London: Phillimore, 1975.

Hollis, Stephanie. *Anglo-Saxon Women and the Church: Sharing a Common Fate.* Woodbridge: Boydell, 1992.

Hollister, C. Warren. *The Making of England, 55 B.C. to 1399.* 6th ed. Lexington, Mass.: D. C. Heath, 1992.

Holt, J. C., ed. *Domesday Studies.* Woodbridge: Boydell, 1987.

Hooke, Della, ed. *Anglo-Saxon Settlements.* Oxford: Blackwell, 1988.

———. *Medieval Villages: A Review of Current Work.* Oxford: Oxford University Committee for Archaeology, 1985.

Howe, Nicholas. *Migration and Mythmaking in Anglo-Saxon England.* New Haven, Conn.: Yale University Press, 1989.

Hunt, Lynn. *The New Cultural History.* Berkeley: University of California Press, 1989.

Hunt, Tony. *Popular Medicine in Thirteenth-Century England.* Cambridge: D. S. Brewer, 1990.

Hurt, James. *Ælfric.* New York: Twayne, 1972.

Hutton, Patrick H. "The History of Mentalities: The New Map of Cultural History." *History and Theory* 20 (1981): 237–59.

Imbart de la Tour, Pierre. *Les paroisses rurales du IVe au XIe siècles.* Paris: A. Picard et fils, 1900.

Jacobeit, Wolfgang, and Paul Nedo, eds. *Probleme und Methoden volkskundlicher Gegenwartsforschung.* Berlin: Akademie-Verlag, 1969.

James, Edwin Oliver. "The Influence of Christianity on Folklore." *Folklore* 58 (1947): 361–76.

John, Eric. *Land Tenure in Early England: A Discussion of Some Problems.* Leicester: Leicester University Press, 1960. Corrected, 1964.

————. *Orbis Britanniae.* Leicester: Leicester University Press, 1966.

————. "The Social and Political Problems of the Early English Church." In *Land, Church, and People: Essays Presented to Professor H. P. R. Finberg,* edited by Joan Thirsk, pp. 39–63. Reading: Museum of English Rural Life, 1970.

————. "War and Society in the Tenth Century: The Maldon Campaign." *Transactions of the Royal Historical Society,* 5th ser., 27 (1977): 173–95.

————. "The World of Abbot Ælfric." In *Ideal and Reality in Frankish and Anglo-Saxon Society,* edited by Patrick Wormald, Donald Bullough, and Roger Collins, pp. 300–316. Oxford: Blackwell, 1982.

Jolly, Karen Louise. "Anglo-Saxon Charms in the Context of a Christian World View." *The Journal of Medieval History* 11 (1985): 279–92.

————. "Father God and Mother Earth: Nature-Mysticism in the Early Middle Ages." In *The Medieval World of Nature,* edited by Joyce Salisbury, pp. 221–52. New York: Garland, 1992.

Jones, A. H. M. *Constantine and the Conversion of Europe.* New York: Macmillan, 1948. Reprint, Toronto: University of Toronto Press, 1978.

Jost, Karl. *Wulfstanstudien.* Swiss Studies in English 23. Bern: A. Francke, 1950.

Joyce, James Wayland. *England's Sacred Synods: A Constitutional History of the Convocations of the Clergy.* London: Rivingtons, 1855. Reprint, Farnborough: Gregg, 1967.

Julia, Dominique. "A propos des sources écrites de la religion populaire: Questions de méthode." *Ricerche di storia sociale e religiosa,* new ser., 11 (1977): 109–17.

Kaplan, Steven L., ed. *Understanding Popular Culture: Europe from the Middle Ages to the Nineteenth Century.* Berlin: Mouton, 1984.

Karras, Ruth Mazo. "Pagan Survivals and Syncretism in the Conversion of Saxony." *Catholic Historical Review* 72 (1986): 553–72.

Kealey, Edward J. *Medieval Medicus: A Social History of Anglo-Norman Medicine.* Baltimore: Johns Hopkins University Press, 1981.

Kee, Howard Clark. *Medicine, Miracle, and Magic in New Testament Times.* Cambridge: Cambridge University Press, 1986.

————. *Miracle in the Early Christian World: A Study in Sociohistorical Method.* New Haven: Yale University Press, 1983.

Keynes, Simon. "The Declining Reputation of King Ethelred the Unready." In *Ethelred the Unready: Papers from the Millenary Conference,* edited by D. Hill, pp. 227–53. British Archaeological Reports, British ser. lix, 1978.

————. *The Diplomas of King Æthelred 'the Unready'.* Cambridge: Cambridge University Press, 1980.

Kieckhefer, Richard. *Magic in the Middle Ages.* Cambridge: Cambridge University Press, 1989.

————. "The Specific Rationality of Medieval Magic." *American Historical Review* 99 (1994): 813–36.

————. *Unquiet Souls: Fourteenth-Century Saints and Their Religious Milieu.* Chicago: University of Chicago Press, 1984.

Kitson, Peter. "From Eastern Learning to Western Folklore." In *Superstition and Popular Medicine in Anglo-Saxon England,* edited by D. G. Scragg, pp. 57–71. Manchester: Manchester Centre for Anglo-Saxon Studies, 1989.

————. "Lapidary Traditions in Anglo-Saxon England." *Anglo-Saxon England* 12 (1983): 73–123.

Kroll, Jerome, and Bernard Bachrach. "Monastic Medicine in Pre-Crusade Europe: The Care of Sick Children." In *The Medieval Monastery,* edited by Andrew MacLeish, pp. 59–63. Medieval Studies at Minnesota 2. St. Cloud, Minn.: North Star, 1988.

————. "Sin and Mental Illness in the Middle Ages." *Psychological Medicine* 14 (1984): 507–14.

————. "Sin and the Etiology of Disease in Pre-Crusade Europe." *Journal of the History of Medicine* 41 (1986): 395–414.

Lacroix, Benoit, and Pietro Boglioni, eds. *Les religions populaires.* Colloque international 1970. Quebec: Les Presses de l'Universite Laval, 1972.

Ladner, Gerhart B. *The Idea of Reform and Its Impact on Christian Thought and Action in the Age of the Fathers.* Cambridge, Mass.: Harvard University Press, 1959. Rev. ed., New York: Harper and Row, 1967.

Ladurie, Emmanuel Le Roy. *Montaillou: The Promised Land of Error.* Translated by Barbara Bray. New York: Scolar, 1978. Originally published as *Montaillou, village occitan de 1294 à 1324.* Paris: Editions Gallimard, 1975.

Landes, Richard. "Millenarismus absconditus: L'historiographie augustinienne et le millénarisme du haut Moyen Age jusqu'à l'an Mil." *Le Moyen Age* 98 (1992): 355–77.

————. "Sur les traces du Millennium." *Le Moyen Age* 99 (1993): 5–26.

Lapidge, Michael. "Surviving Booklists from Anglo-Saxon England." In *Anglo-Saxon Manuscripts: Basic Readings,* edited by Mary P. Richards, pp. 87–167. New York: Garland, 1994.

Lawson, M. K. *Cnut: The Danes in England in the Early Eleventh Century.* London: Longman, 1993.

Leclercq, Jean. "Modern Psychology and the Interpretation of Medieval Texts." *Speculum* 48 (1973): 476–90.

Lecouteux, Claude. "Paganisme, christianisme et merveilleux." *Annales* 37 (1982): 700–716.

Lees, Clare A. "Working with Patristic Sources: Language and Context in Old

English Homilies." In *Speaking Two Languages: Traditional Disciplines and Contemporary Theory in Medieval Studies*, edited by Allen J. Frantzen, pp. 157–80. Albany: SUNY Press, 1991.

Le Goff, Jacques. *La civilisation de l'occident médiévale*. Paris: Arthaud, 1964.

———. "Culture cléricale et traditions folkloriques dans la civilisation mérovingienne." *Annales* 22 (1967): 780–89.

Lennard, Reginald. "The Economic Position of the Domesday Sokeman." *Economic Journal* 57 (1947): 179–95.

———. "The Economic Position of the Domesday Villani." *Economic Journal* 56 (1946): 244–64.

———. *Rural England, 1086–1135: A Study of Social and Agrarian Conditions*. Oxford: Clarendon, 1959. Reprint, 1966.

Lienhardt, Godfrey. *Divinity and Experience: The Religion of the Dinka*. Oxford: Clarendon, 1961.

"The Liturgy and Ritual of the Anglo-Saxon Church." *Church Quarterly Review* 14 (1882): 276–94.

Logan, Donald. *The Vikings in History*. London: Hutchinson, 1983.

Loyn, H. R. *Anglo-Saxon England and the Norman Conquest*. 2nd ed. London: Longman, 1991.

———. "Church and State in England in the Tenth and Eleventh Centuries." In *Tenth Century Studies: Essays in Commemoration of the Council of Winchester and Regularis Concordia*, edited by David Parsons, pp. 94–102, 229–31. London: Phillimore, 1975.

———. *The Governance of Anglo-Saxon England, 500–1087*. Stanford: Stanford University Press, 1984.

———. "The King and the Structure of Society in Late Anglo-Saxon England." *History* 42 (1957): 87–100.

———. *The Vikings in Britain*. New York: St. Martins, 1977.

McDonald, John, and G. D. Snooks. *Domesday Economy: A New Approach to Anglo-Norman History*. Oxford: Clarendon, 1986.

McGinn, Bernard. *Visions of the End: Apocalyptic Traditions in the Middle Ages*. New York: Columbia University Press, 1979.

MacKinney, Loren C. "An Unpublished Treatise on Medicine and Magic from the Age of Charlemagne." *Speculum* 18 (1943): 494–96.

McNeill, John T., and Helena Gamer. "Folk-Paganism in the Penitentials." *Journal of Religion* 13 (1933): 450–66.

Magoun, F. P. "On Some Survivals of Pagan Belief in Anglo-Saxon England." *Harvard Theological Review* 40 (1947): 33–46.

Malinowski, Bronislaw. *Magic, Science, and Religion and Other Essays*. Garden City, N.Y.: Doubleday, 1948.

Manselli, Raoul. *La religion populaire au moyen âge: Problèmes de méthode et d'histoire*. Montreal: Institut d'études mediévales Albert-le-Grand, 1975. Originally

published as *La religione popolare nel medioevo (Sec. VI–XIII)*. Turin:
 G. Giappichelli, 1974.
Mayr-Harting, Henry. *The Coming of Christianity to Anglo-Saxon England*. 3rd ed.
 University Park: Pennsylvania State University Press, 1991.
Meaney, Audrey L. "Ælfric and Idolatry." *Journal of Religious History* 13 (1984): 119–35.
———. "Æthelweard, Ælfric, the Norse Gods, and Northumbria." *Journal of
 Religious History* 6 (1970): 105–32.
———. "Variant Versions of Old English Medical Remedies and the Compilation
 of *Bald's Leechbook*." *Anglo-Saxon England* 13 (1984): 235–68.
———. "Women, Witchcraft, and Magic." In *Superstition and Popular Medicine in Anglo-
 Saxon England*, edited by D. G. Scragg, pp. 9–40. Manchester: Manchester Centre
 for Anglo-Saxon Studies, 1989.
Miles-Cadman, Margaret. "Ælfric and Education." In *A Festschrift for Edgar Ronald
 Seary: Essays in English Language and Literature Presented by Colleagues and Former Students*,
 edited by A. A. Macdonald, P. A. Flaherty, and G. M. Story, pp. 27–39. St. Johns:
 Memorial University of Newfoundland, 1975.
Moore, R. I. "Family, Community, and Cult on the Eve of the Gregorian Reform."
 Transactions of the Royal Historical Society, 5th ser., 30 (1980): 49–69.
Morris, Richard K. *The Church in British Archaeology*. CBA Research Report 47.
 London: Council for British Archaeology, 1983.
Morrison, Karl Frederick. *Understanding Conversion*. Charlottesville: University Press of
 Virginia, 1992.
———. *Conversion and Text: The Cases of Augustine of Hippo, Herman-Judah, and Constantine
 Tsatsos*. Charlottesville: University Press of Virginia, 1992.
Muir, Edward, and Guido Ruggiero, eds. *Microhistory and the Lost Peoples of Europe*.
 Translated by Eren Branch. Baltimore: Johns Hopkins University Press, 1991.
Murray, Alexander. "Missionaries and Magic in Dark Age Europe." *Past and Present*
 136 (1992): 186–205.
———. *Reason and Society in the Middle Ages*. Oxford: Clarendon, 1978.
Nelson, Marie. "An Old English Charm against Nightmare." *Germanic Notes* 13 (1982):
 17–18.
———. "Sound as Meaning in Old English Charms, Riddles, and Maxims." In *The
 27th Annual Mountain Interstate Foreign Language Conference*, edited by E. Zayas-Bazan
 and M. Laurentino Suarez, pp. 122–28. Johnson City, 1978.
———. "A Woman's Charm." *Studia Neophilologica* 57 (1985): 3–8.
———. "'Wordsige and Worcsige': Speech Acts in Three Old English Charms."
 Language and Style 17 (1984): 57–66.
Neusner, Jacob, Ernest Frerichs, and Paul Virgil McCracken Flesher, eds. *Religion,
 Science, and Magic: In Concert and in Conflict*. Oxford: Oxford University Press, 1989.
Ni Chathain, Proinseas, and Michael Richter, eds. *Irland und die Christenheit:
 Bibelstudien und Mission*. Stuttgart: Klett-Cotta, 1987.
Niles, John D. "The Æcerbot Ritual in Context." In *Old English Literature in Context*,
 edited by John Niles, pp. 44–56, 163–64. Cambridge: D. S. Brewer, 1980.

————. "Pagan Survivals and Popular Belief." In *The Cambridge Companion to Old English Literature*, edited by Malcolm Godden and Michael Lapidge, pp. 126–41. Cambridge: Cambridge University Press, 1991.

Niles, John D., and Mark Amodio, eds. *Anglo-Scandinavian England: Norse-English Relations in the Period before the Conquest*. New York: University Press of America, 1989.

Noth, Winifried. "Semiotics of the Old English Charm." *Semiotica* 19 (1977): 59–83.

Oakley, Thomas P. *English Penitential Discipline and Anglo-Saxon Law in Their Joint Influence*. New York: AMS, 1969.

Owen, Dorothy M. "Episcopal Visitation Books." *History* 49, Short Guide 8 (1964): 185–88.

Owen, Gale R. *Rites and Religions of the Anglo-Saxons*. Totowa, N.J.: Barnes and Noble, 1981.

Page, R. I. *An Introduction to English Runes*. London: Methuen, 1973.

————. "Old English Liturgical Rubrics in Corpus Christi College, Cambridge, MS 422." *Anglia* 96 (1978): 149–58.

Page, William. "Some Remarks on the Churches of the Domesday Survey." *Archaeologia* 66 (1914–15): 61–102.

Paxton, Frederick S. *Christianizing Death: The Creation of a Ritual Process in Early Medieval Europe*. Ithaca: Cornell University Press, 1990.

Payne, Joseph F. *English Medicine in the Anglo-Saxon Times*. Oxford: Clarendon, 1904.

Peters, Edward. *The Magician, the Witch, and the Law*. Philadelphia: University of Pennsylvania Press, 1978.

Peters, R. A. "OE Ælf, -Ælf, Ælfen, -Ælfen." *Philological Quarterly* 42 (1963): 250–57.

Pettersson, Olaf. "Magic-Religion." *Ethnos* 22 (1957): 109–19.

Pinto, Lucille B. "Medical Science and Superstition: A Report on a Unique Medical Scroll of the Eleventh-Twelfth Century." *Manuscripta* 17 (1973): 12–21.

Platt, Colin. *The Parish Churches of Medieval England*. London: Secker and Warburg, 1981.

Plongeron, B., ed. *La Religion populaire dans l'occident chrétien: Approches historiques*. Paris: Beauchesne, 1976.

Plummer, Alfred. *The Churches in Britain before A.D. 1000*. 2 vols. London: R. Scott, 1911–12.

Potts, Cassandra. "The Recovery and Reform of Monasticism in Eleventh-Century France: Normandy and Its Neighbors." Unpublished paper, American Historical Association Annual Meeting, Washington, D.C., December 1992.

————. "The Revival of Monasticism in Normandy, 911–1066." Ph.D. diss., University of California at Santa Barbara, 1990.

Price, Richard. *First Time: The Historical Vision of an Afro-American People*. Baltimore: Johns Hopkins University Press, 1983.

Redfield, Robert. *Peasant Society and Culture: An Anthropological Approach to Civilization*. Chicago: University of Chicago Press, 1956.

Reinsma, Luke. *Ælfric: An Annotated Bibliography*. New York: Garland, 1987.

Remly, Lyn. "Magic, Myth, and Medicine: The Veterinary Art in the Middle Ages (9th–15th Centuries)." *Fifteenth Century Studies* 2 (1979): 203–9.

Reynolds, Susan. *Fiefs and Vassals: The Medieval Evidence Reinterpreted.* Oxford: Oxford University Press, 1994.

———. *Kingdoms and Communities in Western Europe, 900–1300.* Oxford: Oxford University Press, 1984.

Richards, Mary P. "Innovations in Ælfrician Homiletic Manuscripts at Rochester." *Annuale Mediaevale* 19 (1979): 13–26.

Riché, M. Pierre. "La magie a l'époque Carolingienne." *Comptes rendus des séances de l'Académie des inscriptions et belles-lettres* 1 (1973): 127–38.

Ridyard, Susan J. "Monk-Kings and the Anglo-Saxon Hagiographic Tradition." *Haskins Society Journal* 6 (1994): 13–27.

Robinson, J. Armitage. *The Times of Saint Dunstan.* Oxford: Clarendon, 1923.

Rodwell, Warwick. *Archaeology of Religious Places: Churches and Cemeteries in Britain.* Rev. ed. Philadelphia: University of Pennsylvania Press, 1989.

———. *The Archaeology of the English Church: The Study of Historic Churches and Churchyards.* London: Batsford, 1981.

———, ed. *Temples, Churches, and Religion: Recent Research in Roman Britain.* British Archaeological Report 77. Oxford: BAR, 1980.

Rollason, David. *Saints and Relics in Anglo-Saxon England.* Oxford: Blackwell, 1989.

Rosenberg, Bruce A. "Folkloristes et médiévistes face au texte littéraire: Problèmes de méthode." *Annales* 34 (1979): 943–55.

Ross, Anne. *Pagan Celtic Britain.* New York: Columbia University Press, 1967.

Rubin, Stanley. "The Anglo-Saxon Physician." *British History Illustrated* 1 (1975): 40–47.

———. *Medieval English Medicine.* New York: Barnes and Noble, 1974.

Rumble, Alexander R., ed. *The Reign of Cnut: King of England, Denmark, and Norway.* London: Leicester University Press, 1994.

Rushton, Peter. "A Note on the Survival of Popular Christian Magic." *Folklore* 91 (1980): 115–18.

Russell, James C. *The Germanization of Early Medieval Christianity: A Sociohistorical Approach to Religious Transformation.* Oxford: Oxford University Press, 1994.

Russell, Jeffrey B. *The Devil: Perceptions of Evil from Antiquity to Primitive Christianity.* Ithaca: Cornell University Press, 1977.

———. "History and Truth." *Historian* 50 (1987): 3–13.

———. *A History of Witchcraft, Sorcerers, Heretics, and Pagans.* New York: Thames and Hudson, 1980.

———. *Lucifer: The Devil in the Middle Ages.* Ithaca: Cornell University Press, 1984.

———. *Mephistopheles: The Devil in the Modern World.* Ithaca: Cornell University Press, 1986.

———. *Satan: The Early Christian Tradition.* Ithaca: Cornell University Press, 1981.

Sawyer, Peter H. *From Roman Britain to Norman England.* New York: St. Martin's, 1978.

————. *Kings and Vikings: Scandinavia and Europe, A.D. 700–1100.* London: Methuen, 1982.

————, ed. *Medieval Settlement: Continuity and Change.* London: Edward Arnold, 1976.

Schmitt, Jean-Claude. "Les traditions folkloriques dans la culture médiévale: Quelques réflexions de méthode." *Archives de sciences sociales des religions* 52 (1981): 5–20.

Scragg, D. G., ed. *Superstition and Popular Medicine in Anglo-Saxon England.* Manchester: Manchester Centre for Anglo-Saxon Studies, 1989.

Searle, Eleanor. *Predatory Kinship and the Creation of Norman Power, 840–1066.* Berkeley: University of California Press, 1988.

Serjeantson, Mary Sidney. "The Vocabulary of Folklore in Old and Middle English." *Folklore* 47 (1936): 42–73.

Shook, L. K. "Notes on the Old English Charms." *Modern Language Notes* 55 (1940): 139–40.

Singer, Charles. *From Magic to Science: Essays on the Scientific Twilight.* London: Ernest Benn, 1928.

————. *A Short History of Medicine.* New York: Oxford, 1962.

Singer, Charles, and Dorothea Singer. "An Unrecognized Anglo-Saxon Medical Text." *Annals of Medical History* 3 (1921): 136–49.

Siraisi, Nancy. *Medieval and Early Renaissance Medicine.* Chicago: University of Chicago Press, 1990.

Smart, Ninian. *Worldviews: Crosscultural Explorations of Human Beliefs.* New York: Macmillan, 1983.

Smyth, Alfred P. *Scandinavian Kings in the British Isles, 850–880.* Oxford: Oxford University Press, 1977.

————. *Scandinavian York and Dublin: The History and Archaeology of Two Related Viking Kingdoms.* 2 vols. Dublin: Templekieran Press, 1975, 1979.

————. *Warlords and Holy Men: Scotland, A.D. 80–1000.* London: E. Arnold, 1984.

Stafford, Pauline. *Unification and Conquest: A Political and Social History of England in the Tenth and Eleventh Centuries.* London: Edward Arnold, 1989.

Stancliffe, Clare. "Kings Who Opted Out." In *Ideal and Reality in Frankish and Anglo-Saxon Society,* edited by Patrick Wormald, Donald Bullough, and Roger Collins, pp. xx–176. Oxford: Blackwell, 1982.

Stanley, Eric Gerald. *The Search for Anglo-Saxon Paganism.* Cambridge: D. S. Brewer, 1975.

Stenton, Sir Frank. *Anglo-Saxon England.* 3rd ed. Oxford: Oxford University Press, 1971.

————. "Types of Manorial Structure in the Northern Danelaw." *Oxford Studies in Social and Legal History* 2 (1910): 3–96.

Stock, Brian. *The Implications of Literacy.* Princeton: Princeton University Press, 1983.

Stoney, Constance B. "The English Parish before the Norman Conquest." *Saga Book of the Viking Club* 9 (1925): 311–32.

Straw, Carole. *Gregory the Great: Perfection in Imperfection*. Berkeley: University of
   California Press, 1988.

Strunk, Oliver, ed. *Source Readings in Music History: Antiquity and the Middle Ages*. New
   York: Norton, 1965.

Stuart, Heather. "The Anglo-Saxon Elf." *Studia Neophilologica* 48 (1976): 313–20.

———. "The Meaning of Old English Ælfsciene." *Parergon* 2 (1972): 22–26.

———. "Spider in Old English." *Parergon* 18 (1977): 37–42.

———. "Utterance Instructions in the Anglo-Saxon Charms." *Parergon*, n.s., 3
   (1985): 31–37.

Stutz, V. "The Proprietary Church as an Element of Medieval Germanic
   Ecclesiastical Law." In *Medieval Germany, 911–1250*, vol. 2, *Essays*, edited and
   translated by Geoffrey Barraclough. Oxford: Blackwell, 1948.

Sullivan, Richard E. *Christian Missionary Activity in the Early Middle Ages*. Brookfield, Vt.:
   Variorum, 1994.

Szarmach, Paul E. "The Vercelli Homilies: Style and Structure." In *The Old English
   Homily and Its Backgrounds*, edited by Paul E. Szarmach and Bernard F. Huppe, pp.
   241–67. Albany: SUNY Press, 1978.

Szarmach, Paul E., and Bernard F. Huppe, eds. *The Old English Homily and Its
   Backgrounds*. Albany: SUNY Press, 1978.

Talbot, Charles H. *Medicine in Medieval England*. London: Oldbourne, 1967.

Talbot, Charles H., and E. A. Hammond. *The Medical Practitioners in Medieval England:
   A Biographical Register*. London: Wellcome Historical Medical Library, 1965.

Tambiah, Stanley. *Magic, Science, Religion, and the Scope of Rationality*. Cambridge:
   Cambridge University Press, 1990.

Taylor, H. M. "The Position of the Altar in Early Anglo-Saxon Churches."
   Antiquaries Journal 53 (1973): 52–58.

———. "Some Little-Known Aspects of English Pre-Conquest Churches." In *The
   Anglo-Saxons: Studies in Some Aspects of their History and Culture*, edited by Peter
   Clemoes, pp. 137–58. London: Bowes and Bowes, 1959.

———. "Tenth-Century Church Building in England and on the Continent." In
   Tenth-Century Studies, edited by David Parsons, pp. 141–68. London:
   Phillimore, 1975.

Taylor, H. M., and Joan Taylor. *Anglo-Saxon Architecture*. 3 vols. Cambridge:
   Cambridge University Press, 1965, 1978.

Thomas, Keith. *Religion and the Decline of Magic*. New York: Scribners, 1971.

Thorndike, Lynn. *History of Magic and Experimental Science during the First Thirteen Centuries
   of our Era*. 2 vols. New York: Columbia University Press, 1923.

———. "Some Medieval Conceptions of Magic." *Monist* 25 (1915): 107–39.

Thun, Nils. "The Malignant Elves." *Studia Neophilologica* 41 (1969): 378–96.

Tierney, Brian. *The Middle Ages*. Vol. 1, *Sources of Medieval History*. 4th ed. New York:
   Knopf, 1983.

Tripp, Raymond P., Jr. "The Effect of the Occult and the Supernatural upon the

Way We Read Old English Poetry." In *Literature and the Occult: Essays in Comparative Literature*, edited by Luanne Frank, pp. 255–63. Arlington: University of Texas Press, 1977.

Tylor, Edward B. *Primitive Culture: Researches into the Development of Mythology, Philosophy, Religion, Language, Art, and Custom.* Vol. 1. New York, 1889.

Van Baal, J. "Magic as a Religious Phenomenon." *Higher Education and Research in the Netherlands* 8 (1963): 10–21.

Van der Meer, Frederik. *Augustine the Bishop.* Translated by Brian Battershaw and G. R. Lamb. London: Sheed and Ward, 1961.

Van Engen, John. "The Christian Middle Ages as an Historiographical Problem." *American Historical Review* 91 (1986): 519–52.

Varah, William Edward. "Minsters." *Notes and Queries* 165 (1933): 148–49.

Vaughan-Sterling, Judith A. "The Anglo-Saxon 'Metrical Charms' Poetry as Ritual." *Journal of English and Germanic Philology* 82 (1983): 186–200.

Vogel, Cyrille. *Medieval Liturgy: An Introduction to the Sources.* Revised and translated by William G. Storey and Niels Krogh Rasmussen. Washington, D.C.: Pastoral Press, 1986.

——. "Pratiques superstitieuses au début du XIe siècle d'après le 'Corrector sive medicus' de Burchard évêque de Worms, 965–1025." In *Etudes de civilisation médiévale, IXe–XIIe siècles: Mélanges offerts à Edmond-René Labande*, pp. 751–61. Poitiers: CESCM, 1974.

Voigts, Linda. "Anglo-Saxon Plant Remedies and the Anglo-Saxons." *Isis* 70 (1979): 250–68.

Vovelle, Michel. "La religion populaire: Problèmes et méthodes." *Le monde alpin et rhodanien* 5 (1977): 7–32.

Wainwright, F. T. *Scandinavian England.* Edited by H. P. R. Finberg. Chichester: Phillimore, 1975.

Wallace-Hadrill, J. M. *Early Germanic Kingship in England and on the Continent.* Oxford: Clarendon, 1971.

——. *The Frankish Church.* Oxford: Oxford University Press, 1983.

Ward, Benedicta. "Miracles and History: A Reconsideration of the Miracle Stories used by Bede." In *Famulus Christi: Essays in Commemoration of the Thirteenth Centenary of the Birthday of the Venerable Bede*, edited by Gerald Bonner, pp. 70–76. London: S.P.C.K., 1976.

——. *Miracles and the Medieval Mind.* Philadelphia: University of Pennsylvania Press, 1982.

Ward, Gordon. "The List of Saxon Churches in the Textus Roffensis." *Archaeologia Cantiana* 44 (1932): 39–59.

——. "The Lists of Saxon Churches in the Domesday Monachorum, and White Book of St. Augustine." *Archaeologia Cantiana* 45 (1933): 60–89.

Warner, Peter. "Shared Churchyards, Freeman Church Builders, and the Development of Parishes in Eleventh-century East Anglia." *Landscape History* 8 (1986): 39–52.

Wax, Murray, and Rosalie Wax. "The Magical World View." *Journal for the Scientific Study of Religion* 1 (1962): 179–88.

White, Caroline. *Ælfric: A New Study of his Life and Writings*. Boston: Lamson, Wolffe, 1898.

Whitelock, Dorothy. "Archbishop Wulfstan, Homilist and Statesman." *Transactions of the Royal Historical Society*, 4th ser., 24 (1942): 25–45.

———. "The Conversion of the Eastern Danelaw." *Saga Book of the Viking Society* 13 (1941): 159–76.

———. "Two Notes on Ælfric and Wulfstan." *MLR* 38 (1943): 122–26.

———. "Wulfstan and the Laws of Cnut." *English Historical Review* 63 (1948): 434–52.

———. "Wulfstan and the So-Called Laws of Edward and Guthrum." *English Historical Review* 56 (1941): 1–21.

———. "Wulfstan at York." In *Franciplegius: Medieval and Linguistic Studies in Honour of Francis Peabody Magoun, Jr.*, edited by Jess B. Bessinger, Jr., and Robert P. Creed, pp. 214–31. New York: New York University Press, 1965.

Wilson, David M. *Anglo-Saxon Paganism*. New York: Routledge, 1992.

———. "The Vikings' Relationship with Christianity in Northern England." *Journal of the British Archaeological Association*, 3rd ser., 30 (1967): 37–46.

Wood, I. N. "Early Merovingian Devotion in Town and Country." In *The Church in Town and Countryside*, edited by Derek Baker, pp. 61–76. Studies in Church History 16. Oxford: Blackwell, 1979.

Wormald, C. P. "The Uses of Literacy in Anglo-Saxon England and Its Neighbours." *Transactions of the Royal Historical Society*, 5th ser., 27 (1977): 95–114.

INDEX

Abbesses: role in conversion, 44, 184 (n. 14)

Abbeys: as proprietors, 53; liturgical reform, 114. *See also* Minsters; Monasteries

Abels, Richard, 38

Absinthium: ingredient in remedies, 136. *See also* Wormwood

Abstract: concepts, 12–13; thought, 22–23, 105

Accommodation: in theory, 2–3, 9–12, 17–18, 21, 24–27, 171–74; in Anglo-Saxon culture, 28–34; Anglo-Saxon and Scandinavian, 36–39, 55; in conversion, 40–46; through local churches and priests, 69–70; in homiletic thought, 72–79, 86; evident in medical texts and charms, 96–97, 106, 115–16, 123–24, 129–31, 132–33, 138, 142–45, 154–56, 160, 163–65. *See also* Christianization; Conversion; Synthesis, cultural

Acculturation. *See* Accommodation

Adaptation. *See* Accommodation

Adders, 124–30. *See also* Poison; Worm

Adjurations: in charm formulas and as exorcisms, 109, 118–19, 145, 150

Æcerbot Remedy. *See* Field Remedy

Ælf, and related compounds. *See* Elf afflictions and remedies; Elves

Ælfgar, Ealdorman of Essex, 49

Ælfhere, Ealdorman of Mercia, 50

Ælfric, Abbot of Eynsham: influence, 47, 48, 51; on priests, 61–69; homilies and worldview, 76–81, 94–95; on miracles, 82–85; on magic, 86–89; on healing, 89–93; views related to charms, 102, 108, 109, 110, 113, 120, 121, 131, 149, 151, 152, 161, 166–67; glossary, 135

Ælfthone: ingredient in remedies, 109, 135–36, 160, 161–62, 166, 167, 204 (n. 9)

Æsir, 28, 31, 127–28, 134, 139–40

Æthelflæd, Lady of the Mericans, 49

Æthelred, Ealdorman of Mercia, 49

Æthelred Unræd, King, 50–51; laws regarding churches, 53, 59; and Wulfstan, 77, 78; hand of God coin, 81

Æthelthryth, Saint (Queen Etheldreda), Abbess of Ely, 83, 85, 184 (n. 14)

Æthelwine, Ealdorman of East Anglia, 56

Æthelwold, Bishop of Winchester, 49, 51, 56, 76

Agate: ingredient in remedies, 153–54, 206 (n. 52)

Agricultural concerns, 23; in local church, 39, 46; in homilies, 70, 83; in charms, 120, 149. *See also* Field Remedy

Aidan, Saint, Bishop of Lindisfarne, 52

Ale: ingredient in remedies, 147, 148, 150, 155, 156, 161, 165, 166–67

Alexanders: ingredient in remedies, 149

"Alfheim" (Elfland), 134
Alfred, King, 35–38, 42, 70; remedy sent to, 151
Allegorical thinking, 13, 43, 82, 195 (n. 46)
Alms, 68; as part of a prescription, 7, 148
Alpha and Omega, 119, 149, 201 (n. 59)
Altar: used in remedies, 7, 93, 119, 122, 148, 149, 155, 157, 159, 161; placement in church, 67–69
Amalgamation. *See* Accommodation
Amulets: Germanic, 45; condemned, 92–93; with words, 109, 145, 149, 150; herbal, 157–58
Angels, 81, 136–37
Anglo-Saxon Herbal, 105, 108–9, 113, 125, 135–36
Animals: blessing of, 6, 87; veterinary treatment of, 130, 134–36, 142–43, 149. *See also* Cattle; Horses; *Medicina de Quadrupedibus*
Animism, 10, 23, 26–28, 45, 67, 82, 89, 95, 102, 127, 171
Anointing the sick, 68–69, 120
Anthropology, 15–16, 101, 176 (n. 2), 201 (n. 65). *See also* Ethnography
Antimonastic reaction, 49–50, 56
Apples: ingredient in remedies, 126–27, 149, 153, 155
Archaeology: of burial, 31–32, 60; of churches, 47–48, 53–57, 67–69
Aristocracy, 46, 49–53, 65–66. *See also* Ealdormen; Thegns
Armelu: ingredient in remedies, 149
Ashes: ingredient in remedies, 127
Ashthroat: ingredient in remedies, 159
Asp, 118. *See also* Worm
Asser, 35–36, 41–43
Assimilation. *See* Accommodation
Astrology, 88, 93

Astronomy, 113
Athelstan, "Half-King," Ealdorman of East Anglia, 49, 56
Attorlathe (one of the nine herbs), 126–27, 135, 147, 148, 154, 165
Augustine of Hippo: influence, 9, 41, 73–74; source for Ælfric, 77, 85, 91, 92; view of miracles, 82, 85, 89
Augustinian worldview, 40, 71–81, 82–95 passim, 96, 109, 113, 121, 131, 170. *See also* Worldview
Ayer, Joseph, 62

Bald's Leechbook. See Leechbook
Baptism: of Guthrum, 35–36, 41–42, 45, 70; in conversion, 41–43; church rights to perform, 60, 62; as priestly duty, 63, 68, 69
Barley: blessed, 8; ear of in remedy, 109
Basilisk, 118
Bathing: in a remedy, 155
Bede, the Venerable, 24, 52; as source, 9, 74, 94; on conversion, 24, 41–44
Bells: used in remedies, 146, 147–48
Benedicite (blessing): prescribed, 7, 117, 160–61
"Benedictio Herbarum," 120
Benedictions, 7–8, 117, 128–29, 139–40, 144, 145, 208 (n. 71). *See also* Benedicite; Blessings
"Benedictio Potus sive Unguenti," 121
"Benedictio Unguentum," 121
Beolone: ingredient in remedies, 207 (n. 64). *See also* Henbane
Beowulf, 15, 29, 133
Beronice, Byrnice. *See* Veronica
Betony (betonica): ingredient in remedies, 135, 147, 148, 149, 153, 154, 155, 157, 158, 159, 160, 161, 166; translation, 204 (n. 11), 207 (n. 55)

236 : Index

Bishops: relationship to local churches, 47, 53, 56, 58–65

Bishopwort (bisceopwyrt). See Betony

Black Mass, 142

Blair, John, 48

Blessings: of fields, 6–8, 21–23, 26; of animals, 87–88; to transfer virtue, 90–95, 120–22, 159, 170, 173–74; in healing, 116, 117, 141, 143–44, 149, 150, 152, 159, 161–62, 202. See also Benedictions

Blickling Homilies, 74–76

Blisters, 127

Blood: in remedies, 109, 128, 139–40

Bloodletting, 108–11, 113, 140

Body: and soul or mind, 75, 76, 80, 93–95, 108, 119, 121, 135, 146, 151, 167; incorruption and corruption, 80, 83, 85; exorcism of parts, 163–64

Boiling: of ingredients in remedies, 127, 139, 149, 150, 155, 158, 159, 160, 161

Bonewort: ingredient in remedies, 148

Boniface, Saint, 25, 44

Bowel problems, 152, 158, 162

Bramble root: ingredient in remedies, 152

Brass nails, 152

Bread: used in Field Remedy, 8, 21; miracle of multiplying loaves of, 83–84, 120; consecrated, ingredient in remedies, 119–20, 122, 155. See also Eucharist

Brooke, Rosalind and Christopher, 14

Brooks, Nicholas, 55

Brown, Peter, 122–23

Burial, 28, 31–32; fees for, 59–60, 65

Butter: ingredient in remedies, 139, 149, 155, 158, 159

Byrhtferth, Handbook of, 105, 107, 110–11

Byrhtnoth, Ealdorman, of Essex, 50

Cædmon manuscript, 110–12

Caesarius of Heisterbach, 82

Calendars and computation, 60, 63, 113, 114

Cameron, M. L., 100, 106, 137

Camomile. See Maythe

Campbell, J., 56

Canons of Edgar, 64, 66

Canterbury, archbishops of, 49, 50

Canterbury Psalter, 81, 136

Castalis, 163. See also Elves

Cathedrals, 22, 57, 59, 104

Catholic Homilies of Ælfric, 77. See also Ælfric, Abbot of Eynsham

Catmint: ingredient in remedies, 166

Cattle: elf attack on, 1, 133, 135; theft, 123

Celandine: ingredient in remedies, 155

Celtic influences, 38, 43, 181–82 (n. 51), 200 (n. 40); in charms, 118, 124, 130, 163

Centralization. See Centrifugal and centripetal forces

Centrifugal and centripetal forces, 38–60 passim

Chants and chanting, 98–99, 109, 125, 167. See also Charms; Enchant

Chapels, 51–52, 59, 67. See also Churches

Charms, 92, 98–99; as middle practices, 3, 11, 74, 89–90, 96–97, 102–3; Christianized, 3, 94, 171; textualization of, 20, 22, 151, 172–73; social context for in local churches, 36, 40, 46, 68, 172; laws against, 92–93, 102; as pagan or superstitious, 94, 100–102, 115, 125–28; historiography, 99–102, 106, 115, 141–42; in medical manuscripts, 103, 113; in liturgical context, 114, 116–18, 123, 151, 174; in folklore, 123–30. See also Galdor

Charms against elves, 1, 133–36; in

the *Lacnunga*, 138–45; in marginalia, 144–45; in *Bald's Leechbook*, 145–54; in *Leechbook III*, 154–67

Cheese. *See* Dairy products

Chervil (one of the nine herbs), 126–27

Chicken pox, 135, 166

Childbearing complaints, 109–10

Chrism, distribution of, 58, 60, 62, 68

Christening: as a miracle, 94

Christianity, theological definitions of. *See* Formal religion

Christianization, 9–12, 15–16, 18, 24–28, 31–33, 170, 171; late Saxon and Scandinavian, 36–40, 41, 43, 45, 54, 70, 71; of worldview, 82; of charms, 93–94, 97, 123–24, 128, 130, 133, 138, 140, 151, 164, 166, 168; of medicine, 107, 109. *See also* Conversion

Chrysostom, John, 117, 145

Churches: local, 10, 39–40, 46–53, 58–67 passim, 72, 132, 151, 172; types, 57–59; revenues, 59–60, 68; consecrations, 60, 62; design, 68–69. *See also* Cathedrals; Minsters; Monasteries

Church-scot, 60

Civilization, 3, 38, 173

Classical: Christian tradition, 72, 151; medicine, 97, 104–8, 110, 113, 135, 151–52; languages, 118

Clergy: and laity, 3, 13, 17, 21, 24, 25, 52, 70, 76, 77, 96, 104, 145, 172; literate, 9, 23, 76; local, 11, 69, 103, 115, 171; collegiate, 52, 63; celibacy of, 64–65. *See also* Churches; Priests

Clerical reform, 62–65

Cloves: ingredient in remedies, 155, 164

Clovis, King of the Franks, 24, 42, 44

Cnut, King, 39, 47, 50–51, 59, 66, 79

Coals: used in elf remedies, 160, 161

Cockayne, Oswald, 153, 157

Colic, 143

Comfrey. *See* Consolde

Command formulas, 109, 116, 144

Confession, 68–69, 75, 78. *See also* Penance and penitentials

Consolde: ingredient in remedies, 165, 209 (n. 75)

Constantine, Emperor, 42, 44

Constellations, 110

Conversion, 41–46; examples, 9–12, 29, 31–33, 35–36, 38–40, 70, 172–73; and magic, 14–18; and popular religion, 24–27. *See also* Christianization

Cosmology: pagan, 31, 134; shift in, 72, 82, 95, 107, 122, 129; Christian, 80–82, 86, 88–90, 94–95, 124, 132–33, 145, 159, 171, 173

Cosmos, 82, 96–97, 110, 113, 146. *See also* Macrocosm and microcosm

Costmary: ingredient in remedies, 148

Crab-apple: ingredient in remedies, 127

Cræftig man (artful man), 8

Craft (art, skill), 92–93, 146–47, 164. *See also* Galdor: *galdor-cræftas*; Sorcery; Witchcraft

Creation, Creator, 80–82, 84, 87–88, 91, 93, 102, 110, 122, 152, 171

Creed: taught, 69; in remedies, 93, 117, 141, 146, 160, 161, 164

Cress. *See* Lamb's cress

Cristalan: ingredient in remedies, 141

Cropleek: ingredient in remedies, 135, 147, 148, 149, 155, 159, 161, 166

Cross (rood): in remedies, 7, 45, 86, 88, 90, 92–94, 119–20, 128, 147, 149, 150, 152, 153, 159, 160, 161, 162, 164, 165; placement of, 24–26, 31, 59, 165, 171. *See also* Trees

Cucumber: ingredient in remedies, 156

Cup: as measure, 117, 150, 155, 156, 159, 161

Curses and cursing, 87–88, 92, 152

Cuthbert, Saint, 85

Cwidol wif (speaking woman), 8

Cynoglossum: ingredient in remedies, 147

Cysts, 117, 123

Dædbote (deed-remedy), 78. *See also* Penance and penitentials

Dairy products: ingredients in remedies, 153; milk, 6, 8, 149, 160, 161; cheese, 155

Daisy, 209 (n. 75)

Danelaw, 36–40, 41, 45, 49–51, 53, 54–58, 63, 79, 85, 172

Dawn, 6, 148, 161

Days: of the week, 28; special, 32, 87–88, 93, 110–13; Monday, 87; Sunday, 87; Thursday, 160–62

Death: worldview, 9, 21, 29, 31–32, 74, 75, 91; symbolic transference, 109; Christ's, 121–22, 165

Deceptions. *See* Delusions

Deities, pagan, 25, 27–28, 102, 134. *See also* Æsir; Vanir

Delaruelle, E., 13–14

Delumeau, Jean, 12

Delusions, 25, 73, 75–76, 86–88, 142, 149, 151

Dementedness. *See* Madness

Demonization: of elves, 11, 27, 136, 142, 164; of pagans, 25, 38

Demons, 79, 81, 86, 89, 95, 103, 122–23, 133–38, 144, 145, 146, 151, 156, 158–59, 165, 167, 171; demonic possession, 123, 147, 151. *See also* Devil; Temptation

Dental remedy, 110

Devil, 31, 83, 86–90, 91–94, 103,

129, 137; God versus, 2–3, 9, 17, 75, 82; magic associated with, 17, 25, 73, 82; expelling, 143–44, 164; sickness, 145, 158, 170; as cause of illness, 147, 157, 158, 159, 166, 167

Devil-worship (*deofolgylde*), 92

Diagnosis, 134–35, 144

Dialectical rapport: in popular religion, 13–14, 24, 40

Diarrhea, 152, 153

Diet, 109, 153

Digelnysse (deep secret), 77

Dill: ingredient in remedies, 136, 164, 165

Dioceses, 37–39, 52–62 passim

Divination, 25, 93

Dock seed: ingredient in remedies, 1, 119, 142, 165

Doctor. *See* Leech; Physicians

Domesday Book, 39, 47–48, 53, 54, 56–58, 62, 65, 66

Domesday Monachorum, 58

Dorchester, see of, 51

Draconitis (gem), 129

Dragon (*dracon*), 118, 129, 137

Dragonzan: ingredient in remedies, 164

Dream of the Rood, 29–31

Dreams, 135, 199 (n. 37)

Drinks: prescribed, 109, 119, 135–36, 140–41, 146–51, 153–59, 161, 163, 164, 166, 167; dangerous days for, 110, 113

Drycræft. *See* Sorcery

Dry disease, 123, 158

Dualities, 3–4, 9–10, 13–14, 18, 25, 38, 76, 84, 108, 135, 146

Dunstan, Saint, abbot, Archbishop of Canterbury, 49–51, 67, 76

Durham Ritual, 121

Dwarf dwosle. *See* Pollegian

Dwarves, 28, 81, 123, 155

Housel, 95. *See also* Bread, consecrated; Eucharist

Housel dish: used in remedies, 119–20, 140–41, 146, 147

Humors, four, 105, 108–9, 110, 152–53, 165–66

Icelandic lore, 134, 181 (n. 51)

Idols, 87

Illiteracy. *See* Literacy

Illusions. *See* Delusions

Immaculate (*unmælne*) person, 141–42. *See also* Virginity

Imposition: of hands, 143; of writing, 163, 164

Incantation, 98–99. *See also* Charms

Incense: used in remedies, 8, 159, 160, 161. *See also* Smoke

Incisions, 110; lance, 140

Incubus, 149

Infections, 127, 140. *See also* Flying venoms

Intelligibility of language, 19, 109, 117–18, 130, 145

Invisibility: visible vs. invisible, 80, 94–95, 99, 108, 151, 168; beings and internal or spiritual ailments, 93, 94–95, 108, 113, 123, 127, 128–30, 134, 144, 148, 159, 165, 170. *See also* Spiritual agencies/powers

Invocations, 10, 20, 110, 122, 139, 143, 144, 149, 150

Irish. *See* Celtic influences

Iron: as specified in remedies, 136, 139

Itch: symptom in remedies, 152, 153

Ker, N. R., 106

Kernels. *See* Nodes

Kieckhefer, Richard, 13, 16

Kinship, 43, 49

Knife: used in remedies, 136, 139–40, 143, 152, 160–61

Lacnunga, 106–7; remedies in, 108, 113–30 passim; elf remedies in, 138–45

Ladurie, Emmanuel Le Roy, 15, 19

Læce-wyrte (medicinal herb), 92

Laity: relationship to clergy, 17, 21–23, 40, 45–46, 69, 52, 70, 76, 96, 104, 172; education and reform of, 25, 28, 46, 47, 64, 68–69, 76; lay ownership of churches, 37–39, 45, 56, 58. *See also* Lay piety; Proprietary churches

Lamb's cress: ingredient in remedies, 127

"Land" disease. *See* Homesickness

Landholding patterns, 48–49, 52, 55, 61

Lard: ingredient in remedies, 158

Latin: relationship with Anglo-Saxon, 4, 18–19, 23, 25, 52, 66, 78, 99, 104, 105, 124, 135, 144, 151, 163–64; intelligibility, 19, 117–18, 145. *See also* Literacy

Laws: regarding churches and priests, 58–65, 76–79; on charms, 99, 102. *See also* Æthelred Unræd, King; Canons of Edgar

Laxatives, 108, 155

"Lay of the Nine Herbs," 125–28

Lay piety, 46, 49, 52–53, 56–58, 71

Leech, 158. *See also* Bloodletting

Leech (doctor), 103, 105, 136, 166; God as true leech, 81, 91–92. *See also* Healer

Leechbook, 106–7, 113, 123; remedies in, 108, 119, 130; elf remedies in, 132–33, 138, 145–67 passim

Leechdom (medicine), 91, 146–47, 152, 157, 165

Le Goff, Jacques, 11

Lent disease, 146–47, 150, 152, 153, 155

Leoba, Abbess, 44

153, 157, 159–61, 167. *See also*
Benedictions; Litanies; Liturgy; Pater
noster; Psalms
Preventative medicine, 153, 157–59
Price, Richard, 4–5
Pricking: in elf remedies, 1, 134, 136,
143, 152
Priests: required in remedies, 7,
119–20, 142–43, 148, 153–54,
164; as teachers, 44, 64, 66, 69;
in local churches, 59–61; training
of, 61–64, 69, 72; and bishops, 62–
65; celibacy of, 64–65; and proprietors, 65–66; and lay congregation,
66–69; and reformers, 71–72,
78–79; in development of charms,
115–16, 122, 142, 143, 150–51,
170. *See also* Clergy
Professionals of culture, 20. *See also* Formal religion
Prognostics, 110–13
Progress model, 36–39, 42–43, 100–
101, 106, 173
Proprietary churches, 51–53, 56, 59,
61, 65. *See also* Churches: local
Psalms: in remedies, 99, 116–18, 130,
141–42, 146, 148, 167–68. *See also*
Litanies; Liturgy; Mass
Psalters, 81, 136–38
Purgation, 108; in elf remedies,
134–36, 140, 143, 144, 147–48,
151–58. *See also* Exorcisms; Smoke
Purity, in persons, 85, 117, 121. *See also*
Virginity
Purity, of Germanic and Christian tra-
ditions, 12–13, 98–100, 114, 121,
140, 166

Quickbeam: used in Field Remedy, 7

Radish: ingredient in remedies, 157
Ram's gall: ingredient in remedies,
150

Rationality, modes of, 16–17, 101,
115; historical, 26, 73, 168; historiographical, 97, 100–107, 141. *See
also* Worldview
Reduction charms, 117–18, 130
Reform: in conversion, 24–26, 32;
in response to invasions, 38–40,
56–58; in local churches, 46–53;
of priests, 61–65, 69; of popular
Christianity, 71–79, 90
Reginsmal, 134
Relics, 43, 52, 83, 85, 89–90, 92–93,
150. *See also* Saints, cult of
Religion: defined, 16–18. *See also* Religion, formal; Religion, popular
Religion, formal, 9–14, 18–27 passim,
33–34, 38, 39, 72, 96, 172
Religion populaire, 13–14
Religion, popular, 9–10; historiography, 12–14; model, 18–24, 171–
73; in relation to conversion, 24–27,
33–34; Viking impact, 37–40, 54–
55, 70–71; popularization in homilies, 72–74, 77; in medical texts and
charms, 104, 145. *See also* Christianization; Churches: local; Conversion;
Middle practices
Religion savante, 13–14
Resurrection: hope of, 80, 83; Christ's,
121–22, 165
Reynolds, Susan, 67
Ritual, 23, 94–95; in popular religion,
12–13, 18, 20–21, 26, 89–93; in
medicine, 116, 123, 130, 135; Germanic and Christian examples of,
142, 147–65 passim. *See also* Exorcisms; Liturgy
Rollo, Duke of Normandy, 42
Roman Christianity, cultural synthesis
of, 17–19, 27–29; in church organization, 51–52; in medicine and
liturgy, 97, 113–14, 148
Romulus and Remus, 29

Thomas, Keith, 16

Thor, 28, 161

Three: as number specified in remedies, 7–8, 78, 88, 110, 117, 125–
27, 128, 144, 148, 149, 152, 153,
155, 158, 160, 161–62, 164, 165,
167. *See also* Trinity

Tithes: distribution of, 59–60, 65

Tongue: making cross marks on, in a
remedy, 153

Toothache, 110

Transference, symbolic, 108–10, 120,
122

Transferential magic, 100

Translations: author's policy on, 4; of
vernacular homilies, 74, 76, 80; of
classical medicine, 105, 124, 135;
problematic, of elf charms, 142,
157, 159

Treaties: in conversion, 42–43

Treaty of Alfred and Guthrum, 35–36,
38, 41–42

Trees: in remedies, 6, 120, 160; pagan
worship at, 25–26, 28, 87–88, 92,
113. *See also* Cross

Trinity: invocation of, 7, 118, 121,
129, 141, 143, 145; referenced in
remedies, 118, 119, 144. *See also*
Three

Twelve: as number specified in remedies, 1, 119, 122, 143, 148, 153,
166

Typhus. *See* Lent disease

Ulcers (theor): remedies for, 118,
157–58, 202 (n. 67); associations
of, with other illnesses, 123

Unction. *See* Anointing the sick; Oil of
extreme unction

Uncuthum sidran (strange custom), 153

Ungemynde (out-of-mind). *See* Madness

Unguents, blessing of, 121–22. *See also*
Salves

Unintelligible. *See* Intelligibility of
language

Utrecht Psalter, 136

Van Engen, John, 13

Vanir, 28. *See also* Æsir

Venomloather. *See* Attorlathe

Venoms. *See* Flying venoms, Poison

Vercelli Homilies, 74–76

Vernacular: use of, to popularize ideas,
74, 77, 80–81, 86, 104, 115–16,
124–25. *See also* Textualization

Veronica: invoked in remedies, 149,
150, 163

Veterinary remedies. *See* Animals

Vikings: impact on churches, 35–38,
41–46, 49–50, 54–58, 78–79. *See
also* Danelaw

Villeins: and priests, 61, 65–66

Vills, local churches in, 51–53, 66–70

Virginity: required in remedies, 117,
141–42

Virtues: as inherent in nature, 82, 89;
proper use of, 93, 95, 168; as acti-
vated in medicine and folklore, 109,
116, 125–27; in elf remedies, 135,
160–61

Visions, fearful: remedies against, 135.
See also Nightmares

Vomiting: induced in a remedy, 155.
See also Purgation

Vovelle, Michel, 13

Wanderer, 43

Warriors, herbs as, 125–27

Warrior values, Christianized, 28–31

Water: holy, used in remedies, 1, 7–8,
94–95, 119–20, 130, 143, 146,
147–48, 149, 150, 153, 158, 160–
62, 164, 165, 166, 167–68; ordinary or spring, 117, 127, 141–42,
155, 159; blessing of, 120

Water-elf disease, 134–35, 157, 165

Wax: ingredient in elfshot remedy, 1, 119, 142
Waybread (waybroad; one of the nine herbs), 125–27; as ingredient in remedies, 135–36, 139, 150, 153
Weapons, spiritual, 29, 87, 128
Weeds, 127
Week. See Days
Weland the Smith, 29
Wells and wellsprings: pagan worship at, Christianized, 28, 32, 45, 67, 87, 95, 171
Wenwort (ingredient in remedies): knotty, 149; cloved, 155
Wergule (one of the nine herbs), 126
White Book of St. Augustine, 58
Wights, 126
Winchester scriptorium, 106
Wine, hallowed: used in remedies, 119–20, 141, 153, 206 (n. 52)
Wisemen and wisewomen, 7, 23, 103, 149
Witchcraft (wiccecræft) and witches, 86–87, 91–93, 99, 102–3, 157. See also Sorcery
Woden: beliefs about, 28, 181 (n. 51); in charms, 125–28, 197 (n. 9)
Wolfscomb: ingredient in remedies, 154, 166
Women: power in speech, 8, 23, 146, 149, 157; role in conversion, 43–45; as healers, 103, 134
Wonder. See Wundor
Worldview: 72; in popular religion, 12–17, 19; modern or scientific,

86, 101, 115; medical, 103, 105, 108–13, 131; in view of elves, 133, 136–38, 141, 151; rethinking early medieval, 169–74. See also Augustinian worldview; Rationality
Worm (wyrm): as cause of disease, 117, 124, 125–27, 128–30, 136
Wormwood: ingredient in remedies, 135–36, 155, 159, 164, 165, 166
Wounds: treatment of, 127, 157–58, 165; elfshot, 134–35, 137, 139, 144
Writing: washed into a drink, 119, 140–41, 146–47
Wuldorgeflogenum (fugitives from glory), 126
Wuldor-tanas (glory-twigs), 126
Wulfstan II, Archbishop of York, 47; authorship of laws, 50–51; on priesthood, 62–65, 68–69; homilies, 74–79
Wundor, 75, 82–86. See also Miracles
Wyrigung (curse), 87; wyrigedum galdrum (cursing charms), 92. See also Charms

Yarrow: ingredient in remedies, 147, 154
Yeast: specified in Field Remedy, 6
Yellow disease, 152, 158, 162
Yellowish membranes, 134, 162
Yewberry: ingredient in remedies, 165
York, archbishopric of, 50–51. See also Wulfstan II

Zedoary: ingredient in remedies, 141

Printed in the United States
5839